ROUTLEDGE LIBRARY EDITIONS
BROADCASTING

Volume 17

COLOUR TELEVISION

COLOUR TELEVISION

Techniques, Business, Impact

Edited by
HOWARD W. COLEMAN

LONDON AND NEW YORK

First published in 1968 by Focal Press

This edition first published in 2024
by Routledge
4 Park Square, Milton Park, Abingdon, Oxon OX14 4RN

and by Routledge
605 Third Avenue, New York, NY 10158

Routledge is an imprint of the Taylor & Francis Group, an informa business

© 1968 Focal Press Limited

All rights reserved. No part of this book may be reprinted or reproduced or utilised in any form or by any electronic, mechanical, or other means, now known or hereafter invented, including photocopying and recording, or in any information storage or retrieval system, without permission in writing from the publishers.

Trademark notice: Product or corporate names may be trademarks or registered trademarks, and are used only for identification and explanation without intent to infringe.

British Library Cataloguing in Publication Data
A catalogue record for this book is available from the British Library

ISBN: 978-1-032-59391-3 (Set)
ISBN: 978-1-032-61985-9 (Volume 17) (hbk)
ISBN: 978-1-032-61990-3 (Volume 17) (pbk)
ISBN: 978-1-032-61988-0 (Volume 17) (ebk)

DOI: 10.4324/9781032619880

Publisher's Note
The publisher has gone to great lengths to ensure the quality of this reprint but points out that some imperfections in the original copies may be apparent.

Disclaimer
The publisher has made every effort to trace copyright holders and would welcome correspondence from those they have been unable to trace.

COLOUR TELEVISION

TECHNIQUES - BUSINESS - IMPACT

Edited by **HOWARD W. COLEMAN**

FOCAL PRESS
London and New York

© FOCAL PRESS LIMITED 1968
SBN 240 50651 0

No part of this book may be reproduced in any form without written permission of the publishers

First published 1968

*Printed and bound in Great Britain by
Staples Printers Limited at their Rochester, Kent, establishment*

Contents

Editor's Preface	7
THE DIMENSIONS OF COLOR Arthur C. Nielsen, Jr.	10

I. *The Techniques of Color Television*

1. THE BASICS OF COLOR Howard Ketcham	21
2. THE ELECTRONICS OF COLOR TELEVISION John W. Wentworth	28
3. COLOR TELEVISION EQUIPMENT: PRESENT AND FUTURE John T. Wilner	37

II. *Producing for Color Television*

4. COLOR PRODUCTION E. Carlton Winckler	53
5. COLOUR IN THE STUDIO A. R. Stanley	66
6. COLOR FILM PRODUCTION FOR COLOR TELEVISION John M. Waner	82
7. PUBLIC SERVICE PROGRAMMING IN COLOR Ward L. Quaal	95

8. COLOR IN TELEVISION NEWS 107
Sheldon W. Peterson

III. The Color Television Audience

9. THE IMPACT OF COLOR 121
(A PROFILE OF COLOR TV SET OWNERS: TELEVISION'S "CLASS" AUDIENCE)
Thomas E. Coffin
Sam Tuchman

IV. Doing Business in Color

10. SELLING COLOR TELEVISION 139
Norman E. Cash

11. COLOR PROMOTION 146
Chet Campbell

12. ADVERTISING IN COLOR 159
Donald F. Coleman

13. THE LOCAL STATION AND COLOR 172
Roy Bacus

14. COLOR IT LOCAL: A SAMPLING OF LOCAL STATION COLOR ACTIVITY 187
Kenneth A. Mills

V. The Sum of the Parts

15. IT'S IN COLOR—SO WHAT? 197
Howard W. Coleman

16. COLOUR TELEVISION SYSTEMS 207
A. V. Lord

APPENDICES 253
GLOSSARY 266
INDEX 283

Editor's Preface

USE of the quotes (real *or* apocryphal) of movie mogul Sam Goldwyn has been fair game in the writing on or of anything remotely connected with the wondrous world of *show biz* for well over a quarter of a century.

But how can one resist, in the context of this book, when the attributed Goldwynism is "I'll believe color is here when I see it in black-and-white!"

Yes, Sam, there *is* a Santa Claus—and he is equipped not only with a snowy-white beard and a cherry-red nose but with a 21-inch sleigh, loaded with goodies of every hue, tone and shade; mauve and orchid and chartreuse and R.A.F. blue and all the rest.

A bearer of gifts? Maybe, maybe not—but there is no doubt about his *presence* in the minds of the people represented here. The contributors to this text attest to widely divergent backgrounds, geographic areas and current employment arenas. But they are at the same time drawn together by at least one common bond, which is explicit in their writings: they *have* seen it in black-and-white, and they *do* know that *color is here!*

Quite obviously, they have many other mutual interests under the overall umbrella of television broadcasting. Since those of us who work in the statistical world of Nielsen are most comfortable with shares and averages and other compilations, these authors might be profiled in this way:

1. Two of them are TV station general managers, and have guided their charges since the first multi-toned flicker went forth from their transmitters . . .
2. Five of them (including this editor) were participants in the

pioneering 1966 *Color Conference* segment of the annual meeting of the National Association of Broadcasters . . .
3. Three of them—two English, one American—presented their materials before the *Color Symposium* of the Royal Television Society in London, in early 1967 . . .
4. Three of them have been researching color since its first pale glimmer; several others exploring its technical intricacies, and a pair developing sales and promotion tools, for a like period in time . . .
5. There is a pride of one time NBC toilers represented here (and, to personalize, one of the contributors is my brother; another, my boss!)

Almost without exception, the group has been in the industry from the day color TV became a practical offering for the public—and in many cases its members were present for the dawn of black-and-white as well. Depending on areas of interest, they have engineered or produced or administrated, bought or sold or promoted or written about, the broadcast industry and its products for a professional total of 329 years!

Assembling the talent and the energies to produce a text on a new and specialized subject is never easy. In his letter of invitation to the participants in this work, the publisher wrote: "It is our intention that the final product should be a thorough going examination of the pragmatics of color telecasting."

And this is the goal we have kept before us, all delays and occasional weakening of the signal to the contrary. During the early stages of assembling materials, a critic of the TV medium grumbled that "You're borrowing and pasting together old speeches, just like your whole industry does when it dreams up new westerns and situation comedies." Let it be understood, then, that 13 of the 17 chapters in this text are the original offerings of the authors (and their staffs as well, in some cases), written to the specific requirements of the work at hand. And written, it should be added, by very busy people employed in a frenetic and fast-moving business, solely to the appeal that their experiences be put down while fresh in mind and for the use of those who follow.

In four chapters, use has been made of materials previously presented, or published in limited circulation. In all four cases the reasoning was the same: we were advised by experts and authoritative industry groups that these were the *very best materials available* on the subjects proposed.

To demonstrate that complexities in communications are not limited to the compatibility of technical systems, we found that we were faced with *English*-English as opposed to *American*-English in manuscript editing—that the *Colour* detailed so authoritatively by British contributors Stanley and Lord agreed in content but differed in style from the *Color* of our American writers. Seeking to avoid an international incident between the Broadcast *Center* in Fort Worth and the BBC's Television *Centre*, we elected to retain the spelling (and style) of the authors—the only proviso being that it agree with the editorial standards of the shore of the Atlantic on which it was created!

It will be noted that there is present a certain amount of divergence of opinion between writers, and some occasional duplication as well. We think this to be all to the good: to paraphrase the standard disclaimer that "the opinions expressed are not necessarily those of the management", it might be said that these differences and re-statements of major issues reflect, *happily*, a wide variety of experience in an ever-changing industry.

In addition to a low bow to the contributing authors, gratitude must be expressed to a generous employer, an ambidextrous secretary, and a patient wife and family. Several members of the Broadcasters Promotion Association and the International Radio-TV Society, many members of the broadcast trade press, and friends in mass communications education, have been generous in suggestions and criticism. And the postal service seldom let us down, even in the rush of the Christmas season!

New York, December 1967   H. COLEMAN

The Dimensions of Color

A. C. NIELSEN, Jr.
President, A. C. Nielsen Company

Color has brought a new dimension to television; turned the gray-scale of early black-and-white video into the rainbow of the 1960's; inspired new programming ideas, incited new concepts in sales promotion, established a new class of "we have color" viewers—and in turn posed problematical questions for the researchers of TV's watching mores and folkways: Do people watch more when it's in color? Do more people watch on a color set? Will they watch something in color that they wouldn't *watch in black-and-white?*

In addressing the subject, Arthur C. Nielsen, Jr., couples a lifetime of research experience (under the guidance of his father, founder and chairman of the board of A. C. Nielsen Company) with high academic achievement and a record of service as a marketing consultant to the United States government.

In the following, he recalls the shifts in audience broadcast interest that he has seen take place, from radio to TV and then from black-and-white TV to the encroaching interests of color. He offers some answers to the above queries, as seen in a given point in time, and speculates as well on the future research needs for color viewing data at the time when color viewing will be considered to be as commonplace as is black-and-white watching today.

THERE can be no doubt but that color television runs a gamut of interest from the largest to the smallest advertiser, from the television fan who says "we're watching even more than before" to the critic who claims that "I never liked it in black-and-white either", from the largest metropolitan markets all the way to our editor's favorite town of Open Switch, U.S.A.

Here in the Chicago area, where colorcasting was pioneered on a large scale in 1956, the merchandising of the medium at the point of sale continues to be a topic of major interest. The nation's largest appliance dealership (Polk Bros., Chicago) is here, and headman Sol Polk has for over a decade cited color television as the "hottest item in my shop".

Polk talks of color as "a great force", one that will aid many other industries, including the chemical and glass and the home furnishings industries. He says that "people will become subconsciously concerned with their furniture after watching color television"; adds that "the carpeting industry should run a banquet for General Sarnoff".

The rapid growth of color can be documented in a number of ways: in the mid-50s, the color program was "special" in every meaning of the word—a 90-minute *Spectacular*, the color origination of World Series telecasts, or a visit by the stars of Chicago's *Zoo Parade* to the Bronx Zoo.

But, by the fall of 1965, there was only *one* half-hour period in the evening programming of the three networks when viewers did *not* have at least one color program to watch. *Finding something in color* was no longer a problem one year later. The fall of 1966 was truly the beginning of *all color* time on the networks. Situation comedies, feature films, dramatic series, westerns and all the rest, were in full color.

Football on network television—NCAA and NFL and AFL—grew from slightly over 50 games per season to almost 90 in the five year period culminating in 1966. And the 1966 outdoor originations were almost universally in color, as were the post-season playoffs and bowl games that carried over into mid-January of 1967.

If—and that's a big and hard-to-define *if*—the viewer sought color for the sake of color, he had more opportunity and more variety than ever before.

In contemplating color television, there are lessons to be learned by looking backward—to broadcasting's brief but rapidly-unfolding history. Radio, particularly the pre-TV network radio we once knew, lost much of its traditional evening audience and most of its financial support with the advent of television. The comedy hours with their guest stars, the dramatic "theatres", the musical programs, the soap operas, all converted to television or disappeared in the early 1950s.

Would their era have continued indefinitely, *without* the intrusion of television? The question is of course unfair in that it is so safe to pose; there can be no answer, in the light of that fast-moving history. But in the way of reinforcing conjecture, radio's audience *was* changing, as the sociological influences of post-World War II living made themselves felt. The independent radio stations, complete with disc jockeys, bright music, informational services (and often 24-hour-a-day operation) were making inroads in the traditional dominance of the network style of broadcasting. More and more car radios, portable sets, multiple sets throughout the home; more leisure time, new and changing styles in music—with greater appeal to an increasingly affluent youth audience; more traveling and outdoor living—all combined to pull sizeable segments of the radio audience away from its traditional listening habits.

And, as we know, television did the rest.

Measuring the Color Television Audience

Now we turn to an exploration of color television, and its influence (and potential for even greater influence) on overall TV viewing patterns.

Television came into our Nielsen sampling of radio listening in the late 1940s, even as the first TV stations went on the air in major markets and as the coaxial cable began to link those stations into networks. Our Audimeters (R)—patented devices for recording and reporting the use of radio—were readily adaptable for the recording of TV usage as well. In this way we saw television grow, from estimates of 3·4 million households TV-equipped in 1950 (an 8 percent national penetration) to 30·2 million households (63 percent) in 1955, 45·2 million households in 1960 (87 percent) and to 56·0 million households (95 percent, and virtual saturation) in our most recent estimate for the fall of 1967.

THE DIMENSIONS OF COLOR

In the same way that television coincidentally entered our sampling, we now find color set households on the roster of our NTI sample—in part as new households brought into the panel turn up with color sets, in another part as existing sample households replace their black-and-white sets with color units.

It is well worth noting that, as of March, 1966, we reported "almost half of upper income households have multiple TV sets". There are strong indications in the electronics industry that, when the color set is purchased, the black-and-white set moves to the bedroom or the recreation room, in turn creating a "multi-set" household. In the above-mentioned report, we found 24 percent of *all* TV households to have more than one TV set. This penetration was strongest in urban ("A") counties, with 35 percent, and scaled down to 10 percent in rural ("D") counties.

In our three groupings under *Household Income* we list *lower* as under $5,000 annually, *middle* as $5-9,999, and *upper* as $10,000 and over. By these definitions, we estimated 43 percent of upper income households with more than one TV set, 26 percent in the middle range, and 8 percent in the lower group.

In that same month—March 1966—we reported color set penetration in this way: "Almost a fifth of upper-income households have color TV sets." We also estimated the percent of *all* TV households viewing in color—a statistic most recently updated (January 1967) to approximately 13 percent. As would be expected, we found greater penetration in urban counties, less in small market and rural areas. In the classification by household income, we found the greatest spread: 17 percent color in upper income households, 8 percent in the middle category, 4 percent in the lower group.

It should be noted that the foregoing data reflect information from our *national* sample; as such, take into account rural areas as well as heavily-populated urban clusters, markets serviced by one or two TV stations as well as those with six or more signals, and geographic areas with a wide diversity in span of income and education.

In the appendix of this text, the reader will note a charting of color TV set penetration on a market-by-market basis, from estimates supplied by our local TV audience measurement service, Nielsen Station Index. In these listings we can find a wide range of color viewing and interest, from lows of around 5 percent to highs approaching 30 percent or more.

Television station history in color effort, market-by-market, sometimes coupled with the promotional urges of TV set distributors and retailers, is tied closely with these data, as is *affluence*—per capita income and the individual urge to "be the first in the neighborhood"—a phenomenon that was observed in the early days of black-and-white TV!

In a pilot study, our Nielsen Station Index service paired Audilog (R) diary reports of TV viewing of households having color sets with households equipped with black-and-white sets only, based on one-week diaries kept by sample households during the four-week period ending 24th March 1965.

Within the metropolitan areas of 29 three-network NSI markets (areas where three stations provide full affiliated service from the ABC, CBS and NBC networks), 961 color set households were matched with a like-sized sample of B & W households.

1. The paired households were in similar geographic locations, in the same postal zones, wherever possible, and in all cases within the same counties.
2. They were measured and compared within the same week to ensure similarity in programming.
3. They were similar in the number of sets owned (single vs. multi-set households).

Approximately 68 percent of the households in each part of the sample had one or more television sets in working order.

Again, in terms of broadcast history, the date of this pilot study must be restated. In those early months of 1965, NBC offered considerably more hours of color programming than its two competitors combined—a factor that no longer exists in network prime time television. Thus the data must be considered solely as they reflect that particular point in time and that competitive situation.

Herewith a composite week assembled from that comparative color and B & W household viewing data, with one program selected in each evening's prime-time, as representative of the color—noncolor scope of the medium:

Evening and Program	Color Households		Black-and-White Households	
	(Rating and share data rounded to whole #s)			
	Rating %	Share %	Rating %	Share %
Monday (Andy Williams)	45	60	28	43
Tuesday (Telephone Hour)	26	38	12	20
Wednesday (Virginian)	40	60	20	32
Thursday (Suspense Theater)	36	56	18	32
Friday (Bob Hope Show)	40	60	26	40
Saturday (Feature Movie)	36	52	23	39
Sunday (Bonanza)	53	68	42	59

With another note of caution regarding time and competitive situation, this survey is offered (as witnessed by other chapters in this text dealing with the local station) because of its meaningfulness in relation to the continuing growth of color and of *local* color telecasting.

A Summary of the Survey

The above-cited roster of programs delivered, in the category of color TV households, an estimated 276 rating points, as opposed to 169 rating points in B & W only households. To go ahead one more step, the average share of audience for those seven programs is estimated as slightly more than 56 percent for the color households, slightly less than 38 percent for the black-and-white viewing group.

From this study, the desirability of advertising within color programming is obvious on a cost-per-thousand, dollars-and-cents basis. For a comprehensive reader's comparison of the worth of these data in relation to later color telecasting (with virtually all prime-time programming offered in color), it is suggested that Ken Mills' chapter in this text—*Color it Local: A Sampling of Local Station Color Activity*—be consulted.

The Question:
How Much Future Need for Color Viewing Information?

The expanding needs of broadcast advertisers, coupled with equally-expanding abilities in electronic data gathering and processing, have combined to produce ever-growing banks of information detailing the use of television in the household.

In addition to the traditional ratings and shares of audience for programs, there are many demographic modifiers: the presence in the TV-using household of the man-of-house and lady-of-house, identified by age group and by further modifiers of employment and size of family; of households by size and income and many other meaningful groupings of data.

By example, we have (in early 1967) introduced a new concept—*Nielsen Product-Media Service*—as a supplemental service of our national reporting of household and person viewing. Here we equate viewing in a very commercial way—as matched with purchases of products and services by various product and service classes, and also by specific brand names.

Obviously, this will in its next step move to a re-classification of those categories in terms of *color households* as opposed to *black-and-white only households*.

Will this next step be necessary; if so, for how long? Here only the television industry and its advertisers can answer, and this in relation to the percentage of color saturation of its local markets and its national market, as each year goes by.

We have come to the moment where virtually all of the networks' prime-time offerings are in color, and where daytime and weekend offerings are moving into that "all-color" status as well. We recognize, as does the television industry, that concepts of "color advantage" are already outmoded on an availability basis. The interest of the advertisers who use color television as the vehicle for their sales messages is keen: for maximum effectiveness, they need all possible information about the viewer at the receiving end of the compatible color—black-and-white TV signal.

That viewer gives every indication of moving rapidly to the status of *color* viewer. In many parts of the country (again, see NSI table in appendix of this text) we have reported color set penetration estimates that have doubled in a 24-month period.

As that viewer moves from B & W to color, so will we make every effort to move with him. At the same time, we anticipate the realities of a situation just a few years away, when we will be reporting viewing in terms that will be *assumed to be* predominantly color (we do now report color versus non-color household viewing on a regular basis), in a pattern that will in turn be as universal in itself as was black-and-white in that yesteryear of just a few seasons ago!

I

The Techniques
of Color Television

1 The Basics of Color

HOWARD KETCHAM
President, Howard Ketcham Incorporated

During the early stages of preparation of this book, I told a friend of my delight at having received permission to include a very authoritative article that had appeared in the 6th December 1965, Television Age. *"Nice," he replied, "but it's too bad you couldn't get something from the* real *authority —Howard Ketcham."*

"This is by Howard Ketcham!"

"Then I'll buy your book!"

Over 30 years ago, Howard Ketcham created a new profession—Color Engineering. Since that time, he has pioneered color planning for automobiles, aircraft interiors, truck fleets, railroad boxcars, hearses, supermarkets, shipping cartons, sunglasses, toothbrushes, boats, and an amazing list of additional products; has set up industry color standards and specifications for dyes, inks, papers, paints, flooring, building materials and plastics.

Ketcham is and has been a contributing editor and consultant for many magazines and publications; has written numerous articles and books, including Color Planning for Business and Industry *(Harper & Row, 1958).*

In this article, Ketcham says that "The electronic processes peculiar to color TV do some highly irregular things to color." Knowledgeability in circumventing, coping with, or even meeting head-on, those "irregular things", is the offering of this chapter . . .

IN the beginning of the world of communications, was the voice. Printing broadened the impact of two-dimensional imagery. Radio added the dimension of sound. Black-and-white television brought motion to the image.

Color television now gives us sound-supported moving images—in the color of the real world about us.

Here is a medium that, ideally, translates reality from one place to another. From the outdoors or the studio to the living room. And the viewer in his easy chair, eyes glued to a color television set he has paid a substantial premium for, fully expects this reality to be faithfully reproduced. Rejection in the marketplace awaits any television advertiser who fails to realize the unique problems posed by the use of color on television.

The electronic processes peculiar to color TV do some highly irregular things to color. Although great improvements have been made during recent years, there are still danger areas that require consideration. For example: red bleeds into other colors, especially lighter, neutral areas. White often looks bluish or yellowish. A bluish white is sometimes an asset when the cleanliness of white is to be emphasized, but it can be a drawback at other times. Pale pastels have a tendency to fade and appear almost colorless, but bright, medium-value pastels appear intensified. Deep reds sometimes lose character and appear brownish.

There is also a marked difference in color reception on different makes of TV sets. Some emphasize the warmer colors, others the cool hues. Thus the same red or pink may appear almost orange on one set and rose or magenta on another. This distortion must be compensated for.

There is also a considerable difference in the color presentation of outdoor scenes and those produced in the studio. Since many commercials feature outdoor scenes, this is an important consideration. The natural green of foliage seldom looks natural for it takes on an olive or faded brownish cast on television. The blue of sky or water diffuses throughout a presentation and is especially hard on the complexion of actors. It can be corrected by the use of judicious lighting but it is something to be carefully watched.

A bright blue sky *can* be a fascinatingly effective background. In this it differs from a bright blue indoor backdrop that can be ineffective and disturbing looking. The difference is one of distance.

A single bright object seen against a sunny sky takes on added vividness, but only when it is isolated from the surrounding landscape. The contrast of great distance must be maintained to prevent the diffusion of blue already noted.

Yellow is the most visible color. It is great for backgrounds but causes reading trouble at close range. After-images can work for or against you. A green shirt, for instance, can make an over-flushed or too rosy complexion look redder; a green-colored cardboard platter, used for displaying meat in a refrigerated display gondola, makes meat look more appetizingly fresh by intensifying its red color.

A good basic rule is to keep color contrast simple, one light value against one dark value, or one bright color with a neutral color.

As in all color advertising problems these basic color rules can be successfully broken by the color specialist who understands thoroughly both color and the technicalities of color TV. I recall a sequence featuring coffee production in which gay china and pottery tableware holding coffee, whip cream, cakes and the like, had various backgrounds of scenery typical of the nations in which the several kinds of coffee were consumed. This broke all the rules of color, composition and photography, but the result was charming and not in the least confusing. The backgrounds stayed back, the featured place settings were exactly right, and the coffee had a convincing and appetizing coffee look.

Knowing what color impressions to expect and how to keep color distortions under control is more than half the battle. Not knowing the basic ground rule regulations as they apply to color control can result in some really appalling results on product color, to say nothing of wasted advertising expenditure. Here are some typical color distortions to be expected on color TV:

1. Preserves turn black.
2. Certain fish reproduce so very white that they look unnatural.
3. Silverware acquires a scintillating halo.
4. Necktie colors look appreciably darker against white shirts than they do against blue shirts.

New problems develop constantly as color-innovations are introduced. In spite of the lavish use of cartoon characters, much of today's color TV advertising relies on people—filmed or alive—to do the selling job. Color TV can be ghastly. When it was in its primitive stage, viewers didn't much mind if a model's dress came through as green instead of pink. They were deeply concerned, however, when her face matched the dress. While much of this has been rectified, stage make-up still won't work 100 percent on color television. Stage footlights necessitate high coloring, while subdued make-up tones reproduce most convincingly on color TV.

But even subtle cosmetic tones tend to reflect color after-images from clothes, and one of the most vexing problems continues to be the overlapping of clothes and complexion.

Following are a few of the most successful clothing-color considerations that typical complexion types can wear to advantage on and off the color TV screen:

Redheads: Medium neutral gray and light gray make them look more vivid; rust gives less appeal; yellow-green adversely affects the redhead's complexion. Faded pinks are splendid.

Brunettes: Medium neutral gray or bright dark blue makes them look more vivid; light gray gives a tanned look; yellow brings out the pinkish tones in brunettes.

Blondes: Medium neutral gray makes them look faded; light gray gives them a darker look; medium tan or bright dark blue adds vividness; yellow gives blondes a violet cast.

White Hair: Medium neutral gray or light gray makes skin coloring of women with white hair look faded; yellow gives a violet cast; light violet-blue brings out fresh pinkish tones; bright dark blue makes these people look sallow. Rose and subdued pink are flattering.

In general, fabric colors whirl around in TV's electronic environment and come out changed. Take that everyday stand-by of the American male, the ubiquitous white shirt. White is still too much for today's color systems. It appears much too bright on the receiver. It takes a gray or blue shirt with one-half the reflectivity of white to look like a white shirt on color TV.

A good basic rule in costuming for color is always to avoid white for large areas. Today's video equipment will gag on a picture with more than 20 percent of its area in white. (Incidentally, the color camera is like the human eye. If the color is too bright, the

FIG. 1. Color influences apparent size. Which of the colored circles fits exactly into the white circle in the black area? Which fits into the black circle in the white area?

FIG. 2. Color influences apparent proportion. The colored area does not take up 70 or 80 per cent of the space within the rectangle as it may seem. The interior block is only 50 per cent of the total area within the rectangle

FIG. 3. Color influences apparent shape. The colored circles are just that—circles, perfect circles. The relationship between the light black lines and the heavy colored circles makes the circles seem lopsided.

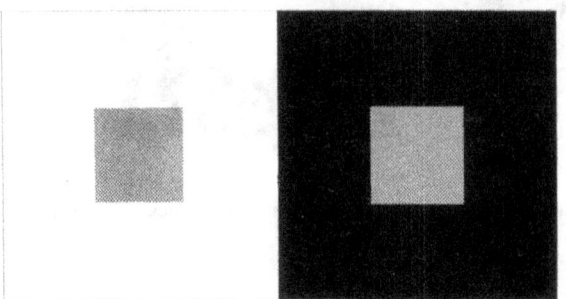

FIG. 4. Color influences apparent values. The neutral grey squares are *not* different in value. They are the same, but on the white the grey seems darker, and on the black the grey seems lighter.

camera blinks. The commercial is thus transmitted with a set of nervous blinks, distorting the visual quality of the presentation.)

A related problem is color saturation. Consider a red shirt against a blue background. The variation of brightness between strong red and equally strong blue will diffuse the transition between the shirt and the background so that the edges of the shirt will appear to smear. Contrasting yellow in place of red against blue will make this particular color transition effective.

Color television puts the product in another selling environment and complicates the problems of window display, and package design in general.

Should the advertiser let his package alone, even though it may look differently on color television and the supermarket shelf? Or should he re-design to create a package that looks the same on a screen as it does on a counter or in a window?

There is no pat solution. All we can do is list the factors that will influence a decision:

1. It is difficult and sometimes costly to develop package colors that will look the same on color and black-and-white TV and "in the flesh".
2. Such a redesign may lose the selling value of carefully established package colors.
3. On the other hand, more and more advertising is originating from the point of sale; if a package is unrecognizable when the camera moves into that supermarket, it has become a very expensive package indeed.
4. Using special colors that simulate a package on TV may or may not produce a convincing replica.

As a rule of thumb, an advertiser will probably fare best by making a brand-new package line compatible with black-and-white or color and point-of-sale viewing, a complex job best left in the hands of the color engineer. If the advertiser retains his old package line, the problems of making it compatible may be insurmountable, and he had better get professional help in trying to simulate his package on TV as closely as possible.

Lighting has an immense job to do with getting an advertising message over to the viewer. Lighting can make or break television colors; it is even more important than lighting for black-and-white.

Lighting for color TV must be comparatively shadowless and extremely bright because the average level of light on a color TV set runs four to six times that of black-and-white. If the originating studio doesn't have color-controlled and color-integrated lighting, small objects with slight color differences—like people's faces—will show up extremely poorly on the home set.

The lighting of a studio, if it is carefully co-ordinated, can do a much better job of presenting an advertising message than natural lighting. The big problem is co-ordinating lighting with the colors to be aired.

The color engineer handles this with a color-and-light correlation chart. Such a chart gives information on the typical color of the conventional studio light sources, the color of the pigment that the light will reflect from, the resultant hue, and whether the value and chroma of the pigment are respectively raised or lowered.

Probably the most important factor in producing effective color TV is to maintain exactly the right amount of contrast and to use the "right" colors together. Too great contrast is not only disturbing but also, and in contradiction to its usual effect, tends to neutralize itself. This is exemplified, for instance, when an announcer in a dark blue suit is shown against a brighter and lighter blue background. His normally healthy tan complexion, a color complementary to blue, becomes pallid by reflection and bleeding of the background into the flesh tones.

On the other hand, too little contrast is just as bad. A charming white kitten on a shaggy white rug (in a commercial advertising pet foods) became a mass of irridescent, reflected colors that carried no impact. In black-and-white with the right light and shadow this picture might have been very striking. In color it was lost. The same white rug behind a red-brown puppy was eye-catching and riveted the attention not only on the puppy, but most especially on the deeper red-brown dog food that appeared rich and succulent, as it should. This is good color advertising and it brings up another point—the effectiveness of simplicity. A silver-gray or yellow kitten would have given the puppy serious competition in spectacular interest.

In a short commercial, three colors are better than four, and two, if they are the "right" ones, are better than three. When the object shown necessarily consists of several colors, as in a brightly hued package, it is especially necessary to show it against a neutral background, but not one that is in such sharp contrast that it distorts the true colors of the display. A neutral background need not be gray or beige. In fact these colors tend to take on undesirable reflections. It can be gray-green or mauve or gray-blue, depending on the color or colors with which it is intended to contrast. But in any case it is apt to be most successful when it is simple, without texture or folds or pattern of light and shade.

When considering colors for TV commercials, remember also that colors traditionally have symbolism. Manufacturers who demand the most exacting standards in their advertising, product or package communication find nothing excels color—it tells the sales story, it sells faster than words—but the colors must be the correct ones.

So far as moods induced by color are concerned, the following associations are valid. Note that different values and intensities of the same color often have quite opposite connotations.

Light reds induce cheerfulness, but very dark or very bright reds are more likely to induce depression and irritability.

Soft pinks are associated with femininity, but bright magenta pinks suggest frivolity.

Light orange looks clean and appetizing, but when this color is grayed to a tan shade, it merely looks drab.

Pale yellow and ivory suggest daintiness, but deep, strong yellow suggests boldness, virility and gaiety.

A clear, fairly light yellow-green is associated with young growth and freshness, but the same color darkened and subdued to olive brings to mind an impression of decay.

Light sky blue is a tranquil color; deepened to indigo, it becomes depressing.

Color controls the very world we live in. It is bright and gay and happy, or cool and calm and restful, or irritating and painful. The entire range of human involvement and emotion has a color identity —and this must be equally well presented in the commercial counterparts projected on color TV to be effective and rewarding to all concerned. Color must attract, not distract.

2 The Electronics of Color Television

JOHN W. WENTWORTH
Manager,
"Current Concepts in Science and Engineering" Program,
Radio Corporation of America, Camden, New Jersey

John Wentworth writes, in the introduction to his theme, that "decision-making people in all facets of the broadcast industry should understand at least the basic principles of the technology on which our industry is built." And it was exactly because of his expertise that he was sought for this topic!

University of Maine graduate John Wentworth joined the Radio Corporation of America in 1949. Initially assigned to development and design work in color TV, he subsequently became an engineering manager, responsible for directing design work on a section of RCA's broadcast studio equipment product line. Since 1959 he has devoted most of his attention to the field of educational technology. As manager, CCSE Program, he is responsible for developing "Current Concepts in Science and Engineering", a program for the continuing education of RCA managers and leaders.

He is the author of Color Television Engineering *(McGraw-Hill, 1955); has published more than a dozen papers on broadcast engineering and educational technology; has lectured extensively throughout the United States. In London (in 1963) he worked with the European Broadcasting Union Committee, studying color TV systems; is also the producer, writer and studio teacher of* "Electronics at Work", *a course in basic electronics based on a series of 90 instructional TV programs.*

THE objective of this chapter is to review and interpret the major technical concepts involved in color television. Decision-making people in all facets of the broadcast industry should understand at least the basic principles of the technology on which our industry is built.

While matters of technical detail can properly be left in the hands of a station's engineering department, a broadcast enterprise can be most effective and most profitable when station management and program production personnel understand television technology well enough to appreciate both the capabilities and limitations of the medium, and know how to talk intelligently with their engineering colleagues.

No one can become a technical expert on color television without months of study, but this brief chapter should give you a general impression as to how it works and acquaint you with many of the technical terms you will encounter frequently in connection with color TV.

The Role of Primary Colors

In essence, color television is a "marriage" of television technology and the art of reproducing color images by means of primary colors.

Virtually everyone in the television industry has at least a superficial understanding of the basic television techniques that make possible "vision at a distance". These techniques include the scanning process and the handling of electronic signals through processes generally similar to those used in radio broadcasting. It is also common knowledge that a wide range of colors encountered in everyday life can be matched by an appropriate combination of three so-called "primary" colors.

All practical processes for reproducing color images, including color photography, color halftone printing and color television, are based on the primary color principle. That is, the final image in each of these processes is produced by combining a minimum of three primary color images. The specific primary colors used for color television are red, green and blue.

One of the most significant differences between *color* television and *monochrome* television is the necessity for handling *three independent picture signals* to produce color images. In some parts of the color system, it is easy to see the relationship between these three signals and the values of red, green and blue light needed to form the final color image. In other portions of the system, the signals may be transformed or processed in such a way that their relationship to the primary colors becomes obscure to the non-engineer, but there must always be at least three degrees of freedom in the signals at any point in the system. In principle, one could transmit color images by operating three monochrome television systems in parallel, using a separate channel for each of the primary colors. In practice, the problem becomes much more difficult because it is necessary to fit all three primary color signals into a single broadcast channel.

Color Cameras and Picture Tubes

A color camera must provide some means for subdividing an optical image into red, green and blue components so that independent signals can be developed for the primary colors. Most of the color cameras now in service employ three separate pick-up tubes in association with a light-splitting optical system to develop red, green and blue signals.

Many of the newer camera designs employ a total of *four* pick-up tubes to provide improved image quality. At the receiving end of the system, the picture must be displayed on a device that provides independent control of three primary color images. The most popular type of color picture tube is the so-called shadow-mask tube, in which three separate electron beams are used to control red, green and blue images consisting of many tiny dots of light-emitting phosphors.

The Encoding/Decoding Problem

Because of the very limited number of available television channels in the broadcast spectrum, the FCC made it clear in the early stages of color television development that it could consider only those color television systems capable of operating within the same 6-megacycle channels used for monochrome broadcasting. Thus, much of the engineering work on color television was directed at the problem of *multiplexing*: that is, the problem of processing the primary color signals in such a way that they could share a common transmission channel. Multiplexing is actually accomplished by *encoding* and *decoding* techniques. When the three color signals provided by a 3-tube camera are *encoded*, they produce a single 3-variable signal which contains all the required information "packaged" in a new form. The encoding device is commonly called a *colorplexer*. A group of *decoding* circuits must be used in each television receiver to recover the original red, green and blue signals from the 3-variable signal which is available at the receiver's input terminals.

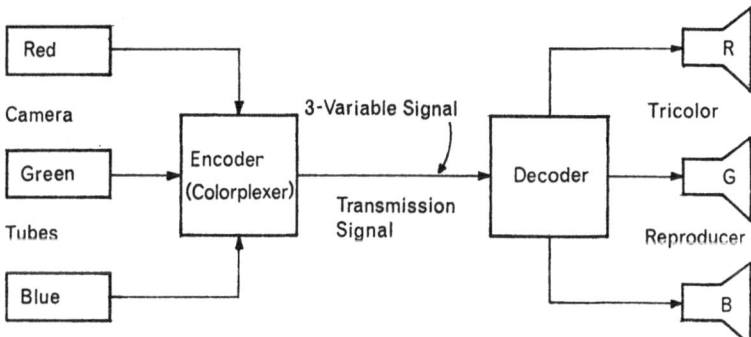

Fig. 1. Simplified block diagram of a color television system.

Encoding and decoding in a color system are also necessary to solve the *compatibility* problem, which has great practical and commercial significance for the broadcaster. Thanks to the *compatibility* feature in our color television standards, our color broadcasting service can "live in harmony" with the existing monochrome broadcasting service. The encoding process is handled in such a way that one component of the final signal is almost identical to an ordinary monochrome signal; this signal component is therefore able to render very satisfactory service to monochrome receivers. Conversely, color receivers are so designed that ordinary monochrome signals produce good monochrome pictures. As we shall see presently, a color signal must contain some extra information, over and above that contained in its monochrome component, but this extra information is "packaged" in such a way that it does not interfere with the normal operation of monochrome equipment.

Four basic electronic techniques are involved in the encoding of color television signals.

These techniques are known as matrixing, bandshaping, two-phase modulation and frequency interlace. Let us now review briefly what is involved in each of these techniques.

Matrixing and Bandshaping

A basic solution to the compatibility problem in color television is provided by simply adding the three primary color signals in a matrix circuit in the proportion of 30 percent red, 59 percent green and 11 percent blue. This particular combination of the red, green and blue signals forms a so-called *luminance* signal that is, for all practical purposes, equivalent to the output of a monochrome camera. This signal is often designated by the letter M (for monochrome), although sometimes the symbol Y is used. Since it requires a minimum of three independent signals to produce a color image, however, we must employ additional matrix circuits to produce two other signals (usually designated by the arbitrary letters I and Q), each of which must be a different combination of red, green and blue. The I and Q signals convey *color-difference* or *chrominance* information; that is, they indicate how the colors being transmitted differ from a neutral or gray of the luminance value designated by the M signal. At the receiving end of the system, the M, I and Q signals are again *matrixed* or cross-mixed to recover the original red, green and blue signals.

The matrixing technique not only solves the basic compatibility problem, but also makes possible the exploitation of a very important property of human vision. It is now well known that the human eye has much poorer acuity (or resolving power) for chrominance differences than for luminance (or brightness) differences, and that the resolving power for certain color combinations is much poorer than for others. The composition of the I and Q chrominance signals has been carefully chosen so that bandwidths allotted to these signal components can be greatly reduced without adversely affecting the final picture quality. In a television system, reducing the bandwidth has the effect of reducing the effective resolution, because the very rapid changes in signal voltage needed to reproduce fine details in the picture are no longer transmitted. In a color system, the bandwidth of the I signal is deliberately reduced to about ⅜th of the normal monochrome value, and the bandwidth of the Q signal is even more drastically reduced to about ⅛th of the normal monochrome value. In other words, most of the information related to color differences

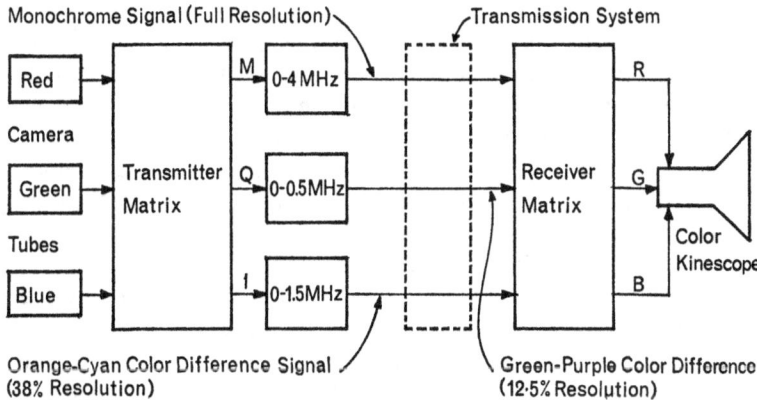

Fig. 2. Block diagram of a color television system, showing matrixing and bandshaping techniques.

in the fine details of the image is deliberately thrown away. This loss is of little importance, since the eye cannot utilize the discarded information at normal viewing distances anyway. The bandwidth reductions help to simplify the *multiplexing* problem; however, it would be far more difficult to fit the I and Q signals into the same channel occupied by the M signal if we were unable to employ the bandshaping technique.

Two-Phase Modulation

An important step in forming the single 3-variable signal required in a compatible color television system is the generation of a so-called *color subcarrier* by the two-phase modulation of the I and Q signals. We cannot simply add the M, I and Q signals for transmission through a single channel, because the three signals would lose their identities; that is, there would be no way to separate them again. If we modulate the I and Q signals upon *subcarriers*, however, we can transform them to time-varying waves which occupy different frequency bands so that they can be added together and later separated by tuned circuits or *filters*. Because of the very limited spectrum space or bandwidth at our disposal, however, it is desirable to process the I and Q signals in such a way that they form two *different* modulated waves at the same basic frequency. This type of signal transformation is made possible by two-phase modulation. Through a balanced modulator circuit rather similar to the modulator in a radio transmitter, the I signal is made to vary the amplitude of a carrier wave of approximately 3·6 megacycles. Meanwhile, the Q signal is applied to an identical modulator circuit where it produces amplitude variations in another carrier signal at precisely the same frequency (derived from the same electronic oscillator). There is an important *timing* difference between the two modulated waves, however; the carrier wave fed to the Q modulator is delayed by one-quarter of a cycle relative to the carrier wave supplied to the I modulator. Thus the peaks of the two carrier waves occur at slightly different instants in time, so it is possible to separate the two signals even though they are added together at the output of the modulator circuits.

Because precise *timing* information is needed in every color television receiver to separate the I and Q signals from the combined modulated wave, a special type of *synchronizing* circuit is required. Every color television receiver must have a *subcarrier oscillator* that is precisely locked in both frequency and phase to a master oscillator at the transmitting end of the system. The necessary synchronizing information for the receiver oscillator is transmitted in the form of a *burst*, a brief sample of the output of the master oscillator with a known time relationship transmitted shortly after every horizontal synchronizing pulse (during the horizontal retrace period). A special circuit in the receiver compares each burst signal with the output of the receiver's subcarrier oscillator, and makes any correction that may be required to keep the oscillator in synchronism with the incoming signal.

Frequency Interlace

The final technique involved in encoding a color signal is *frequency interlace,* a technique which makes possible the simple addition of the two-phase-modulated I and Q signals (that is, the color subcarrier signal) to the M signal without objectionable interference between the several signal components. Frequency interlace is accomplished simply by selecting a subcarrier frequency that is an odd multiple of ½ the horizontal deflection frequency, and then holding this precise frequency relationship by means of electronic counting circuits within the sync generator. The actual subcarrier frequency specified in the FCC standards is 3·579545 MHz, and the horizontal scanning frequency is related to this value by a factor of 455/2.

Frequently interlace is actually a means for taking advantage of the "persistence of vision" effect so as to make possible the transmission of two independent signals in the same frequency band. The color subcarrier frequency is so chosen that the *polarity* of the modulated wave added to the monochrome or M signal is automatically reversed during every other scan of any given area in the image. Thus, any undesirable effect that might be caused by the

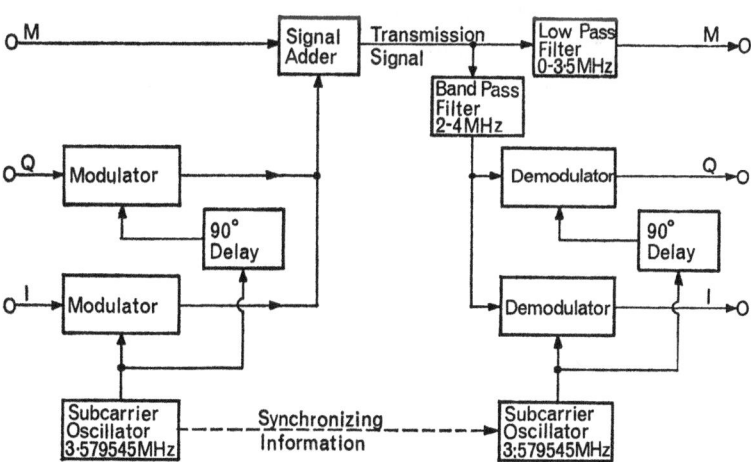

Fig. 3. Block diagram illustrating the two-phase modulation technique used in color television.

presence of the modulated wave is effectively cancelled out by the equal-but-opposite wave that appears in the same image area $\frac{1}{30}$th of a second later.

Handling the Color Signal

This brief survey has, hopefully, given you some insight into the manner in which a color signal is put together. Development of the color signal specifications was clearly a major landmark in communications engineering—few systems of any type have exceeded the spectrum efficiency of the American color television system. Experience over the past decade has shown that the technological foundation for color television is solid indeed. The system works, even in the demanding atmosphere of the American broadcast industry. It should be emphasized, however, that the price we have to pay for the efficient manner in which color television uses the broadcast channel is a high level of excellence in all signal-handling equipment. Signal distortions that might go unnoticed in a monochrome system can produce very objectionable degradation of a color image. The required quality standards are readily attainable, however. Those broadcasters who have always insisted on high engineering standards will have little difficulty in serving their audiences and sponsors with the improved type of service made possible by color television.

3 Color Television Equipment: Present & Future

JOHN T. WILNER

Vice-President for Engineering, The Hearst Corporation

In several introductions in this text, the term veteran *has been used to ascribe professionalism and maturity to the author of the piece at hand. Nowhere could we find better use of the ultimate* veteran's veteran *than in the case of John Wilner, who undertook this summation of color TV equipment. He was, from 1937 to 1949, a member of the CBS Laboratories, under Dr. P. C. Goldmark. During that time the original CBS flagship television station in New York was constructed, and the sequential color television system was developed. Also, a UHF transmitter was constructed, to demonstrate the feasibility of color television operating in the UHF spectrum.*

From 1949 to the present, John Wilner has been vice-president for engineering for the Hearst Corporation broadcasting stations, headquartered at the WBAL Stations in Baltimore. Station WBAL-TV, it should be noted, has operated with the present NTSC color system since the day the Federal Communications Commission approved that system!

In the following, Wilner brings into focus the rapidly changing developments in color TV engineering equipment today, and offers an informed picture of the compact, solid state future...

COLOR television may be described as black-and-white television with two additional parameters added, hue and saturation of color. Unfortunately, these two additional requirements cannot be added to just any black-and-white television system because of the stringent specifications that must be met to carry the color signal. Black-and-white television, while capable of transmitting excellent pictures, nevertheless has such a wide margin of error that the system must be optimumly adjusted in order to reproduce color faithfully. The only way to ensure that the television plant is capable of satisfactorily handling the color signal is to measure routinely and adjust the system with adequate test equipment and to do this often enough to take care of the drifting of critical circuits and the aging of the transmitter tubes.

A review of the possible causes of color distortion in a transmission system is in order. Some of the more important of these are: 1. frequency response; 2. phase characteristics; 3. envelope delay; 4. compression; 5. differential gain and phase.

1. *The frequency response* of the complete transmission system up to the transmitter should be flat to at least 6mc. In order to achieve this, each component part of the system should be considerably better. This is necessary in order to keep the phase distortion down at the critical color frequencies around 3·58mc. In monochrome, a loss in bandwidth at this frequency will only have a softening effect. In color, variations in response around 3·58mc could result in a marked effect on color fidelity. This will show up as a loss of color saturation and could possibly cause ringing.

2. *Phase characteristics.* A proper color television system depends upon the passage of all frequencies that are contained in the complex signal to have the same time delay. A system having poor frequency response can also have poor phase response. If the component frequencies do not have equal time delays the resulting color picture, after going through such a system, will have misplaced edges on the sharply defined vertical edges of the luminance portion of the signal. It will also affect the chrominance part of the picture, but this requires explanation of several additional causes of distortion which follow.

3. *Envelope delay.* Whenever there is a departure from linear phase or time delay in an RF system, there will be envelope delay distortion. This delay results from the unequal transmission of the upper portions of the modulated waveform. This results in an A.C.

shift at the axis causing phase shifting of certain frequencies. Envelope delay shows up as the separation or misregistration of the color part of the television signal from its luminance counterpart.

4. *Compression.* Non-linear transfer characteristics of a television system can be separated into two groups. The first is the system which is simply overloaded, i.e., too much signal being applied. In monochrome, the dynamic range of the transfer characteristic does not have to be as great as in color because in the latter the chrominance signal adds to the luminance, resulting in a greater amplitude. Thus, for example, the saturated yellow signal results in an overall signal which is 40 IRE units above 100 percent. Obviously, if such a signal is passed through an amplifier which was designed for monochrome, only this portion of the signal would compress and cause color distortion.

The second example of overload is where the transfer characteristic is not linear for an appreciable part of its dynamic range. This is typical and causes differential gain and differential phase distortion as explained in the following paragraph.

5. *Differential gain and phase.* A system which is capable of passing small amplitude signals in a satisfactory manner may, nevertheless, be unsatisfactory when a high frequency signal rides on a low frequency signal under various modulation conditions. Thus, if a 3·6mc frequency is added to a stair-step signal, it will be seen that if the transfer characteristic departs from the straight line, the 3·6mc signal will not be linearly amplified. This type of compression, called differential gain, is simply the ratio of the high frequency signal at various parts of the modulation characteristic. Differential phase can result under these conditions. Since these can occur during the non-linear portions of the transfer characteristic, at either high or low modulation, it is important that equalization be included to cancel these distortions. Differential phase affects the hue of a color as it appears under various levels of saturation. An example might be a person's face which may be adjusted for satisfactory skin tones, but will change in color if the intensity of the studio lighting is altered.

At this point it will be interesting to describe just how much distortion can be allowed when only one of the above parameters was changed, all other parameters being held to optimum adjustment. The amount that any single item could be changed before the observed picture degraded from "excellent" to "good" is listed as follows:*

(a) The primary color amplitude can be changed by ± 20 percent.
(b) The subcarrier amplitude could be changed by ± 30 percent.
(c) The M & I amplitude could be changed by $+40$ percent and -20 percent.
(d) The Q amplitude could be changed between $+60$ percent and -55 percent.
(e) The maximum phase error could be changed by $\pm 11°$.

Although it would seem from the above that the NTSC color system can tolerate large amounts of error, it should be remembered that the percentage of allowable errors falls drastically when simultaneous errors are present in a system.

Much of the equipment at a typical television station has been, up until recently, of the tube and external power supply variety. The introduction of transistorized circuits and soon-to-come integrated circuits brought to the broadcasting industry undreamed-of performance in circuit stability, reduction in size, and improved operation. While the older color components, by and large, are still capable of performing satisfactorily, they do so only with undue expenditure in maintenance and alignment time. The chief engineer, therefore, must face the inevitable decision as to when the best time to replace his equipment will be.

The remainder of this chapter will try to bring out the improvements in the following areas: 1. the transmitter and antenna system; 2. the program switcher; 3. video generating sources; 4. the drive and video amplifier system; 5. color monitors; 6. test equipment.

Audio equipment will not be discussed because of its relatively little effect on color. However, audio equipment components have also kept pace with the rapid improvements in stability and size and represent vast improvements over equipment that was available to this industry just a few years ago.

---

*Wiess IRE—September, 1954 *Significance of Some Receiver Errors to Color Reproduction.*

The Transmitter and Antenna System

Because of the relatively long life and expense of a modern television transmitter, few improvements have been made in this area in the typical television station. Thus, almost constant attention and adjustment are necessary to keep the transmitter in proper working order. Since just about all of the amplifiers in the modulator and RF stages are tubes, the constant deterioration in emission and transconductance mean that the greater drive and modulation levels need constantly be supplied, with the result that a battle between bandwidth and power is continually being waged. This battle results in variable frequency response, differential gain and phase, envelope delay, sync compression and power output. These conditions are more serious in the high band transmitters where higher frequencies and power levels are encountered.

Many of today's transmitters were installed during the time when monochrome was the typical signal being transmitted and many modifications had to be made for color. Some of the more important were:

1. *The clamping circuit.* The hard clamp on the back porch in the modulator had to be modified in order to preserve the 8 cycles of color subcarrier. Usually this subcarrier was removed, then the back porch clamped, and finally the color subcarrier was reinserted after clamping.

2. *Hum and noise.* In monochrome transmission the presence of hum and synchronous noise was not usually objectionable because it stayed in step with the 60-cycle power frequency. The advent of color meant that this type of noise had to be attenuated to at least −45 db because the sync generator was now locked to the non-synchronous color subcarrier. This required better regulated power supplies and usually a change from A.C. to D.C. on critical amplifier tube filaments. The next generation of transmitters will rely heavily on solid state amplifiers, eliminating much of the filament and hum problem in all but the highest modulator and RF stages.

3. *The transmitter.* The present day transmitter was originally designed for monochrome. This meant that the modulator characteristic was usually not good enough to take care of the greater

color signal swing, and the rigid requirement of lower phase distortion. Some pre-distortion in the opposite polarity was necessary to keep the differential gain and phase within allowable limits. It will be appreciated that the transmitter represents the area where the greatest video swings occur and voltage swings of 600 to 700 volts are not unusual. There are some transmitters, of course, which have lower modulation swings and are followed by RF amplifiers. In these transmitters, the major distortion is in the envelope delay area because of the additional RF stages. Differential gain and phase compensation usually takes place either in a stabilizing amplifier or the transmitter modulator itself and consists of the transfer characteristic being abruptly changed at three or four different places to cancel out distortion in the transmitter. This type of correction will probably remain in later transmitters. It is paradoxical that two uncomplementary requirements must be met in a television transmitter. In one case an extremely wide band response is desired and in the other rapid attenuation at certain frequencies is necessary to prevent out-of-band radiation. In order to satisfy both requirements, bandshaping filters are necessary, and the use of phase pre-equalization is mandatory in order to maintain satisfactory envelope delay characteristics. These equalizers only partially compensate and some distortion will remain. Equalization is also necessary to compensate for the sound-notch in the typical home receiver. It is more economical to pre-equalize for this condition at the transmitter than at individual receivers.

4. *Parallel operation of transmitters.* It has been found that the parallel operation of two half-power transmitters, instead of a single full power transmitter, results in a better transmitter from several standpoints. First, it is more reliable. If either half fails, uninterrupted service is maintained at a lower power. Second, such a transmitter is usually less expensive than a separate main and standby. Finally, and probably the most important, lower distortion of the transmitted signal is obtained. The frequency response, phase and gain errors can be additive or canceling, and it has been proven that the overall specifications of such a transmitter are better than the performance of either.

5. *Antenna system.* The commonly accepted SWR of 1 to 1·1 of the antenna system has proven satisfactory for color. With today's

COLOR TELEVISION EQUIPMENT 43

better antenna and transmission line manufacturing techniques and better test equipment it is relatively easy to obtain such a match. However, since most of the energy in a television system is contained in the region immediately around the carrier, it is now generally agreed that the best possible match should be at or near the carrier and a linear rise of SWR to 1·1 at the edge of channel can be tolerated.

The Video Program Switcher

The transmission of color through the studio plant results in several problems which were not present in monochrome. A few are summarized:

1. *Drive delay.* In the encoder the requirement that a filter be used in a luminous channel results in a delay of approximately 1·2 μsec. This requires that the sync which is added to non-composite color signals after switching, must be delayed by an equal amount. If monochrome signals are also present in the same switcher, all drives delivered to these cameras must be similarly delayed.

2. *The use of color* in an integrated switching system means that the sync generator locked to the 60-cycle power frequency can no longer be used. The sync generator must be locked continually to the color subcarrier and these drives must be delivered to both color and monochrome cameras, otherwise color and monochrome signals would be non-synchronous with each other and it would not be possible to superimpose these signals.

3. *In fading from color to monochrome,* color bursts or black burst must be provided as an input to the switcher, otherwise the fading of the color signal to black will result in a gradual loss of the subcarrier and the color will be lost during the fade. Some new video mixing equipment has automatic provision for maintaining proper burst during mixing and effects.

4. *Timing.* The timing between drives and video sources was touched upon above. In multiple studio operation or in a switcher in which various mixers and special effects are fed back into the switcher, it is important to time the system properly. The greatest

delay exists in the effects equipment, followed by the mixing equipment and, finally, the distribution amplifiers. If the output of a mixer or special effects is re-entered into a switcher, careful attention must be paid to provide proper time delays in the various paths of the system. If the path lengths are different, signals from various path lengths would appear displaced and could exhibit hue changes. Re-entry of mixer and effects signals in a switcher is very complicated and requires either switchable delays or automatic cross point reversing circuits.

Tomorrow's video switching system will be very sophisticated. The switcher will be unusually flexible and will contain audio control, video control, machine control, cut-bar operation, will operate during the vertical blanking interval, will automatically handle non-synchronous signals, will automatically maintain proper sync amplitude, will automatically maintain proper burst amplitude, and will work in conjunction with a memory system as part of an automated system.

Video Generating Sources

These will include the color film camera, the color live camera and the color videotape recorder. The greatest advance in these areas has been the introduction of solid state circuitry. Even in monochrome cameras and tape machines, the advantages have been striking. In the older tube type cameras, alignment had to be accomplished daily or even hourly. In the new cameras, alignment will be maintained for days and even weeks. The elimination of tubes and their resulting heat has made modular type construction feasible, which is now standard practice. These advantages, together with the better regulated power supplies, temperature compensated deflection systems, and the use of feedback have resulted in a hundredfold improvement in stability. It is entirely practicable for one man to operate as many as six film and live cameras.

These developments have also provided the same dramatic improvements in color cameras. All of today's color cameras have, to a greater or lesser extent, the following improvements:

(a) All are vastly more stable. Once aligned, these cameras

will stay in alignment all day long with only minor touch-ups.
(b) All are smaller, making it possible to place the camera controls closer.
(c) All use modular construction, making for simplified maintenance.
(d) All require less power, resulting in less heat.
(e) All are simpler to operate.

However, here the similarity ends. Of the four major color camera manufacturers, only one uses a $4\frac{1}{2}$ inch image orthicon tube as a separate luminance channel to achieve the best monochrome picture and to achieve the best sensitivity and resolution for the color luminance channel. The chrominance channel makes use o three vidicon tubes. The separate luminance channel provides for better registration and better monochrome transmission.

Of the remaining color manufacturers, all make use of the newly developed plumbicon pick-up tube developed by Philips of Holland. One camera uses three such tubes and a very simple color-separation optical system is possible. A minimum of in-camera circuitry is necessary. This camera is modularized and the camera control equipment takes up little space. The plumbicon tube, being more like a vidicon than an image orthicon, has the advantage of better signal to noise, lower dark current (minimum shading problems), and simplified control circuits, resulting in ease of operation. It suffers, like all vidicon tubes, from a somewhat softer picture, and does not have the agc type of action of the image orthicon. Horizontal and vertical aperture compensation can be used to improve the resolution, but at the expense of signal-to-noise ratio.

Other plumbicon cameras use the fourth plumbicon tube as the separate luminance channel. The fourth channel makes the camera somewhat more immune to misregistration difficulties. Offsetting this, however, is the fact that less light is available because of the additional optical splitting. The additional circuitry required for the fourth channel increases the complexity of the camera.

All four color cameras have been demonstrated to provide excellent color pictures with a marked reduction in lighting as compared to the original three-image orthicon type of color camera.

The two major color film camera manufacturers have used the same design philosophy. Both use a four-channel camera, both vidicons, which have become the film pick-up tube work-horse in the U.S.A.; both use automatic features such as black-and-white level control and have limited agc video gain control. Neither has truly automatic video gain circuits which will accommodate the extreme contrasts that exist in the available films and slides used in a typical television station.

Even more dramatic improvements have been introduced in videotape recorders. From the original recorder introduced less than ten years ago, that could only play back tapes made on the same type of machine, could not record in color, could not be locked to the station's sync generator, could not use any electrical editing, has come the present-day recorder which can do all the above and more. The present recorder is much smaller, is completely solid state, and produces superior results in every area. Tomorrow's recorder will see a switch to all high-band recording. This recorder uses a higher modulation and demodulation swing, resulting in an improved signal-to-noise ratio. This permits making dubs into the fifth generation or more. Improved color compensation circuits automatically correct for tip penetration, mechanical aberrations of the head and shoe, correction for minute variations of headwheel velocity, and others. This practically eliminates color banding and hue shift. The industry still requires, however, improvements in better headwheel assemblies and videotape.

The Drive and Video Amplifier Distribution System.

Today's distribution amplifiers are also completely solid state. Each has a multiplicity of outputs and is source-terminated to absorb possible reflections returning from the load. The drive amplifiers also have pulse reforming circuits which correct for deteriorated drive signals. These amplifiers are modularized, and a defective unit can easily be replaced. Input circuits have been compensated to cause minimum discontinuity in the line. The amplifiers usually have self-contained power supplies.

Typical results which can be obtained from today's pulse and video amplifiers are compared to those used previously:

	New Equipment	Old Equipment
Gain	1±6 db	1±1 db
Differential Gain	½ percent or better	2 percent—3 percent
Differential Phase	¼ percent or better	4°—5°
Frequency Response	10 mc ± ¼ db	10 mc ± 1 db
Power Requirements	2·5 watts	25 watts
Rise Time & Delay Time	100 n sec	250 n sec
Size	App. 100 cu. in.	200–500 cu. in. inc. P.S.

In some of today's color cameras the drive requirements have been simplified and only composite sync, blanking, burst flag, and subcarrier are required. The camera itself produces the remaining drives that it requires. Also, in some cameras the front porch of the output signal is compared and automatically inserts the proper delayed sync in its output signal. This eliminates the need for delaying the drives to the monochrome cameras. Modern sync generators can now accept composite video from external sources for gen-locking purposes. These sync generators can also be locked to an external subcarrier. Sync generators are available which take up as little as 1¾" of rack space. Only a few years ago a sync generator took up one full rack of space. Equipment is now available in which complete sync derivation is obtained from a single composite signal. All of the drive required for the cameras is obtained from this one signal. This allows for a simplified sync generator genlock and switching system.

Color Monitors

Up until recently it was common practice not to have more than one color monitor in a control room or studio because of the difficulty in making two color monitors look alike. The old color monitor suffered from the same problems as that of the older encoder. The NTSC color system depends upon separate signal circuits that are used for many of the processing functions. All of these individual paths are then combined into a single signal such as the encoder or separated as in the decoder. Hence, it can be seen how important it is that the phase and amplitudes of each separate path have the same phase and gain characteristics, otherwise the circuits could drift because of temperature or voltage instability. Today's color monitors have incorporated solutions to these shortcomings.

Test Equipment

Even a short treatise on color television would not be complete without some comments on adequate test equipment. It should now be apparent that the maintenance of the television plant requires test equipment and procedures of the highest order. A brief review at this point would be helpful.

1. *Sweep alignment.* In today's circuits where we deal with responses to within a $\frac{1}{2}$ db or better, a dual trace scope, an electronic switch, or a differential amplifier must be used to achieve this kind of precision. By looking at the output as well as the input at the same time and introducing known amounts of attenuation into one channel, this kind of response can be measured.

2. *Differential gain and phase.* A vectorscope or the stair-step generator technique can measure this type of distortion to about 1 percent and 1°. A Kelly test set, or its equivalent, will be necessary to go below these values. A fair approximation of how good amplifiers can be, would be to measure the differential phase and gain of approximately six amplifiers in cascade using the first procedure. Caution should be used in this interpretation because differential gain and phase do not necessarily add.

3. *Transient response.* A sine square wave and window signal is extremely useful to measure and adjust phase equalizers in a television system. The same sine square pulse is also useful to determine the condition of the entire video system. The sine square pulse should be adjusted for the correct width so that it can be faithfully passed through a 4mc system. Any deterioration in bandwidth, or poor phase characteristics, will show up as ringing of the sine square pulse.

A square wave generator delivering a 100kc square wave can also be used to adjust the phase equalizers at the transmitter. The harmonics of the 100kc square wave extend well beyond the pass band of the 4mc television system, causing ringing to take place. The equalizing equipment at the transmitter should be adjusted, one unit at a time, for equal amount of before and following ringing. This will provide the optimum adjustment to the system.

4. *Low frequency response.* The low end of the system should be good down to 60 cycles square wave per second. A 1 percent tilt in a 60-cycle square wave is considered satisfactory for minimum smear. With modern video distribution amplifiers a low frequency response to 10 cycles sine wave should easily be achieved.

5. *Signal to noise.* The use of a wide band VTVM capable of measuring in the mv range will be useful in making noise measurements. In some equipment it will be necessary to filter out certain frequencies which are contained outside of the band of the system in order to prevent erroneous readings.

6. A digital frequency read-out is a great help in making measurements on the single side band filter, traps, and point-by-point responses in the RF pass band. An FI set covering the particular channel will be necessary.

7. The remaining test equipment, such as tube and transistor checkers, general purpose oscilloscopes, a test set to provide multi-burst signals, sine square signals (referred to previously), window for smear measurements, a polaroid camera for taking reference pictures, are those found in a well equipped television station and will not be amplified further.

Tomorrow's Television Equipment

It has been pointed out how dramatically television equipment has changed to the present time. What about the future? Transistors and other discreet circuit components are now the standard design building blocks. Density of packaging has allowed shorter signal paths, making for better and more compact equipment. This has been obtained at the expense of maintenance cost and time. With tomorrow's integrated equipment, it will be all but impossible to repair most of these items. Throw-away boards will of necessity have to be used simply because the manpower cost of repair will make it more economical to replace the defective circuit.

Integrated circuits are just beginning to be used in sync generators. The sync generator certainly will be part of the future color camera and a single line will lock the cameras to the internal or external system. Integrated circuits will also drastically reduce the size of the future color camera, making it smaller than today's monochrome cameras.

With smaller and more reliable equipment, the television station of the future will be constructed around a basic package consisting of the switching system, the drive system, the audio, the machine control, the mixing and effects equipment and the memory system to store the day's program segments. Each of these subdivisions will be capable of unlimited expansion and flexibility. The live cameras, film cameras, videotape recorders, audio controls and monitors will merely be connected to this basic package. Self-checking circuits will tell the engineering department exactly what equipment needs attention.

The future television transmitter will be solid state up to the final amplifier. The sound and picture signals will probably be amplified in a single output stage, eliminating the sound transmitter completely. The transmitter will be remote-controlled from the studio with metering and logging being done automatically. Automatic alarms will instantly warn the operator that some part of the transmitter or signal needs attention.

The saturation and hue controls of monitors and home receivers will become automatic and this will be accomplished by automatic circuits at the station for precise control of the color phase. This will eliminate the annoying adjustments that still must be done at the home color receiver.

With tomorrow's television equipment getting so complex and compact, the chief engineer and his staff will have to become more technically oriented, with the result that the staff will have to be split into two categories; one: the technical men who will design, install, modify, and maintain this equipment; two: the others who will only operate the equipment and possibly be closer to the program operations than engineering.

II

Producing for Color Television

4 Color Production

E. CARLTON WINCKLER
Director, Production Standards and Practices,
Operations Department, CBS Television Network

A prominent TV industry researcher dramatized the problems of computer usage in processing audience measurement data with the slogan of GIGO—"Garbage In—Garbage Out!" The result, in other words, can be no better than the elements assembled to make up that result.

The lesson is particularly applicable in color television; the finest technical equipment at the point of program origination, and the best quality home TV sets at the receiving end, are of little use if the elements that make up the picture being taken and transmitted are of less than equal caliber.

E. Carlton Winckler, as director of production standards and practices for the Columbia Broadcasting System, has a major responsibility in the control and maintenance of that quality for his network. Before joining CBS (1951), he served as program director and production manager of ABC's western division, and in a similar position with the Mutual-Don Lee network in Hollywood. He came to television with a wide variety of theatre and motion picture experience, including stage production for the Paramount, Capitol and Roxy theatres in New York, and technical direction for 96 Broadway shows and several seasons of the Ringling circus.

In early 1967, on behalf of the CBS-TV operations department, Winckler presented the following materials before the Royal Television Society in London...

It should be noted that these words are offered on behalf of the Operations Department of the CBS Television Network, and represent the opinions and experiences of that group for contemplation and possible use by the reader.

It has been our experience that those encountering color television for the first time tend to exaggerate production problems out of all proportion to reality. Guidelines for color production practices have been fairly well established to help us in our planning. It is our purpose here to underscore these guidelines and so help to avoid production problems *before* they occur. (It is always hard, incidentally, to define "production", because every organization in our industry would seem to use different terminology to describe the various production functions.)

Guideposts in Color Production

In discussing production procedures for color, in noting things to avoid, or in setting up guideposts based on color experience, we ask the reader to remember that all of these points apply equally to film production, live programs, or to commercials—color reacts in the same way, regardless of its origin or purpose.

We must keep in mind that color is an added tool in television—providing a broader field of programming, making possible a more effective sales job, helping to hold audience attention more firmly, and increasing the impact of all of our presentations. *But* it is a tool—not a new world.

In pointing out that color problems are less complex than might be anticipated, and that most of them can be avoided, we do not wish to convey the impression that there are *no* production problems! There are. One of these problems is in teaching ourselves to look at color properly and to relate what we see to the eventual picture on the home receiver. Most home sets are not as carefully registered as the studio monitors, nor as well color tuned and balanced. This means that our mistakes are *magnified*, and it emphasizes the importance of being aware of some of the guidelines and rules for color television production.

Some readers have had extensive experience. Some have already learned that things which are of marginal quality or even just acceptable on the control room monitors under ideal conditions are definitely not good enough on the home receiver, and that the risks of using such marginal material should be avoided. We can pinpoint these things as an aid to future judgment.

Also, in our enthusiasm for color and exciting color pictures, we must not allow ourselves to forget the black-and-white picture which is seen by the majority of our audience!

Predicting the Color and Black-and-White Picture

As a starting point, let us state firmly that there is *no* mystery about how color reacts on the color television system or about how the color picture will appear on black-and-white receivers. This is entirely predictable—predictable *before* any material is brought into the studio. To do this you do not have to *un*learn anything you have gained by B & W experience—you simply add to this knowledge.

The color camera is actually three black-and-white cameras combined; performs very much like that earlier B & W unit. It is subject to the same rules and limitations. But it is still a *machine*; it has no imagination, no creativity, it only produces what it sees— the image you provide for it. No matter how good a camera is, the picture cannot be any better than the subject you devise.

The very fact that the color camera reproduces what is actually there—*without* any imagination—presents to the producer, the director, the designer, some important problems. Unlike the camera, we (our eyes) do not always see what is there—we see what we *think* is there! We have in our physical make-up a quality known as "approximate color constancy". Translated, that means that we are very stubborn—that we are determined to see familiar objects the way we *think* they are, regardless of how they *actually* are.

The familiar white shirt is the standard example of this.* We all know what a white shirt looks like and we always see it as white. Of course, the light illuminating that shirt may cause it to appear as one of several other colors: normal room lighting will probably make the shirt yellow; daylight will, of course, make it blue. But we still insist upon seeing it as the same white.

---

*In his chapter on *The Local Station*, Roy Bacus makes a good point of this, and with practical reasons.

The color camera does not have this "approximate color constancy" factor, and it sees the shirt as it actually is—*yellow* under the warm room lighting, *blue* under daylight conditions. When the camera presents these facts to us, we say that it is not reproducing the color properly—and all the time the fault is ours and the color system is just doing its job too well.

As we come to be more closely associated with color, we are very much surprised by some of the things we learn. We find that colors used on the color television system react in exactly the same way as colors used anywhere else. One color is affected by the color adjacent to it, or by the color in back of it, and by the temperature of the illumination.

The Awareness of Color Around Us

It is necessary for us to learn to look at color both on the television receiver *and* in everyday life. In life we rarely look at a whole scene; our eye leaps from place to place. We look at a single person, a sign, a car, a flower, but rarely at the whole panorama. When we attend a movie we rarely look at the entire screen. We tend to concentrate our vision on the star—her costume, a bit of ornament. Even when we talk to people we tend to look only at their eyes, their lips, or their ties.

However, when it comes to the small television screen we look at it as a single unit and we concentrate on it—and suddenly we see many things we never saw before. We see that the background appears softer than the foreground. We see the colored shadows. And we find, too, that face colors change sharply as the person moves about in front of different colored backgrounds or in different colored lights. All of this has been happening all of the time in real life, and we just didn't notice it and won't believe it when we *do* see it.

Testing on Camera: Fact or Fallacy?

Designers and producers are always asking to look at a color swatch or a costume on-camera, but considerable experience has proven that such so-called tests are entirely meaningless. The camera will reproduce the color of the costume or the color swatch almost exactly as it appears to the eye and, therefore, testing it on the color camera is purely a waste of time.

In making camera tests of any kind, the color in which you are interested should be surrounded by all of the other colors with which it will be used, and skin tone should always be included in the picture. Testing in this way is meaningful in that the viewer may now judge the total effect of surrounding colors upon each other and, in turn, upon the faces of the actors in the foreground.

There has been a great deal of discussion to the effect that the colors which can be reproduced by the color television system are very limited, and that many colors cannot be reproduced at all. This statement is, of course, entirely erroneous and without any basis of fact. Give or take small variations of the system and minor limitations in the response of the viewing tube phosphors, the color television system can reproduce quite faithfully almost any color which is presented to it. Recent developments in camera circuitry have removed many of the earlier limitations of color reproduction, and as these advances are being effected on a continuous basis, the results come closer every day to equating the response of the human eye.

Setting the Color "Mood" for the Audience

In presenting a color program on television, you encounter one element not present in movie house film or printed media: your audience, through set adjustment, can remix your colors! But don't be alarmed. In planning production for the tint TV system, simply bear in mind that skin tone is of paramount importance—this is used by the home viewer for adjusting his receiver.

Camera exposures, lighting (either natural or artificial), costumes, backgrounds: all should be considered in relation to their ability to complement the skin tones of the people appearing in the scenes. While it is obvious that there are many different kinds of skin tones (and all home viewers don't see them the same way), skin tone is still the only ingredient in a picture on which there can be some area of reasonable agreement. While the viewer's interpretation of the skin tone varies, this variation will be within a sufficiently limited range so that when using skin tone as a reference point in adjusting his receiver, he will not get too far away from original picture balance.

After all, the home viewer has no way of knowing the exact shade of the blue dress or red backdrop, and we must give him *some* point of reference.

Varying Coloration for Effect

If the program or commercial requires the skin tone color to be distorted for an effect, such as blue moonlight or the ruddy glow of a camp fire, *do* explain (visually) the source to the audience, so that they won't injure themselves falling over chairs in an attempt to get to their set to make a correction for a fancied defect that is—in reality—a fanciful *effect*. (Obviously, in the case of commercials, the faithful reproduction of the product color overrides the importance of adjacent skin tones.)

We must be aware that a bright color acts in the same way as a bright light; that is, it tends to become the center of interest in any scene in which it is used. Therefore, the bright color should be reserved for the center of interest in your scene—which is, usually, the action area or the area in which the product is presented.

All other areas of the scene should be slightly subdued in relation to the center of interest. This does not mean, however, that bright colors *must* be used in order to create a center of interest. This can be done naturally and subtly with the design of the set, the placement of the action, and the proper adjustment of the lighting.

Understand: we are *not* saying that bright colors should not be used. Often they are very effective and very natural; too, a diet of subdued colors can be dull—and if continued through scene after scene without strong color highlights and accents, the subdued colors become a bore. Conversely, a picture in which *all* of the colors are extremely bright and of maximum saturation has an almost monochromatic effect—because there is no opportunity for accents to increase visual excitement when every color in the scene is already at its highest key.

Use color as a music arranger uses an orchestration for creating

COLOR PRODUCTION

a romantic mood or one of gaiety, or in building to a smashing climax. Color is a wonderfully flexible tool when it is used with thought and understanding.

Use color naturally to produce a satisfying result for the viewers and to enhance the dramatic impact for the audience.

The Color Contrast Range

There is one very important point that we tend to overlook in thinking about color production, either live or on film—the matter of contrast range. The color television system has a very limited contrast range—about 20 to 1—and this is a most rigid restriction.

This contrast range of 20 to 1 means that the brightest spot in a picture must not be more than 20 times brighter than the darkest spot that you wish to reproduce legibly. To exceed this contrast range on the high side—to introduce pure whites or very bright reflective surfaces which exceed the top limit of the range—will almost invariably cause those areas to bloom or, at best, to lose all detail, in the same manner as black-and-white television.

Even if you decide to accept the loss of detail and to risk the bloom effect of pure white, the adjacent areas—especially faces and other important detail—will appear very dark in comparison and almost always adversely affect the scene. In color, this bloom will tend to be a wavering bright violet color of no particular form. Obviously, special care must be taken with high reflectance whites.

In place of pure white, use television white—which is actually a light gray with a maximum 60 percent light reflectance. (We have been doing this in black-and-white for years.) This will appear white on the color television system and on the resulting B & W picture. Don't forget that light yellows, light pinks, light blues and light greens are also high reflectance items—and that polished surfaces which *appear* very bright can range from starched or satin finished fabrics to chrome.

A side comment: it is interesting to note that jewelry—always a major problem in black-and-white—is quite practical in color, as the bright points of light are small and do not tend to disturb the system. Surprisingly, the black-and-white picture resulting from the color picture of jewelry is also acceptable.

Before leaving the matter of contrast range, it should be emphasized that the 20 to 1 range includes *everything* in the picture—the scenery, the costumes, the actors, *and* the lighting. This means that designers cannot individually avail themselves of the full range, but must allow room for the contribution of other elements so that the total effect remains within that 20 to 1 contrast ratio limitation.

Co-ordination for Net Result

Experience has shown that producing a good color picture is a co-operative operation between the video man, lighting director, and the design personnel. In order to permit each of these areas to make the most effective contribution to the final result, it is essential that the need for adjustments in any area be made a readily discernible factor to the person responsible.

The best procedure for making it possible for these craftsmen to do their job effectively is to set the cameras at the first rehearsal at a normal lens opening, adjusting the video properly for this lens setting, and then *not* making video compensations or corrections until the various craftsmen have had an opportunity to observe their problems.

For example, if the lighting director has an over- or underlighted area which will cause color picture problems, the video operator should not correct for this problem when it appears on-camera during the early fax rehearsals, but should leave the video setting at its normal point and allow the lighting director to correct his intensities for proper picture presentation.

Similarly, the various design groups should have an opportunity to make their corrections—rather than having the video operator attempt to make the adjustments for them. It is not possible for the video operator in color to correct for all of the production elements in a scene which may not be in satisfactory harmony: in attempting to make these corrections, the video man is forced to provide a series of compromises that cannot possibly result in maximum picture quality.

While the final result of this procedure will be a better color picture with fewer broadcast hazards, it does impose upon the director of the program the discipline of looking at a less-than-perfect picture in the early rehearsal stages!

Color versus Brightness Contrasts (The Lost Blonde!)

Continuing the study of contrasts, there is another point of which we must be very aware: color versus brightness contrasts.

Everyone will admit that red and blue are contrasting colors, and will appear so on color television. However, if both the red and blue selected happen to be of the same brightness value—that is, if each reflects the same amount of light—they will appear on monochrome as the same shade of gray. It is very important that the hues selected as components of your picture differ in both color and brightness value—something so basic that it sounds like everybody's speech on color television. But such problems of translation of color to black-and-white really do occur, as in this actual example:

The subject was a glamorous and well-known star—honey blonde hair, peaches-and-cream complexion, dressed in a soft gold lamé gown, standing in front of a blue background, flanked by two yellow and two pink panels. This made a strikingly lovely color picture and we were all delighted until we looked at the black-and-white monitor, where we discovered that the honey blonde hair came out a No. 3 gray; the peaches-and-cream complexion was a No. 3 gray; the gold lamé gown was a No. 3; the blue background was a No. 3; and both the yellow and pink panels were Nos. 3!

In actual fact, the black-and-white screen was nearly blank, having only rather vague shadows moving about.

This was our own fault, because there is no mystery in how colors are going to reproduce on the monochrome system. The various color notation systems—especially the Munsell Color Notation System—relate all of the colors directly to the standard gray-scale values: through the use of these systems, comparing the colors in our designs in the planning stage with the Munsell gray-scale equivalents, we can tell fairly accurately how our monochrome picture is going to look.

If we do not wish to go to the trouble of running down each color in the Munsell system, approximately the same result can be achieved by making an accurate color sketch of our plans and having samples of costume fabrics on hand; then viewing sketch and fabrics for comparison with a gray-scale through a 2·0 density glass, which effectively reduces all of the colors to reasonable equivalents of the gray-scale and makes comparison not too difficult. (Incidentally, do not attempt to use the density glass under fluorescent light. *No* color judgments should be made under fluorescents—either in selecting colors or in viewing results on the tube. Fluorescent light has an interrupted color spectrum; as a result it tends to distort color response.)

Color Production Co-ordination

In planning the color production, it is recommended that one of the show staff, knowledgeable in color, be appointed as a co-ordinating agent, to assure a unified and harmonious approach. The need for greater communication and co-ordination between all of the contributing areas in the production of a color program should be obvious, since all items in the color picture are related and interdependent.

Unless each contributor is well aware of every contribution of his associates, clashing colors and major inharmonies are bound to result. The best way to avoid this is to talk to each other and keep each other fully advised of plans and of any changes made in them. Even though a preliminary meeting has been held, and designs and color schemes selected, there are many times when the execution of these designs is undertaken and the material is being obtained, when some element—such as a costume—will prove to be unobtainable in the color desired. The costume which *is* available in the proper size, period and material may be of a contrasting color. This means that the background planning may have to be changed; this change may, in turn, affect the dressing or other elements of the production. It is well to approach production planning by determining any objects in a scene which are beyond your control, and making those uncontrollable objects the key to the color design.

For example, the clothing of your principal personality may determine the background to be used; or some familiar object—such as a Coca-Cola machine which is of a particular brilliant red—may be the uncontrollable object and determine the surrounding decor. If your program area is to be recorded on videotape, it must be noted that any large area of a highly saturated color may tend to

COLOR PRODUCTION 63

show visible banding. Less-saturated color or simple design inventions will usually avoid this problem.

Color Lighting

Lighting for color is of extreme importance, but no different from that required for black-and-white except that a consistent color temperature of approximately 3,100° Kelvin—plus or minus 250° Kelvin—should be used and, of course, a higher volume of light is required for the color camera. The volume of this light will depend upon the type of camera being used.

As in black-and-white television, and all types of film work, close attention should be paid to shadows. Hard shadows—that is, shadows into which you look and see no detail—should be avoided as they represent a hole in the picture and may be subject to a deposit of spurious color, or may take on the complementary color of the surrounding area. All shadows should be transparent: that is, shadows into which you look and see some detail. Converting a hard shadow into a transparent shadow is extremely easy, as it involves only the addition of a small amount of fill light.

Color Commercial Production Points

In designing commercials, it is of basic importance to remember that the representation of the product or the product's name must be the center of interest and must be highly visible. Good, strong contrast between these items and the background is essential. At least two steps of brightness contrast and of color contrast are recommended. No spot of color brighter than the product should be in the frame with the product, or the bright color will be the center of interest rather than the product. Rather high contrast is recommended for commercials: surveys by leading optical organizations have pointed out that high contrast tends to increase the apparent legibility.

Particular attention should be paid to the size of the lettering or objects. On the color system, objects less than eight percent of the vertical screen height are not sure of legible reproduction.

Most commercials will be produced on motion picture film, and good quality film reproduces very well on the color television system. Naturally, in film commercials, the objective should be to produce good skin tone, so that the home viewer may properly evaluate the other colors present. Other than times when a special effect is called for, it is well to avoid scenes which are too dark; they will appear dark on the system and the commercial will lack visual impact.

In making any film product, it is essential that the same film stock be used throughout: the different film stocks—Ektachrome, Commercial Ektachrome, Kodachrome, Anscochrome, Technicolor—have different dyes, and when intercut will present very distinct color differences.

The maker of film commercials should be especially aware of the film standards published by the networks and adhere to them carefully, as the effectiveness of his commercial is greatly affected by its adjacencies. He may well give serious thought in his production planning to the problem caused by adjacent film which, in most cases, will not be under his control. Most of the problems encountered to date with film commercials have been caused by the preceding film rather than by the quality of the commercial production.

An outstanding example of this adjacency problem was the case of a network special in a cartoon format: a long snow and ice sequence of great brilliance was followed instantly by a commercial that opened with a night exterior, with the camera moving slowly into a candlelight party. While the commercial production and film quality were excellent by comparison with the bright preceding scenes, the whole commercial appeared so dark as to be ineffective. This might have been helped by starting in black for a few seconds and fading up to the night scene. But starting a commercial with a night scene without a goodly proportion of light areas is usually dangerous, unless the adjacent film is carefully understood and the transition planned in advance.

In Summary

Color television is not mysterious; the rules are quite clearcut. The key to success on the production side is simplicity and good taste, with plenty of pre-planning and full communication between all concerned.

In color, it is the final result that counts—the overall production result—the harmonious, inter-related whole that brings the intent of the scene to the viewer with strength, force, and, finally, pictorial beauty.

5 Colour in the Studio

A. R. STANLEY
Project Engineer, Television,
British Broadcasting Corporation

In many of our introductions "pioneer" has been used to dramatize the industry veteran status of the contributors. For the North American reader, the term evokes images of wagon trains, Indians on the warpath, the fording of rivers and the panning of gold.

Londoner A. R. Stanley—some thousands of miles removed from the Rocky Mountains and with his scalp intact—nevertheless must be identified as one of our band of broadcast pioneers. He has been with the British Broadcasting Corporation since 1944, except for two-and-one-half years' Royal Navy service as an instructor on airborne radar.

From the Sound Control Rooms of the BBC, Stanley moved to the Alexandra Palace television operation in 1949. In 1952, as experimental engineer, he assumed responsibility for introduction of technical innovations and non-standard technical requirements; in 1955 was put in charge of a team assigned the development of operational and production colour television techniques. (Editor's note: due not *to pioneer status but to place of birth, Mr. Stanley is one of two contributors permitted to write "color" as a six-letter word.)*

In the late 1950s, Stanley assisted in the technical planning of the BBC Television Centre at White City; in 1960 returned to colour activities. When the start of the British Colour Television Service was announced, he rejoined the

BBC's television projects section to help plan the development of colour facilities.

In the following, he has distilled experimentation logged, lessons learned, skills to be employed, for anyone approaching the production end of colour television...

Introduction

Most people seeing colour for the first time are enthusiastic and when they come to do their first colour programme, become first hypnotized and then obsessed by the colour. There is a definite tendency to use far too much colour indiscriminately and to ignore completely the fact that for many years yet the majority of viewers will be receiving the compatible black-and-white picture. Because of these viewers it may sometimes be necessary to abandon special colour effects, or to modify certain shots which may be exactly right in colour, but meaningless or very poor in monochrome.

In trying to make a general comparison between colour and monochrome production it might be as well to consider some of the specialist skills which go into the making of a television production and try to highlight some of the differences and similarities between the special requirements for colour and monochrome.

Lighting

The two main requirements of lighting for television, colour or monochrome, are to create the atmosphere demanded by the production, and to meet the technical requirements of the system: it is essential to meet the second in order to achieve the first.

Because the light entering the camera is to be shared between its three or four tubes, the colour camera is less sensitive than a monochrome camera and higher lighting levels have to be used in a colour studio. Modern colour cameras are considerably more sensitive than they used to be, but even today it is necessary to use two to three times as much light for colour as for monochrome. This in itself presents problems, as the higher lighting levels are more difficult to achieve and control, but provided that the increase in level is not more than two or three times, e.g. from 50 foot candles to 150 foot candles, it is possible to achieve by the substitution of bigger lamps: to use 5kW spot lamps instead of 2kW. Unfortunately, higher power lanterns are bigger and heavier, thus increasing the difficulties and time spent in rigging and setting. Recently more efficient quartz iodine lamps have become available and because of their increased efficiency, smaller size and weight for a given output, this particular problem may be somewhat eased. Many modern cameras now employ plumbicon type tubes (these tubes are not currently used in most monochrome television studios). With such a camera which has a linear characteristic, there is no fixed point of correct exposure and, within reason, if more light is available, it is possible to use it either by stopping down the lens and gaining a greater depth of field; or by reducing the gain of the amplifiers in the camera channel which results in a "cleaner" or more "noise-free" picture. The converse is equally true—if less light is available the camera can be correctly exposed by opening up the lens aperture and suffering reduced depth of field, or by increasing the gain of the camera channel and suffering a "noisier" picture. It is not possible to apply this principle at very high or very low light levels, as at high levels there might be insufficient beam current to discharge highlights, and at low levels the picture becomes degraded not only by "noise" but by an increased tendency to lag.

Some colour cameras suffer from polarization error; that is, they have a different colour response according to the plane of polarization of the light entering the lens. The most troublesome effect of this failing is a miscolouration of hair or polished surfaces, onto which the light is falling at an acute angle. In particular, back light glancing off the hair into the lens can be so polarized that the hair appears to be green. This is such a disturbing effect that it has been suggested that back light should not be used for colour productions. This, however, is a defeatist attitude and is in any case unrealistic, for what is a back light from one camera position becomes the key light for another camera position. It is usually possible to correct this camera failing by the inclusion of a "quarter wave plate" in the main optical path, and in any case this polarization error only occurs in some colour cameras. Good lighting requires back light to rim the subject, to give depth, added contrast and definition. This is true for photography and black-and-white television as well as for colour.

Lack of back light makes both the compatible black-and-white picture and the colour picture flat and lifeless. They both lose sparkle and depth, although this is more noticeable in the black-and-white picture, which does not have the additional information given by the colour. As with monochrome, backlight intensity is mainly dependent on the subject and it is quite possible for the backlight of a certain subject to equal or exceed the intensity of the main key light.

The need to match cameras is common to both black-and-white and colour, but the requirement for colour is much more critical. If lighting intensity varies over the acting area, movement within this area necessitates iris compensation to maintain correct exposure on the person moving. All static components of the scene however, which might well include other artists, will either be under- or over-exposed according to the direction of the iris compensation. This may result in colours at the extreme ends of the luminance range undergoing a colour shift, whilst the intermediate values are subject to a brightness change. Even illumination is more difficult at the higher lighting levels needed for colour.

A fully flooded 5kW lamp will give 300 foot candles at a distance of 13 feet with a coverage of approximately 11 feet. Whereas a 2kW light gives 50 foot candles at a distance of 26 feet, with a coverage of 27 feet. From these figures it can be seen that lighting to the higher levels required for colour demands lamps closer to the subject and/or several powerful hard sources perhaps, to cover an area where one would be sufficient in a monochrome studio. To achieve the higher intensities required for colour by moving a few feet nearer the source can result in an intensity change of 100 foot candles, and the use of graduated wires may be found necessary to even out the light distribution. With the lower level lighting for black-and-white, lamps can be placed further away, giving more even illumination of the acting area.

Other ways in which lighting could cause mismatching are:

1. Spill from coloured light sources falling onto the acting area.
2. Uneven illumination of a backing intended to have an even reflectance value and colour.
3. Lens flare causing the picture to "sit up".
4. Reflected light from painted floors.

5. Reflections from highly saturated surfaces falling on the face.
6. Variation of colour temperature over the acting area.

Points four and five are mainly a design problem, but a slight shift in the angle of a light can at times make a great improvement. In point six we referred to "colour temperature". Energy leaving a heated "black-body" has a distribution dependent on the temperature, and at certain temperatures some of the radiated energy falls within the visible light spectrum. An incandescent lamp may be regarded as a "black-body" and its energy distribution may be described by its "colour temperature" expressed in degrees Kelvin. At low temperatures there is a lot of energy at the red end of the spectrum and not much blue energy. As the temperature increases, the amount of red energy falls and blue increases. Typical colour temperature values are about 1,950°K for an ordinary candle, 2,500°K for a domestic 100 Watt tungsten filament vacuum lamp, 3,150°K for a typical studio spot light, 3,400°K for a photoflood lamp. Daylight colour temperatures can vary greatly, but in average, noon, direct sunlight may be about 5,000°K and average daylight about 6,400°K.

The colour of an object is dependent on the spectral distribution of the light source illuminating it. We have seen that this spectral distribution may be expressed in terms of the colour temperature. If there is a variation of colour temperature between lamps illuminating different areas of a scene, a noticeable colour shift will occur as the camera moves between the two areas. Under critical conditions it is possible to detect a colour change due to a difference in colour temperature of 100°K; however, under normal conditions a difference of at least 150°K is needed to produce a noticeable difference. Modern television studios are equipped with lighting consoles, and dimmers are used extensively for controlling the light output of luminaires. With filament lamps, control is exercised by varying the voltage: reduction of voltage reduces the operating temperature of the filament, resulting in a reduction of colour temperature. With 240 volt tungsten filament lamps, a 15 percent drop in voltage reduces the colour temperature by about 150°K and the light output by approximately 40 percent. Although we use dimmers for special effects and lighting changes in monochrome; for the most part, they are used to adjust the contrasts in the picture, and to balance background and artist lighting. If the back lights are too intense, or the background is too light or too dark with respect to the artist, the appropriate lamps may be dimmed down until a more pleasing picture is obtained.

Within the technical limitations of the system, either the lamps illuminating the background or those aimed at the artist's face may be adjusted. In colour the artist's face is all-important, and only limited variations of colour temperature of the lamps illuminating the face can be permitted. So in balancing the lighting, greater use is made of the dimmers controlling lamps lighting the background. In balancing the picture by use of dimmers, the need for even illumination must not be forgotten, for, as we have seen, the lighting director cannot rely on the iris to even out variations in the lighting level over the acting area to the same extent as in black-and-white.

Even illumination should not be interpreted as flat lighting. Although the level of illumination must be uniform, the lighting contrast may be controlled to give the required variation between highlight and shadow. To achieve even illumination the lighting director must know the exact action within a set. Pre-planning of a production is of crucial importance. It should be accurate and observed more strictly than in a comparable black-and-white production, as a change of plan takes longer to deal with because of the heavier lighting rig. Above all, the understanding and co-operation of the design and production staff are essential.

Make-Up

The viewer has little or no knowledge of the actual set or costume colours in the studio, and as long as they are reasonable and pleasant, even if incorrectly reproduced, they will be acceptable and the errors will not be immediately apparent. However, flesh tones are known and recognized by the viewer and if these are not reproduced satisfactorily, the whole colour picture will be judged unsatisfactory. Make-up for colour is thus more demanding than for black-and-white, as many more factors are involved in the correct reproduction of skin tones.

Unless it is excessive, variation in skin type between artists is accepted more readily in colour than in black-and-white, although a close-up of a dark skinned man and a fair skinned girl will accentuate on the screen the difference in flesh tone. In the colour picture such things as "five o'clock shadow" and discolouration under the eyes are less worrying than in monochrome, where they create dark shadows, but they will probably need attention because of picture compatibility. A bad five o'clock shadow may tend to become blue and over-emphasized by the colour camera. Colours concentrated into the small area of the television screen can appear stronger than is natural. In particular, a red, bucolic, male face faithfully reproduced can appear most unrealistic. The problem of male make-up in general is difficult, for if a man's face needs to be completely made up, it requires skill on the part of the make-up artist and also a great deal of time, if the man is to appear natural and not look "made-up". If a male make-up does not look natural, it would probably have been better not to use make-up at all. In general, male make-up must be approached with caution and only attempted where essential. One kind of make-up for men, however, which is required for colour and not for monochrome, is ear make-up. Back light falling onto the artist can often illuminate the ears from behind and make them appear excessively red, and make-up is required to eliminate this effect—with women the hair usually covers the ears and this is not necessary.

A summer tan usually reproduces well, but the more delicate "pink-and-white" complexion can sometimes be troublesome. Usually with this sort of colouring the skin texture is very fine, blood rises to the surface more easily and the pinkness is exaggerated. Whilst it is usually sufficient to make-up faces only for black-and-white, it is often necessary for colour to make-up neck, arms and hands also.

Skin of course varies from person to person and also in difficulty of accurate reproduction. If a foundation has been on the face for some time, skin acidity may change the colour to give a "muddy" look. Eye shadow needs to be applied more sparingly; in particular, blue and mauve eye shadow appear over-exaggerated and these colours should be only used with care. Red in the skin often tends to be exaggerated. The natural red content itself can rise, due to nervousness, or warmth from the lighting. Skin tones can also be affected by coloured light reflections from nearby colours—perhaps a bright dress or a scarf. This can be acceptable if the object causing the reflection can be seen by the viewer, or if its existence has previously been established. Skin tones and, in fact, any colours, look different when surrounded by other colours, especially if these are strong. Skin tone appears to be biased towards a complementary colour. For instance, a cherry-coloured background tends to make skin look greenish, whilst a strong blue background makes it appear yellow.

The cost of make-up for colour is inclined to be higher than for black-and-white, due to the need for better and finer foundations, lipsticks and eye shadows. The cheaper ranges of cosmetics tend to be garish and must be avoided. Fashion changes particularly affect lipsticks and eye shadows, and stocks of these need to be changed frequently to keep up-to-date.

Although it is a little easier to conceal wig joins for colour, the matching of texture and tone of extra hair has to be more accurate with finer gradation of colours. This calls for more time in the making of hair pieces and consequently earlier booking of artists.

Greater liaison between make-up specialists and those in design, lighting and costume, is advisable in colour, as many different effects can be achieved by the change of background or colour of lighting and, of course, the actual clothes the artist is wearing. In make-up, as in every other field, the requirements of the compatible picture limit the degree of control which can be applied to the colour picture.

Costume

The costume supervisor's job, like everyone else's, is more exacting for colour than for black-and-white. For black-and-white it is only necessary to match costumes and accessories in terms of the grey-scale. For example, pink gloves may be used with a blue dress and, although the colours are different, they appear the same tone on the black-and-white screen and are quite acceptable. In colour the mismatch is immediately obvious. The costume supervisor is well aware of the time and money that can be saved in black-and-white by the use of unmatched colours of a similar tone, which appear matched on the black-and-white screen. This is not possible for colour. Furthermore, it is quite possible that certain colours which appear as an approximate match to the eye may appear most unsatisfactory on-camera.

For the designer, the colours chosen must fall within the contrast handling capacity of the system. It is obvious that costume colours cannot be considered in isolation, but must be chosen in close collaboration with the set designer. Early discussion and planning are essential to avoid costly mistakes. Dirty or faded costumes, which might be quite acceptable in monochrome, look just what they are in colour. Artists must be dissuaded from wearing their costumes to the canteen. The odd spot of gravy on the corsage of a beautiful ball gown does show in colour; in fact, all sorts of detail seem to show more through the colour camera. Possibly because of the extra depth and realism, wayward shoulder straps, uneven hems, dark underwear shadowing through light blouses, bulging suspenders under tight skirts, all seem more obvious.

In many instances it is necessary for artists to wear their own clothing. In these cases it is highly desirable for the costume supervisor to see the clothes for herself. To be given a verbal description of the colour of a dress in such terms as "shocking pink", "poppy red", or "grass green" can be very inexact and may mean entirely different colours to different people. If it is necessary to describe a colour to someone, it should be done by reference to an approved colour notation, such as the Munsell system, and the same notation should be used by the set designer and other members of the production team. Although it is said that the dominant colours should be worn by the artist to attract attention, strong colours must be used with restraint, due to the problem of reflections affecting flesh tones.

Design

Besides providing a suitable setting, as with lighting, the designer must help create the mood demanded by the production, and work within the technical requirements of the system. It is common for the designer faced with colour for the first time to expect the addition to complicate his job to an alarming extent. This it should not do. Black-and-white television is almost invariably designed in colour; it is only that the choice of colours is more critical for colour television. In choosing his colours the designer must bear in mind the contrast range of the system. Although the contrast range for colour is approximately the same as for black-and-white, the effect of exceeding the contrast range is far more marked in colour. The camera is normally exposed for correct reproduction of the artist's flesh tones, and if excessively bright, high reflectance colours or objects are used, these will be over-exposed. This over-exposure can affect the three or four channels of the colour camera differently and so give rise to false colours in highlights. In a black-and-white studio the exposure on the artist's face is less critical and if such over-exposure does occur, it will generally only result in "burning out" and loss of detail of the over-exposed area. Many modern colour cameras employ plumbicon tubes, and under certain circumstances when such cameras are panned across any area giving an excessive over-exposure, the highlight becomes stretched out into a form of elastic comet tail. This can be particularly disturbing if the comet tail is different for the three or four tubes, thus giving rise to a coloured comet tail. At the other end of the scale there may be lack of detail in the darker toned colours in black-and-white, but in colour, incorrect reproduction of the colours is also very likely. There may be occasions when colours, materials or objects outside the normal range have to be used. If differential lighting can be employed between the acting area and set walls, the lighting director can often be of great assistance by reducing the amount of light on areas which are too bright, or increasing the light on areas that are too dark.

Any strong colour which appears in the colour picture attracts the viewer's attention and is liable to become the centre of attention. Therefore, the use of strong colours must be considered very carefully. This can, of course, be used for effect, by deliberately choosing brilliant or strong colours for areas where emphasis is required. Problems can still arise: take for instance a scene where an artist in a fawn costume is sitting on a grey settee. In long shots the use of brightly coloured scatter cushions could look quite natural and pleasing, but if the camera now takes a medium close-up of the artist including one cushion, the cushion will become the centre of attention instead of the artist. It is unlikely that such a thing could happen in black-and-white, unless perhaps the cushion had a particularly bold and striking pattern. Except for deliberate effect, relatively subdued, subtle or neutral colours should be used for sets, with the colour concentrated on the artist. This is particularly important for drama productions where the object is realism: if strong colours intrude, realism is lost.

In choosing a colour scheme for a particular production the designer must bear in mind that there is considerable variation in colour taste between individuals. There is no "ugly colour" or "beautiful colour" except in the eyes of the beholder. Fortunately "taste" in colour, as in anything else, is governed by fashion, so we tend to get a majority agreement, but we are left always with some divergence of opinion. If a designer employs a very unusual, modern colour scheme, he may well find that it does not agree with the taste of the majority of the viewers. However, the viewer may be unprecise in attributing his dislike to the colour scheme and may refer to the whole picture as a bad colour picture. Indeed his dislike may become even more general and he may react against the programme as a whole. In other words, we have introduced another possible divergence from the "all popular" programme.

In selecting his colour scheme the designer needs to remember that the colour receiver should be balanced to a colour temperature of about 6,500°K. If viewed in isolation in a completely darkened room the eye rapidly adjusts to this, as it does when one goes from artificial lighting into daylight. However, if the viewing room is illuminated with normal incandescent lights and the eye is adapted to the lower colour temperature of these, the colour receiver is likely in comparison to appear too blue.

The designer must be prepared to soften down props and dressings which become obtrusive when seen through the colour camera. This could mean covering a white tablecloth with black net, or moving a colourful vase of flowers to a more distant, shadowy part of the set. This is only an extension of the normal activity of the designer in black-and-white television, where he is constantly on the look-out for objects obtruding unnecessarily into the picture. With colour it is not only the shape and position of objects, but their colour and colour contrast with their surroundings, which have to be watched. Props and dressings which have to be selected with particular care, are gilt objects—furniture or picture frames for example —which may tend to appear green rather than gold. Leaves of any greenery which appear too dark may need to be sprayed for a more realistic effect.

Much can be achieved, especially in light entertainment, by the use of coloured lights, but for maximum effect close co-operation with the lighting director is essential. Reflections from highly coloured surfaces may affect make-up, although the effects may be alleviated by lighting. Apart from the need to concentrate attention on the artist, the colours of set and costume must be complementary and must not clash. So once again we see the need for much more pre-planning and co-operation than is necessary with black-and-white. The designer must, like everyone else, be constantly aware of the effects he is producing on the compatible picture as well as on the colour picture.

Production

Once again attention must be shared between the colour picture and the compatible black-and-white picture. It is quite possible to compose a colour picture, to balance the composition with dominant colours—and produce a completely unbalanced compatible picture. However, the converse is much less true. A picture that is well composed in black-and-white almost invariably produces satisfactory colour composition. It is therefore no great disadvantage to find that the colour cameraman is supplied with a black-and-white viewfinder, although it is necessary for the director to remember not to give his camera directions with reference to the colour, "Pan to the girl in the red dress". There are occasions when the moods of the colour picture and the compatible picture can appear very different. Apart from the obvious cases where a green cast may be used to create a sinister mood, blue a cold mood and red or yellow a warm mood—all of which are completely lost to the compatible viewer—this can be equally true of a picture which contains a fair amount of colour, such as a sky exterior viewed through a window. This may appear as a nice blue, typical of a sunny day, in colour; whereas in black-and-white it may appear dull and stormy, due to the low luminance of blue.

The higher intensity of lighting required for colour and the necessity for even illumination make the lighting director's task more difficult. It should be complicated as little as possible by last minute changes of camera position, shooting angles or artists' positions. In both monochrome and colour there is always the problem of matching cameras so that, in cutting between them, vast changes are not apparent. Nowadays a very high standard of matching is achieved for black-and-white cameras, but even closer matching is necessary for colour, as the eye is far more critical of colour changes. Apparent colour changes are not necessarily caused by differences between cameras. They can be due to a number of subjective effects. A pale foreground object may be biased towards a complementary colour, when placed against a stronger coloured background. If the next camera shot is a close-up which largely eliminates the colour background, this subjective colour bias will disappear and an apparent colour change may be noticed. Similarly, two cameras cross-shooting with different coloured backgrounds may produce a different subjective colour bias on the same foreground.

It is possible to maintain the interest in a colour production with fewer changes of shot, presumably because there is more information to absorb the viewer. Cuts from one scene to another, especially if they contain different strong colours, can produce a shock effect. This should be avoided, unless shock is the intent. Mixes are equally satisfactory in colour and black-and-white, and although superimposition produces a mixture of colour, this is objectionable only very occasionally. It is perhaps easier to differentiate the two separate pictures in colour than in black-and-white.

Programming

Although these points must be borne in mind for a colour production, they cannot be allowed to affect the pace and style of a production too much or the compatible production will suffer. This apparent difference in pace may turn out to be one of the stumbling blocks to achieving colourization of existing monochrome productions. A compatible black-and-white picture is likely to be less "contrasty" than that obtained with black-and-white cameras (lower gamma). In attempting to achieve a satisfactory colour production, the nature of the compatible monochrome production may be changed. *The Black and White Minstrel Show* relies quite heavily on high contrast pictures with bright whites and deep blacks, although these are just as often achieved with coloured costumes as with true black and white. The contrast range is a deliberate strain on black-and-white cameras and needs to be modified slightly for the colour cameras. This, together with the less contrasty reproduction of the compatible picture, produces a somewhat different, although perhaps equally acceptable, result.

The same production makes extensive use of effects lanterns which cast sharply defined patterns and shadows on the floor or backcloth. These particular lanterns are not powerful enough to produce a satisfactory effect at the higher intensities required for colour; either alternative lanterns of increased power must be found or this particular type of effect will need to be produced by other means or abandoned.

When a *Come Dancing* programme was televised in colour, the need for more pre-production planning and supervision was very apparent. Yellow must have been a very fashionable colour at this time, for both teams of formation dancers chose an almost identical yellow for their costumes, and amongst other dancers taking part, there was a fair sprinkling of lime green to yellow dresses. When people were not dancing, they sat around the dance floor and their dresses tended to form a yellow out-of-focus background. The overall effect was somewhat confusing, boring and lacking in colour contrast, with everything tending to look yellow.

When considering which programmes should appear in colour, most people think first of gay, light entertainment. There is no doubt that these programmes benefit greatly from the addition of colour and they are probably the easiest programmes to produce satisfactorily for as long as the colour is harmonious, it need not be absolutely exact. A satisfactory compatible picture may not be so readily obtained. Programmes on subjects such as cookery and art are much improved by the addition of colour, but it must be remembered that the additional information is no more present on the compatible picture than it was when the programme was produced in black-and-white. Drama is probably the most difficult field for colour television, since the aim must be realism and the intrusion of unnecessary colours will destroy this illusion. This applies equally to situation comedies and documentaries, which are very akin to drama in this respect.

Production Problems: Film

It is common practice to insert film sequences into studio productions: in black-and-white it is seldom obvious to the viewer when he is watching filmed or live action, or when the producer cuts from one to the other. Colour reproduction obtained from the various film stocks all vary slightly, and all are different again from that obtained from a colour camera. 35mm. film is normally used in black-and-white for insert work because the quality is higher than 16mm. However, the cost of colour filming is so much more expensive that there is a very strong bias towards the use of 16mm. film to offset some of this increased cost. A great deal of work is currently being carried out on methods of improving the basic film stocks and the colour reproduction of these stocks. One correction can vary any colour bias in the film, at either the dark end or the light end of the scale, independently, whilst another form of correction can improve saturation and correct luminance errors. By the use of these devices, it should soon be possible to match film to studio almost as well as in a black-and-white production, although no correction can be applied for badly shot, wrongly exposed film. There is still the problem of the inferior quality of the 16mm. film stock which is being partially offset by improved film stocks with better resolution and less grain, and also by improvements to the film scanners. Although it is unlikely that 16mm. film will ever equal the quality obtained from 35mm., it is hoped that the degradation will only be slight. There is of course another factor in the use of film and that is the much reduced sensitivity of colour film stocks compared with black-and-white stocks. The limitation of this is quite obvious: it is necessary to use wider lens apertures with restricted depth of field and higher lighting levels.

Production Problems: Back Projection

Another aid to production commonly used in the studio is back projection, either still or moving. Due to the lower sensitivity of the colour cameras, more powerful and efficient projectors need to be used. A large increase in power is seldom possible and it is therefore necessary to restrict the size of the screen. Fortunately, recent improvements in the sensitivity of colour cameras mean that screen widths of up to about 15 feet are possible with more or less normal monochrome projectors, and this is large enough for most productions. There is a definite problem in matching back projection film or slides into the studio foreground and several approaches are possible, i.e. specially balanced prints, use of coloured filters or low colour temperature carbons and even the use of coloured screens. So far, separate experiment and balancing have been necessary every time back projection has been used. No clear advantage for any one method of correction has become obvious, and it is possible that the eventual solution may be the combination of all three methods.

There is no doubt that everyone's job is a little more demanding in colour and the automatic response is a plea for more time and more staff. Although some slight increases may be necessary, every effort should be made to meet the extra demands by greater efficiency. By careful pre-planning and better, closer and more complete co-operation between the various departments, costly and unnecessary mistakes can be avoided. A colour production is bound to cost more than its black-and-white counterpart, but by careful planning and more efficient operation the extra cost should not be more than 10 percent to 25 percent depending on the type of production, and the production should give at least a corresponding increase in pleasure to viewers.

6 Color Film Production for Color Television

JOHN M. WANER
Eastman Kodak Company, Motion Picture Film Dept.
Chairman of the Color Committee
Society of Motion Picture and Television Engineers

In the very early planning stages of this text, we came to the realization that a chapter on color film vis-à-vis the TV medium was of utmost importance. "Definitive, authoritative, encompassing the knowledge and experience of the entire industry," we wrote to three different expert sources, asking each to suggest a person or persons who could produce the desired information in this degree of professionalism and completeness.

When all three sources said, in effect: "Why don't you use that report made by John Waner and his group before the SMPTE?" we could only conclude that there was but one path to follow.

The following chapter, as credited to John Waner and associates on the Color Committee, represents the happy result of this search. It appeared in the May, 1964, Journal of the Society of Motion Picture and Television Engineers *(Vol. 73, No. 5), and is reproduced here with the permission of the editor of the* Journal.

The report first was made before the April, 1964, Technical Conference of the SMPTE, in Los Angeles, by Edward P. Ancona, Jr., for John M. Waner, chairman of the SMPTE Color Committee and executive with the Hollywood Motion Picture Film Department of the Eastman Kodak Company.

Representing the eighteen-man sub-committee, the Waner report is as follows . . .

COLOR FILM PRODUCTION FOR COLOR TELEVISION

THIS presentation is intended to furnish practical suggestions for the production of color motion pictures for color television, and is offered to enable production personnel—such as directors of photography, set and costume designers, etc.—to ensure a more effective translation of their skills and artistry into the final picture as received on the home television set, irrespective of whether the reception is in color or black-and-white. It is only by proper understanding and control at all stages in the production of color film for television that the optimum relation of the photographic art with the technical requirements of television can be achieved.

Much of this material is equally applicable to photography with black-and-white films for presentation on black-and-white television systems.

These suggestions take into account the limitations of the systems involved in the process of reproducing an original scene onto the home receiver while still permitting the use of economical procedures throughout.

Considered use of these suggestions should contribute to the accomplishment of the following:

1. better and more consistent gray-scale reproduction on home receivers.

2. enhanced sharpness and detail rendering on the home receiver.

3. minimized need for corrective video adjustment in transmission.

4. minimized variations in the negative in order to simplify production of quality prints.

5. better matching of color balance and contrast among various types and sources of prints.

6. the presentation of pleasing pictures with as wide a brightness and color gamut as possible.

The procedures to be used in making color motion pictures for television are similar to those used for theatrical production, but with certain variations. As in theatrical film production, the best professional guidance, equipment and methods are to be recommended if successful results are to be obtained.

Television System Characteristics

From a technical standpoint, it is important to recognize certain properties of the television system that necessitate control in the making of a film print suitable for color television transmission. Among these are the following:

(a) Control of transmission (video control) is directly related to the extremes of highlight and shadow densities of each scene of the print. The control of these densities must be exercised at various stages of production, starting with the design of sets and costumes, followed by lighting of the scene and exposure of the camera film, to the making of the print.

(b) Lowlight (shadow) reproduction suffers in television transmission and reception through a combination of effects: flare in the projector optics; incorrect "black-level voltage" adjustment; flare in the receiver picture tube; but primarily, incorrect receiver brightness setting by the home viewer, and ambient light falling on the home picture tube, tend to degrade the delineation of detail in the darker areas of the images. Careful control of the print shadow densities by use of proper techniques in stage practices and photography will improve detail of these darker areas.

(c) Home color television viewing utilizes characteristically small viewing angles in which the eye can make extremely critical color judgments; furthermore, the high degree of color saturation available in the television system often tends to exaggerate any color mismatches. Additionally, because of constant reference room illumination, usually not a factor in theaters, the home viewer cannot readily accept changes in program color balance, thus necessitating increased accuracy in color balance from show to show, or even from station to station. Therefore, color prints for television demand scene-to-scene color timing at least as accurate as the high standards applied to theatrical release prints.

Color Film Characteristics

Conversely, certain properties of color films and the manner of their use in television affect the degree and type of controls that can be applied.

(a) In a black-and-white print, printer exposure (print density) and the extent of development (contrast) may be altered to assist in obtaining a density and contrast range optimum for television. In color printing and processing, such modifications are not easily available, or controlled, and may produce undesirable side effects, such as changes in color balance or saturation and failure to produce a uniform gray reproduction from white to black.

(b) The problem of consistent color balance throughout an entire show becomes particularly acute in some instances; for example, in reel-to-reel balance, and particularly in those cases where commercials, trailers, etc., which are printed at one laboratory are undercut into the main body of a show printed at another laboratory or printed on a different type of release print material.

Observations of trained technicians indicate that undercut print material, including reel-to-reel differences, should be within approximately ± 0.04 log E (approximately a ± 0.05 color correction filter) in color balance differences and ± 0.04 log E (approximately ± 1 printer point) in density variations.

Recommendations for color balance for the various intercut components of the show (or from show to show) cannot be made in terms of densitometric readings of a neutral test chart, since various dye systems represented by different film products will rarely result in the same visual appearance of a neutral object when faces have been timed to match, and, conversely.

An approach to the solution of this problem of balancing intercut print material includes correlation among laboratories by means of exchange of representative material or careful co-ordination by the consumer among his several sources of supply.

(c) It is important to recognize that the reproduction of the original scene by the film in regard to hue, saturation and brightness range is not necessarily required to be exact; it is usually required only that it be "pleasing". Where more exact color reproduction is required, as, for example, in commercial product packages, it is suggested that a photographic test be made. The test should include the product package, a normal face and a gray-scale, if possible. Ideally, the evaluation of such a test would include closed-circuit viewing of a timed color print, either from the original negative or from a duplicate negative if a duplicate is required to produce the commercial.

Since there are certain colors and combinations of colors which cannot be accurately or even approximately matched by a film-and-television process, it may be found necessary, if a close match is required, to photograph a "dummy" object (with changed or enhanced color) to obtain a reproduction which matches the color of the original.

(d) In the day-to-day production of television films, a great number of variables enter into the images appearing on the negative from which the final prints are to be made: shooting may be done in bright sunshine, or on overcast days; different types of lighting units may be utilized from time to time on different sets; an almost infinite variety of sets, set decoration and wardrobe will be encountered; and a wide assortment of different flesh colors will be seen in the various actors, guest stars and extras appearing in the scenes. Superimposed on all this are the different artistic expressions in lighting and staging which are employed by the photographers and directors; and the economic and time limitations which may, in the last instance, influence and sometimes limit the scope and quality of the final result.

Additionally, there are usually variations in camera exposure, small variations in color balance or contrast between different emulsions or between different film manufacturers' products and variations in processing from day to day.

Obviously, the particular densities of various areas shown in a color print, which is a record of the brightness and color of corresponding subject areas, are not a property of the print alone; they are the end-product of a sequence beginning with the materials (that is, wardrobe and set selection, make-up, etc.) on the stage, and including the intensity, type and distribution of lighting, negative exposure, negative processing, printing and print processing.

Color prints are timed and balanced in a laboratory on the basis of subjective viewing by direct projection. However, in view of the few controls which it is feasible to employ in color printing (primarily density and color balance for scene-to-scene correction), it is the intent of this chapter to emphasize that *the most effective way to control the quality of a television print is to exercise control in the stage practices.* Therefore, the following includes a description of some practical stage techniques and procedures that will make possible production of prints that will meet the limitations of the complete system.

Stage Practice Recommendations

The images on a color film may be considered to consist of two independent *visual* components: first, the gray-scale or brightness (luminance) values, and, second, the color (chromaticity) values. Of the two, the brightness component is the more important factor to be controlled in the photography for optimum television reproduction. This brightness component becomes the signal displayed by black-and-white receivers tuned to a color broadcast, and it is the chief parameter monitored during the picture transmission by the video operator. Therefore, if high quality picture transmission (video operation) and optimum gray-scale rendering (good highlight and shadow detail and effective placement of face tones) are to be easily obtained, then the integral density range of the print must be controlled within a certain range as dictated by the limitations of the color film and color television systems.

The film densities are a direct function of the reflectances of the elements that are photographed, of the intensity and distribution of light and of the camera exposure. Control of these factors results in a negative from which satisfactory prints can be made.

Reflectance of wardrobe, set decoration and title artwork materials should be controlled to eliminate or "gray down" the lighter whites and to avoid the darker tones where any texture or detail is to be seen. For color television photography using professional color motion-picture films, it is recommended that the reflectance of important fully-illuminated objects be held between 60 percent maximum and 3 percent minimum.

Neutral reference material of these reflectance values* are useful for evaluation of wardrobe, set, or artwork reflectance values.

The brightest element in any scene (excluding a few glints or areas smaller than about 1 percent of the area of the photographed image) becomes the "reference white" of that scene, and is adjusted

---

*Such reference material can be obtained from the Munsell Corp., 2441 N. Calvert St., Baltimore, Md.; and Container Corporation of America (Ostwald), 11 S. Dearborn St., Chicago, Ill. Approximately 60 percent reflectance is equivalent to a Munsell N8.0/ or an Ostwald C. Approximately 19 percent reflectance is equivalent to a Munsell N5.0/ or an Ostwald G. Approximately three percent reflectance is equivalent to a Munsell N2.0/ or an Ostwald P.

by the video operator or automatic video control to 100 percent signal voltage.

The recommended maximum reflectance of 60 percent is intended to apply to any fully illuminated white object which will be the "reference white" of the scene. (This might, for instance, be a white collar in a medium close-up, a white tablecloth in a long shot, etc.)

If the reflectance of this element has been properly controlled *during photography*, then face tones and other scene elements will have good placement on the gray-scale and will have optimum color saturation.

If any object in the scene becomes brighter than the recommended "reference white" it will either lose texture and detail in its reproduction or will, by action of the video control, become an improperly high "reference white", causing the remainder of the scene to be reproduced unnaturally dark and with low contrast. On the contrary, if the scene does not contain a "reference white", action of the video control may choose an improper reference point, causing the scene to be reproduced unnaturally bright and with too much contrast. (*Note:* this factor is more important in systems using automatic gain control.)

Almost any scene will have shadowed or unilluminated black areas, and these black areas (excluding areas of less than about 1 percent of the photographed area) become the "reference black" of the scene and are normally adjusted by the video operator or automatic video control to zero percent picture signal voltage.

The recommended minimum reflectance value of 3 percent is intended to apply to any fully illuminated dark areas or objects in which detail is to be seen and which are to be identified as *lighter* than "reference black".

If the brightness of the dark areas in which detail is to be seen is properly controlled *during photography* with respect to the darkest (unilluminated) blacks, then the shadow detail of the image will have good visibility on the receiver. In a scene containing a proper "reference white", any objects or areas darker than a fully illuminated 3 percent reflectance object will be reproduced with little or no contour or detail and will not be distinguished or separated from the unilluminated blacks.

Furthermore, with "whites" and "dark areas" controlled as

outlined in the preceding paragraphs, the resulting color print will transmit with a minimum of picture transmission (video operation) problems.

One of the most important considerations that arises in shooting color films is that, at least in the next several years, a majority of the receivers tuned to a color broadcast will be black-and-white receivers. It should be noted that materials which have contrasting colors might have similar brightness values in their reproduction on a black-and-white receiver, and therefore, have very little effective separation or contrast. In addition to providing good color separation or "color contrast" on the stage, therefore, care should be taken to provide good brightness separation in lighting and in choice of set decoration and wardrobe.

Effective brightness values of colored materials may be estimated after some experience by viewing the materials through an approximately 2·0 neutral density filter. The effective brightness values that will actually appear in a black-and-white receiver can of course be seen by a closed-circuit evaluation from a timed color print.

If dailies (rushes) are made on black-and-white release print stock from a color negative, it should be noted that this stock produces what is, in effect, a "blue separation" equivalent and, therefore, does not give any indication of the tone or gray-scale reproduction to be seen later on black-and-white receivers as transmitted from the final color print. Additionally, such dailies are an inadequate medium from which to judge make-up, wardrobe and other color values. For day-to-day evaluation of exposure, set color values, lighting, etc., it is suggested that color Cinex (or timed pilot) tests be obtained if color daily rush prints are not made. To answer questions with respect to overall photographic quality of the production, that is, with relation to costuming, make-up, etc., it is often desirable to make timed color dailies on selected scenes.

For television generally, and color television in particular, faces are the dominant point of interest, and the small viewing angles require that the natural highlighting and contours of the faces be preserved. Make-up should enhance these natural features of the face, and excessive flatness of make-up is neither necessary nor desirable. Even though, in real life, people have flesh tones of greatly different color and intensity, there is less viewer tolerance for such differences under the restricted conditions of home color television viewing. Therefore, make-up should also be used to reduce such differences except, of course, where racial or other particular characteristics are involved.

It is not within the province of this chapter to state rigid specifications for such a highly subjective factor as flesh tones; however, as a guide line it can be stated that, for effective color television reproduction, the average reflectance of properly made-up flesh tones will be approximately less than one-half of the recommended value of 60 percent reflectance given for the "reference white". Thus the film densities (or range of video voltages) produced by face images would be near those produced by images of 18 to 25 percent reflectance reference materials which were photographed in the same illumination.*

Lighting Recommendations

A "fully lighted" day interior scene should employ a lighting ratio of about 2 to 1 (key light plus fill light, to fill light alone) in the key position. This ratio is somewhat lower than that typically used for theatrical photography (although still commercially acceptable for theatrical release) and is advisable to control contrast range in order to avoid a loss of background shadow detail in television transmission and reception.

To assist reproduction of facial detail, backgrounds should generally be held down in brightness, i.e., to be less bright than the face tone. This means that background illumination in a set of average reflectance should be about one-half of the foreground illumination.

The low lighting ratios and restricted subject reflectance that have been recommended are not meant to imply that the picture should be "flatly lighted". Higher lighting ratios can be employed for effect: night scenes may use very high ratios, and backlight and modeling give a sense of sharpness and saturation to the picture. The use of specular, rather than diffuse key light, will provide better highlight detail and enhance image sharpness. Therefore, it is

---

*For a more detailed description of make-up techniques, a suggested reference is *Elements of Color in Professional Motion Pictures*, published by the Society of Motion Picture and Television Engineers.

suggested that the two types of key light should not be interchanged between scenes, particularly on cut-back scenes. Although the range of recommended *subject brightness* is somewhat limited, the photographic artist can have a wide freedom to employ many different lighting effects. Whenever the actors are walking around on the set, it is advisable to keep the faces in as constant illumination level as possible; when a departure from this condition exists, it is preferable to have the faces pass through an area of lesser rather than greater illumination.

Exterior day scenes will contain many elements of uncontrolled brightness, such as white clouds and unilluminated shadow areas. Here it is essential that supplementary lighting be used to bring face tones or other points of interest up to correct relationship with the brightest parts of the scene (the "reference white"); this will then represent the best compromise for control of this type of situation. The color temperature of this supplementary lighting should approximate that of the surrounding daylight illumination.

Night effects are best obtained by adjustment of the lighting contrast rather than by shooting "day for night" and "printing down" (overprinting). The ideal night effect photography for television would result in prints that have the same density range as a print for a day scene. The use of little or no fill light on the key position, sketchy background illumination, lighted windows, etc.— all create the *effect* of a night scene without the necessity of "printing down" the particular scene. This technique will eliminate the need for special cueing and minimize the need for making video adjustments.

Although "day for night" scenes are generally not recommended for an optimum night effect on television, economic and physical limitations in production will often prohibit the shooting of the more effective but more expensive "night for night" scenes. Therefore, the following paragraphs outline procedures which can achieve effective results from "day for night" scenes.

(a) To create the illusion of night, two of the essential requirements for any exterior night scene are that the sky should appear dark and that shadow areas appear generally without detail. In black-and-white photography this is partially accomplished by the use of a filter that darkens the blue sky. In color photography, the sky can be darkened in some instances with a polarizing filter. Other techniques would include the use of a graduated (or "wedged") neutral filter, or selection of a camera position that avoids having the sky in the frame. (These techniques might limit the staging, but should be strongly recommended by the cinematographer if the illusion of the night scene is to be maintained.)

(b) The color negative should be under-exposed from one to two stops and the natural or supplementary lighting should create an effect of high-contrast lighting. The inclusion of a lighted window or lamp (or warmer color) in the scene will assist in creating the illusion of night. It is desirable to "break up" the direct sunlight and artificial illumination with random patterns to emphasize the lighting contrast subjectively associated with night.

(c) It is often traditional to print night scenes colder (blue) to enhance the night effect. If this is desired, it is best done by print timing in the laboratory and not by omitting the recommended daylight conversion filter during the photography with tungsten balanced films. In some combinations of 16mm. photography and printing, scene-to-scene color timed prints may not be readily available, and the cinematographer should consider this in his original photography.

It is important that the different sources of illumination which are used to light and fill the faces are essentially equal in color temperature. The exceptions would constitute the cases of special effect lighting, such as "warm" firelight or "cold" backlight in night scenes.

The use of a professional color temperature meter is helpful and advisable; however, care should be exercised in reading light sources which have emission characteristics different from tungsten lamps, which have a continuous or "black-body" type of radiation. In particular situations where unusual types of light sources (such as fluorescent lamps) are employed, it would be desirable to make a photographic test.

In the event that special color lighting effects are desired, unless a "normal" reference of proper illumination is included in the scene, the final print will generally be color timed to eliminate the desired effect, or the effect could be inadvertently eliminated by the video control operator or home viewer.

COLOR FILM PRODUCTION FOR COLOR TELEVISION

Title artwork and animation exists in one plane and is lighted with completely flat illumination. Here, subject reflectance alone determines the subject contrast and the artist should use nothing lighter than a 60 percent neutral reflectance material and, where "shadow" detail is to be seen, nothing darker than a 3 percent reflectance material. Areas darker than 3 percent reflectance (equivalent to unilluminated areas in a stage setting) may be used for effect and should be used in at least a small portion of every scene to establish a "reference black" for the video operator.

Titles often use "burn in" letters over artwork or an action scene. These "burn in" titles are considerably lighter than a *photographed* 60 percent neutral reflectance material and, therefore, constitute an improperly high "white reference" that can result in a desaturated or flat reproduction of the underlying artwork or action scene. If effective reproduction of the underlying scene is considered to be important, the title letters should be printed as a *color* or as a white no brighter than the recommended "reference white".

Although the above has described procedures which are most adaptable to day-to-day television film production, it is not intended to imply that more extensive controls should not be applied in photography, printing or television transmission. Photographic exposure and lighting contrast could be controlled to a high degree of accuracy by use of a spot photometer; the laboratories could apply densitometric control of scene-to-scene highlight densities; contrast control of color films may be made practical some day; or specialized systems of video control could be developed.

Conversely, it is realized that in day-to-day production, owing to physical or script limitations, it is not always possible to adhere completely to these recommendations. Under such conditions, the photography should follow the recommendations as closely as possible.

There is no sharp dividing line between color prints which would be generally regarded as acceptable for television and those which would be considered unacceptable. The particular recommendations for color television films which are described above represent observations taken from films with scenes which did reproduce well on a typical color television system. Deviation from these recommendations should be accompanied with caution and should be undertaken only if a particular effect is desired or if tests show that good color television reproduction can be obtained from such films and that they can be printed and intercut properly with films which are known to transmit successfully.

Summary

Certain factors in color television film transmission and reception have a direct bearing on the effectiveness of the reproduction of a color motion-picture film.

Considering these factors, it is desirable (1) to limit the density range of the color print and (2) to include a "reference white" and "reference black" in the scene.

The recommended maximum and minimum reflectances of fully illuminated materials which are to be reproduced with good detail are 60 percent for whites and 3 percent for blacks (with existing film products and techniques).

For a fully lighted day interior scene, a lighting ratio of 2 to 1 is recommended. Higher ratios may be used for special effects and night scenes.

It is emphasized that the most important, practical and effective way to control the density range of the color print is in the *staging* and *photography*, rather than in the final printing.

7 Public Service Programming in Color

WARD L. QUAAL
President, WGN Continental Broadcasting Company

Entertainment and public service programs produced at the WGN Continental Broadcasting Center in Chicago are seen in all sections of the nation and in many foreign countries as well—parts of a continuing effort in all areas of programming that has brought WGN to a position of dominance among the country's television stations.

Ward Quaal came to the leadership of the WGN stations in 1956, continuing a distinguished career that included service with the Crosley Broadcast group and a period of industry service in Washington. Under his guidance, WGN has achieved an enviable place in the ranks of commercial television outlets, be they network affiliates, O & O's or independents, and acquired a roomful of awards and trophies for service to the public and to the industry in doing so.

Of the trunkful of Quaal personal credits, I am stubbornly insistent in citing his willingness to assume the presidency of Chicago's Broadcast Advertising Club, and his quick revitalization of the group, shortly after his return to that city!

In the following chapter, Quaal calls on the experience of several WGN associates in "documenting the documentary", detailing his station's actions in the creation and production of a number of award-winning public service programs.

THE advent of color brought a new magic to television programming *along with* new problems and a need for larger budgets—especially in the all-important public service area where the "stage" offers the challenge and where remote originations and film are involved.

Color has great appeal for the public service program producer as well as for the public. Color television multiplies the impact of anything he does, and—in exactly the same way—it multiplies his problems.

To address the realities of the subject, I have called upon several of my associates who must cope with and resolve the challenges of those problems on a wide variety of assignments. Writer-director-producer Frank Hart comments here on a few typical ones:

"The problems develop from every phase of production activity, ranging from the simple business of moving a cumbersome color camera from one position to another during a show, to the intricacies of 'gray values' when a show will be seen both on color and black-and-white sets. Two very simple and basic situations which occurred in the early days of color broadcasting on WGN-TV will illustrate the sort of hidden problems a producer finds and solves only by experience.

In one case, a simple science experiment on a children's show failed miserably. The principle behind the demonstration was an elementary matter of air convection currents moving a paper spiral when it was held over a lighted table lamp. The demonstration worked beautifully in rehearsal; it flopped on the air. The difference lay solely in the fact that, during the broadcast, the force of the air currents set up by the bright lights required for color television overwhelmed the currents set up by the table lamp.

On another occasion, a piece of humorous business in the same show hinged on the obviousness of a phony control button, painted salmon color, on a gray machine. To the eye and the color camera, the button was perfectly visible from 50 feet across the studio. To the color-blind black-and-white set, the button was completely *invisible*. The gray machine and the brilliantly-tinted button had exactly the same gray value. Even in a close-up, the button was invisible. Since the payoff of the sketch hung on a marionette accidentally bumping against the button and starting the machine, the entire episode would have been meaningless to the viewer with a black-and-white set.

The dozens of details like these are, of course, solvable; experience teaches all personnel where to watch for them and how to handle them when they arise. But like any problem in any industry, they add to costs, manpower requirements, time—and general wear and tear on the producer's nerves."

Color brought a delightful new dimension to all of our television programming, but in the area of public service originations it has posed some very perplexing problems for writers, directors, producers, cameramen, and the engineering department. Primarily these involve lighting and the placement and movement of equipment.

Our *Chicagoland Church Hour* series of remote originations from churches within the Channel 9 signal area encounters some basic problems which we are obliged to solve in one way or another on every assignment. Woodrow Crane, WGN Television's chief engineer, notes them as follows:

"Most churches are 'black'—meaning that they have grossly insufficient light for our purposes. Ideally, to save unnecessary expense and work, we try to park our huge semi-trailer color remote truck within 150 feet of an electrical power source. Also, because our color TV cameras are connected by cables to the truck, we prefer to be within 250 feet of the church.

Then we must determine how best to microwave our signal from this point of origination to the reception 'dish' back at the studios.

And finally we must make sure that the heavy (325 pounds) and bulky color cameras can be moved into the 'staging' site. Since it takes four men for each camera—each one handling 80 dead-weight pounds—we must avoid long hauls and steep, narrow stairways and tricky turns.

However, provided sufficient electrical power and a proper location for our remote truck, TV cameras and extra lighting gear, we can deliver a picture from anywhere, even though the 'stage' is pitch black. It should be pointed out here that a color television camera is more sensitive than a color film camera; as a result we can get an acceptable picture with less lighting.

The same basic problems prevail for virtually all remote originations."

In a television studio and in most modern indoor and outdoor public arenas, adequate lighting (and power for lighting) is available, handy and controllable, and there are special provisions for the placement and mobility of the equipment.

Public service "specials" and documentaries captured on color film offer more promise for the future than any other type of television programming today. This type of program is not only gaining in importance, but is commanding more and more of our prime-time periods. "Specials" and documentaries of all sorts are being applauded by the critics and welcomed by the audience.

Here again, to be truly competitive the feature on film must be in color—and with color we are achieving greater dramatic impact as the art day-by-day is advanced by experience.

Under the most ideal circumstances, a public service "special" or documentary filmed in color must of economic necessity be produced on a limited budget—"limited" by the standards of Hollywood and the large film production companies. Yet ironically, *what* we produce is judged by the highest standards of the film industry, where by comparison there are generous time schedules and almost unlimited budgets.

For the color feature on film the "stage" provides the initial challenge, whether that "stage" is a hospital, an art institute, a university, a government installation and operation, a seaport or an historical site.

Since film, generally, is used for out-of-studio productions—frequently outdoors—light is an endless problem. The high overcast sky which looks so good in black-and-white is a disaster in color production. Indoors the problem is multiplied: perfectly acceptable lighting to the eye can record on color film darker than that infamous Black Hole of Calcutta.

Writer-director-producer Hart relates some experiences in color filming a full hour program in co-operation with the Chicago Art Institute in 1964, *before* many of the later developments in color film and film processing were available to television film crews. Titled *Point of Contact*, the program was designed to foster and sustain an informed interest in modern art. Frank Hart notes:

"*Point of Contact*, filmed at the Art Institute of Chicago, required that the Institute's electrician be with us almost constantly. Even though we drew power for our lights from outlets as much as 150 feet away from the picture we were photographing, we blew fuses in a steady stream. (Lest this seem a criticism of the Institute's wiring, let me add that on another assignment we blew the fuses in the brand new control room which governed the flow of all electric power for north-eastern Minnesota. The superintendent was highly embarrassed, though he should not have been: to light for color film the 25-by-40 foot area of that control room required more power than any designer would ever dream of putting into an electrical wiring system for even the most modern office area.)

This problem of light—indoors or out—is one of the main causes of the added cost of color in any filming project. Another, of course, is the added cost of color film stock and processing. The simple decision to do a film in color, rather than black-and-white, will at least double the cost of the production; in some cases, it may triple or quadruple it.

In the production of public affairs programming in color—whether it be film or studio—the priceless and mandatory ingredient is a naive and stubborn faith that no problem is completely unsolvable. If it won't work one way, try another.

For the Art Institute film, it took almost three weeks of experimentation with various types of lights, three different types of film, and unorthodox techniques for lighting, before we were able to reproduce centuries-old paintings on color film. The solution, we finally discovered, lay in a special daylight film developed originally to film missiles for NASA. This was probably the only time a connection was ever established between 11th century art and 20th century space science.

And yet, that is exactly the meaning of public affairs and educational television. Twentieth century science is being used to achieve what men have been trying to do for millennia: discover new ideas and communicate them to each other."

Frank Hart continues:

"Called *Treasures of Faith*, the film was planned to give Chicagoans a survey of the art in the churches, synagogues and convents of the area.

The project was started during the winter for use in the spring, but my film cameraman was completely frustrated by the vast, gloomy areas that had to be lit artificially. With the exception of a North Side synagogue, extremely modern in architecture, even a bright sunny day didn't give adequate light through the small (often stained glass) windows to achieve the result we were seeking.

Even had we been able to supply economically the huge number of lights needed, the electrical systems of the buildings could not supply the necessary power at the points needed. The breaking point came the day we blew twenty-three fuses in a small English Gothic church in Wilmette.

But again, a producer is paid for his ingenuity in getting around problems. We abandoned film for interior work and went to colored slides. The finished one-hour production used well over 350 slides, in addition to film footage. The huge number of slides did not precisely endear the producer to the projectionist, but it got the job done. The film and slides were then combined with music and voice track on color videotape.

WGN Television's production, *The Light Here Kindled** which has become a Thanksgiving standard for our station, as well as a TV syndica-

---

*Awards won: 1965, Chicago Film Festival, award of merit; 1966, Religious Heritage Award; 1965, ONDAS competition in Barcelona, Spain (with several other WGN Television entries), special recognition for excellence in programming; 1965, New York International Film & TV Festival, Grand Prize in category of Public Service TV Program, single program produced by a local station; 1966, Mayflower Commemorative Medal; 1965, Freedoms Foundations George Washington Honor Medal Award.

tion product and a successful item for educational film sales, ran into the same problem of power source.

It was shot at 'Plimoth Plantation' in Plymouth, Mass., a re-creation of the original Plymouth settlement, and aboard the Mayflower II. One of its big scenes is the familiar Sunday morning march to the church-fort.

We had arranged for about 50 actors—members of the regular staff of 'Plimoth Plantation'—to appear in the scene. But when they showed up in costume, it was pouring rain. Since we had them on the scene, we had to use them or waste a considerable amount of money. So the entire two-week shooting schedule was thrown out, and for 15 hours we filmed interior scenes, dragging lights, cables, cameras and people from one Pilgrim house to another, slipping and sliding through the mud of the hillside.

Obviously, a Pilgrim village doesn't have electricity, so all our power came from a 500 foot cable from a single power outlet. Late that night, still in a driving rain, the producer discovered exactly what is meant by the 'huge power requirements' for color film lighting. As he unplugged the power cable, the rain shorted the connection and he found himself, half stunned, sitting in a mud puddle 6 feet from the outlet.

It takes a lot of power to light a Pilgrim hut—and he can prove it!"

Continuing are other reports on and appraisals of major color film projects, in the words of the men responsible for them.

*Halls of Mercy.** The assignment: To tell the story of a hospital supported by public funds and beset by serious problems. A bad image and a severe help shortage combined to threaten the hospital's accreditation.

Steve Schickel, writer-director-producer, comments:

"Our crew went into the entire operation of the hospital with only one point of view in mind. That was to make our 'report' a factual representation of what actually existed there. There was to be no editorial comment either pro or con, and the viewer was to be left to his own conclusions.

The hospital maintained its accreditation because what the camera saw was good.

On this assignment, we captured the natural sound, the natural light and the natural color, because we did not want the 'report' to be editorial in word, content or staging.

---

*Awards won: 1964, New York International Film & TV Festival, silver first award; 1964, San Francisco International Film Festival, Certificate of Acceptance in the Film as Communication category; 1964, Cook County (Ill.) Board commendation; 1965, Illinois State Medical Society Journalism Award for "outstanding medical documentary"; 1965, Illinois Associated Press Radio-TV Award in Best Documentary Program category.

To do this, most of the footage was shot with a hand-held camera. Sound posed a problem, so we made a makeshift audio pick-up 'studio' on a hospital emergency cart and achieved the mobility that was needed for the tour.

Because lighting equipment could not be moved into sterile atmosphere and areas where explosive gases were used, we had to shoot with available light. This increased laboratory costs, as they had to push low-speed film to a higher ASA rating and correct under-exposed scenes."

On a problem-laden assignment such as this, optimum results and the quality of picture reproduction must be sacrificed for the "story". News assignments and documentaries rely for their appeal on dramatic subject matter—made so important by current events that technique often is of secondary importance—while educational or public service documentaries must utilize the highest quality film techniques.

Passport to Export. A trip to several foreign countries may sound fascinating, but for a reporter and a cameraman it poses all the usual problems *plus* some special challenges to be faced and overcome.

This color film report documented what the government of a state was doing to increase the sale of products made in that state in new overseas markets. Among the countries visited were the Philippines, Japan, Formosa and Australia. Steve Schickel, the reporter, notes:

"Some of the major headaches were the transportation of the necessary equipment and the resultant overweight fees, the time-consuming customs office hassles, the variable procedures for handling film in other countries, and the lack of repair services.

It is of prime importance to take along a variety of adapters and plugs for the various electrical systems with which you will have to work. Also be prepared to do everything for yourself, because these services are just not readily available. The key element is the ability and talent to improvise. A documentary crew must be able to overcome any given obstacle at any time or place. No situation is ever the same as the previous one. There are no set solutions.

Clearing film through customs can be a harrowing experience. On one occasion they opened a can of exposed film, searching for jewels and dope. On another, they threatened to examine the film under X-ray, which would have destroyed it."

When you are filming abroad you must be a real Boy Scout—*be prepared* for every conceivable type of problem.

Operation Italia. From the beginning, this was an extremely unusual challenge in that the writer-director-producer, Arthur (Bud) Churvis, first learned about the project only 16 days before actual air date.

Including this color film feature in the public service category indicates the broad interpretation of public service assumed for this chapter. *Operation Italia* was a half-hour color feature designed to show how television could serve a major retail store. The crew was assigned to follow one of the store's international promotions from Chicago's State Street to Italy and back.

Come along with Bud Churvis as he reports some rich examples of the challenges and problems faced and solved in an extraordinary color film project such as this:

"In a period of sixteen days we had to research the subject, conceive the approach, write the script, shoot scenes in Chicago and Italy, return and have a completed, edited production.

We saw the project for what it was—a living study of the frenzy involved in the world of merchandising and high fashion. Our immediate decision was to allow the camera and the microphone literally to serve as the 'writer' of the film. We took a hotel room across the street from the retail store; had a projector, typewriter, rewind and viewing equipment moved in.

With a fond goodbye to our families, we shot night and day for a solid week. The cameraman unloaded his magazines at the end of each shooting day and deposited the rolls of film in the Eastman night chute. Early the next morning a co-operating laboratory picked up the processed original and made an immediate black-and-white print. Whenever we had a break in shooting we would return to the hotel room and screen the rushes from the previous day. It would have been more to our advantage to have seen a workprint in color, but here again time was the all-important factor, and an entire day was saved by working with the B & W print.

Another highly co-operative service took each day's quarter-inch audio tapes (the entire production was filmed in sync sound) and transferred them to 16mm. magnetic film. In this way the producer was able not only to check his daily film output, but was able also to maintain control over the quality of the sound.

Each night after a hasty dinner I would write a little more script for the minimal narration used in the production, and format the sequence of events as we went along. Thus we avoided wrestling with the resulting 8,000 feet of film at the last minute.

After shooting all the Chicago scenes, we took off for Italy on a night flight. At this point it was important to travel with as compact an equipment package as possible. Not knowing exactly what we would run into in the way of weather or lighting facilities, we decided to take along one extremely important piece of 50-pound luggage: a transformer to recharge the portable Sun Guns, which, as the project developed, proved to be the sole source of interior lighting for the Italian scenes. Fortunately, our planning and preparation paid off, since Milan was fogbound for the two days we were there and the Sun Guns were vitally necessary for 'fill', even on the exterior scenes.

Since we were dealing throughout the production with the vibrant colors to be found in merchandising and high fashion, we chose ECO as our basic outdoor emulsion, with the new Eastman EF for interior scenes. The compatibility of the two was found to be nearly perfect, with no noticeable boiling of grain.

From previous experience with EF, we were aware of its inherent tendency toward green, and were well stocked with all the necessary filters to compensate.

Live sound was used throughout the entire film in order to capture the realities that existed in each scene. People were directed to be themselves, and 'staging' was so subtle that every scene came off with naturalness and believeability.

At this juncture, the observation should be made that the difference between a polished production and one that has amateurish overtones is very often the difference between a director who knows his medium and one who does not. Non-professionals, who are generally the sole 'cast' of a documentary, must be guided and motivated in such a way that what ends up on film is real, natural and unposed.

Also, a good director must have a feel for scene sequence and screen direction. He must keep in mind how one scene will play against another in the finished product. Only in this way can he come up with a totally fluid production without the standard annoying narrator clichés which are so often used as crutches.

Arriving back in Chicago (we were gone three days), we were met by a courier who rushed the Italian footage to the lab for processing. Late that night, and for the next four days without interruption, I worked with my film editor and completely edited the picture. After a master-mix of the sound tracks on the fourth day, the original track was flown to the West Coast for optical transfer, and the now-conformed 'A' and 'B' rolls turned over to the laboratory for timing.

The sound track was back in 24 hours, during which time the laboratory in Chicago had completed preliminary timing and color correction. The following morning the first answer print was turned over to me, and 12 hours later the airprint—with additional color and density corrections indicated—was ready for the station's projection department.

All in all, the entire project was achieved from 'Point Zero' in just 16 days—and to the gratification of all involved received glowing acclaim from both the public press and trade reviewers."

Seaport of Chicago. With this assignment, writer-director-producer Churvis faced a whole new set of problems. The purpose of the 30-minute documentary was to show Chicago area people something that they had had for years and didn't realize: a major deepwater seaport and logical connecting link with the St. Lawrence Seaway. We had to give our audience some of the history of this seaport's development, without sounding historic. The solution, in the words of Bud Churvis:

"For this assignment we utilized a tremendous amount of air-to-ground footage, and were fortunate in that the WGN helicopters were available on short notice. Much of our footage was shot during the extreme heat of summer, flying along the Lake Michigan lakefront. We discovered that in summer air can be more turbulent than in winter, and found ourselves buffeted around nine-tenths of the time.

We also spent much time in tug boats, freighters and fire boats, in all kinds of summer weather.

This was a story that called for sweeping panoramas, which were difficult to film because of the haze that summer heat creates. Heat also plays havoc with raw color film stock; overall, our basic problems included helicopter vibrations, haze and heat.

To protect our film we carried it in a beer cooler—and in one instance (aboard a tug) actually had to use dry ice to make up for the fantastic heat reflecting off the steel deck and bulkheads.

After our first trip in the helicopter we found tremendous vibrations due to air currents around high-rise apartment buildings along the lakefront. To compensate, we decided to shoot all scenes from the air at 48 frames per second, to achieve a certain amount of reduction in camera vibration from the rotors and currents.

We also knew we would have to devise a cushioning for both camera and cameraman that really worked, since we would be flying at low levels much of the time, weaving our way through smoke stacks and sometimes under and between the open arms of a drawbridge. For one shot, we hovered next to a grain elevator as our camera looked down the hatch at grain being unloaded.

We managed to intrigue a foam rubber manufacturer with our problem, and he made form-fitting pieces to cushion cameraman Mel Rathmann's body, feet, elbows and camera.

Once on the water, we found that summer heat played havoc with color balance. Hard to believe, but we learned that the sky in Chicago in summer is more often white than blue, Lake Michigan is more often brown than green or blue, and the world of the seaport is replete with *glaring yellows* (mounds of bulk chemicals), *glistening white* (winter salt storage in bulk) and *dirty reds and browns* (rust).

In this documentary we also had a skin-tone problem. Longshoremen in Chicago are almost exclusively Negro, whereas the sailors are almost all white. We found that in most cases in a scene involving both, shooting for the Negro skin-tone was our best bet, with color corrections to bring down the white skin in the final print. We also chose not to use fill light on exterior scenes in these cases.

As to the haze, when shooting panoramic scenes there was very little we could do other than live with it.

A producer should always know well in advance exactly what scenes he wishes to use for the background of his opening titles and closing credits. Even more care should be taken in photographing these scenes than in any others, to avoid titles and credits with a grainy, amateurish look. Ideally, these scenes should be shot in 35mm. color negative, and the burn-through or aerial image of cells or crawl done on 35mm. format. This can then be reduced to 16mm., and the result will be finer definition in background footage.

We waited until we had the most perfect summer day from a photographic standpoint—a rare day when the winds had blown away all traces of industrial haze from the skyline. When we found it, we immediately contacted the Port Authority, and were placed aboard a British freighter three miles out and approaching the Chicago port.

Once aboard and with cameras set up on the bridge, we were able to take our time shooting scenes exactly as we wanted them for the opening titles and closing credits. By using a polarizing filter we were able to reduce the glare from the sun, and make it work to our advantage. The result was a color film of such perfection and brilliance that the aerial image titles and credits matted against the scene stood out almost as of another dimension, and background grain was almost totally absent.

The sponsor of this film received one important fringe benefit—prints of the feature are made available free of charge to civic and fraternal groups and schools."

Public Service in Color: A Postscript . . .

We are constantly on the alert for new developments in film, processing, equipment and techniques. Great progress is being made in these areas, and today's tools may well be—all for the good of the industry—obsolete tomorrow. Throughout this chapter the reader has undoubtedly noted considerable repetition, as engineers, writers, directors, producers and reporters addressed themselves to the subject—producing public service and related programs in color. We feel most strongly that this repetition is justified, if for no other reason than to emphasize the importance of these factors.

You have probably also noted the disproportionate amount of space devoted to color film programming, as opposed to studio and remote originations. This is by design because, as mentioned earlier, "specials" and documentaries captured on color film continue to grow in acceptance as we advance the art and earn the right to more and more prime-time positions in a station's schedule.

And those who serve, as a licensed television station must serve, have the obligation of availing themselves of the very best at all times—*not* limited to a studio, or even a city or a particular area. They must be mobile, creative, inventive, unencumbered.

We are discovering that high quality "specials" and documentaries produced in color, and with highly professional techniques, are beginning to interest advertisers who seek something different and meaningful. In some cases, they are even willing to commission special projects of this nature in advance. This is a healthy sign for our industry, and will encourage more production in the future.

More important than all this, however, is the fact that television stations throughout the country are finding a new, rich area of competitive programming to explore. Public service programming in color represents a challenge to creativity and ingenuity. And, finally, it provides welcome opportunities to produce quality programming of dignity, stature and purpose.

8 Color in Television News

SHELDON W. PETERSON
Time-Life Broadcast Inc., New York

Sheldon Peterson has been an active practitioner and a leader in electronic journalism for over 20 years. In the journeyman tradition of most journalists, he served with NBC News in Chicago, with the KLZ Stations in Denver, and with the WTCN Stations in Minneapolis-St. Paul (the latter two station combines both in the Time-Life Broadcast group). His credits during that period follow in the same journalistic tradition: writer, copy editor, on-the-air interviewer, program producer, news and public affairs director.

He moved to the New York headquarters of Time-Life Broadcast in 1964, in time to take over supervision of news preparation for the giant electric news boards spotted around the grounds of the New York World Fair. Most recently, he undertook another "on loan" assignment, guiding news policy and presentation for Channel Six-*closed-circuit TV news and information service in many of New York's leading hotels.*

Peterson is a past senior officer of the Radio-TV News Directors Association, and continues to serve that group as chairman of its Ethics and Standards Committee.

In this chapter, Sheldon Peterson offers seasoned personal expertise plus technical knowledge on both the advantages and pitfalls of TV news in color . . .

THERE are many definitions of news. One which has rather wide acceptance is that news is timely information about an unusual event that interests people. Whatever definition may be preferred, it is certain that news on television gains greater audience appeal with the addition of color.

You may test the effect of color upon yourself by walking into a room where there are two television sets, both of them tuned to the same news program, one a black-and-white receiver, the other a color receiver. Note how irresistibly your eyes are drawn to the tinted pictures. The attraction to color would be the same were the program of any other type. Color television has a naturalness about it that parallels an individual's emotional experience of viewing the world as it really is.

It should be pointed out that color does not make the reporting, writing, editing or quality of the photography any better. In fact, it has been charged with some truth that color has been used in an attempt to make news where none existed.

Heated debates frequently take place in newsrooms concerning the extent to which color should be permitted to influence the selection of news. Often hard-bitten newsmen view with scorn those who let color sway their judgment in deciding story coverage. However, the debate has waned as the movement toward total color has increased. When the conversion has been completed, it is likely that the same criteria that determine whether a story should be covered in black-and-white will prevail in color.

The swing to color in television news started in the 1950s when the National Broadcasting Company began televising color and individual stations modified their equipment to run the network programs, both live and on film. Not only did NBC pioneer in electronic color generally, it also was the first of the networks to use color film in news. It is a little remembered fact that color film was used three or four times a week in 1955 and 1956 on the John Cameron Swayze news program on NBC, one of the first of the network TV news programs. It was film shot the same day, too, a feat which latter-day news producers have not always found easy to accomplish.

The extensive use of color news film on the networks was not achieved until 1965. That was the year when the majority of the network programs were televised in color and when the consumer demand for color sets surged ahead of the supply.

In making the switchover, television newsmen quickly adapted to color all of the visual devices and techniques they had perfected in the monochrome medium. The list includes film; videotape; still pictures, including front and rear screen projections and 2in. × 2in. slides; graphics, including maps, charts, graphs and cartoons; and remote originations.

Of these five vehicles, film is the most frequently used. Its utilization is the most difficult to master, and it is the most costly part of the news operating budget; *but* it has the greatest flexibility and it is usually the most effective method for telling the story. It is logical, then, that film should receive the greatest emphasis in this chapter.

The newsfilm cameraman changing over to color film faces many problems that never confronted him with black-and-white film.

One of the first bitter lessons is that color film is a hard taskmaster, allowing much less exposure latitude. In shooting black-and-white film, over- or under-exposure of one or even one and one-half stops could be compensated for in the processing and sometimes in the control room. There can be little or no compensation in the processing of color film or the colors will be seriously altered.

It is possible to do some toning or "painting" of poorly exposed film by control room technicians when it is put on the air. However, such a practice is not recommended for it is difficult to reset the controls for the good film which is to follow.

A better method of "doctoring" up poorly exposed film is to put it through the system, note the scenes where exposure corrections are required, and then transfer it to videotape. The best practice is for the cameraman to use his light meter constantly and make sure that his film is properly exposed in the first place. Once the adjustment period from black-and-white to color film is over, the cameraman should be expected to deliver with consistency film that is properly exposed. If he cannot, then there is no place for him in color television.

Indoor lighting is the great spoiler of good exposures. In the period B.C. (before color), a film crew could set up a couple of incandescent photofloods and the shooting could start with little delay. It isn't that simple now. The light source must be carefully analyzed. Fluorescent lighting is extremely difficult to measure and can be disastrous to color photography.

When fluorescent lighting is present, several compensating filters are available to balance out the film. However, an experienced cameraman much prefers to extinguish the fluorescents if possible and substitute his own photoflood lights. If the fluorescents cannot be turned off, then the cameraman should boost his tungsten lights so as to overpower the fluorescent source.

Most film crews now carry with them quartz iodine lamps which have a color temperature rating of 3,200 degrees Kelvin.

Color temperature in degrees Kelvin is often used as an approximation for an illuminant's color. It is based on comparing an illuminant to a carbon block called a "black-body" heated to a specified temperature.

For example, a 3,200 K tungsten lamp has the same spectral quality, wave length by wave length, as the carbon block heated to 3,200 K. Normal daylight approximates that of a carbon block heated to 6,000 K. The higher the temperature, the bluer the color appears. Other examples are clear sky light that approximates 25,000 K and an early morning sun approximating 5,000 K.

It is important to fit the color film to the proper illuminant. If this cannot be done, adjustment must be made to correct the mismatch in the film/light system.*

For visual purposes, the color quality of a light source is evaluated in terms of the color of a perfect radiator, or "black-body", heated to a certain temperature. This temperature is expressed in degrees Kelvin (K), obtained by adding 273 to the temperature in degrees Centigrade. When the light source matches the black-body in color, it is said to have a *color temperature* equal to the actual temperature of the black-body in the Kelvin scale.

The color of light is bluer with higher and yellower with lower color temperatures. *Note that color temperature refers only to the visual appearance of a light source and does not necessarily describe its photographic effect.* For example, one type of "white" fluorescent lamp is rated at 3,500 K, but the spectral distribution of the light it emits produces photographic results quite different from those produced by a tungsten lamp operated at the same color temperature. *Color temperature values for various daylight conditions also tend to be misleading when they are applied to color photography.* Tungsten lamps, however, have spectral qualities closely resembling those of black-body radiators, and in this case, color temperature is a reliable indication of photographic effect.†

Unlike incandescent lights, which begin to deteriorate after

---

*From *Color Motion Picture Film and Color Television Seminar*, General Aniline & Film Corporation, p. 2.

†From *Color As Seen and Photographed*, Eastman Kodak Company, 1950, Second Edition—Third Printing, 1966, pp. 46-47.

about one-third of their life has been expended, quartz iodine lights remain at full brightness until they burn out. However, one factor which can cause a variation in the quartz lights is the alternating current which energizes them. A variation of five volts, either below or above the rated voltage (usually 120 volts in modern buildings) can cause a change in the color of the film.

A film crew is apt to encounter other puzzling indoor lighting situations. For example, what should be done when an event must be filmed indoors with daylight streaming into the room from one or more windows? If the cameraman is shooting tungsten film, the best procedure is to draw the window shades and use tungsten lighting. If the daylight cannot be shut out, then the only course is to shoot the story with the proper filter.

Manufacturers have greatly improved the quality of their films in recent years to meet the exacting requirements of newsfilm cameramen. Until the mid-60s it was commonplace for a cameraman to carry at least two types of film if he were to cope with the various lighting situations he was likely to encounter. One was a tungsten type, the other daylight. This is not to say it was not possible to get by with only one film; that is, a fast tungsten that could be cut back with a filter for daylight shooting. However, the results were not always the best. When a story was to be shot in daylight, most photo chiefs preferred that their men used a slower, finer-grained film.

As this book goes to press, cameramen have given widespread endorsement to two films on the market, each suitable for tungsten and daylight illumination. One of them is the Ektachrome EF type 7242 produced by the Eastman Kodak Company. The Kodak Wratten filter No. 85 is recommended for this film for daylight shooting. The film carries a tungsten ASA rating of 125 and a daylight rating, with recommended filter, of 80.

The other film is the Anscochrome T/100, manufactured by the General Aniline & Film Corporation. An 81A filter is recommended to balance the T/100 film for daylight. This film carries a tungsten ASA rating of 100 and a daylight rating, with recommended filter, of 64.

No one is better qualified than the man behind the camera to testify as to the convenience of being able to shoot all types of stories with a single film. It is time-consuming and mistakes are more likely to be made if, for example, in going from a governor's indoors news conference to an outdoor daylight parade, the cameraman must change film types. It can be wasteful, too, for often a story shot with one kind of illumination doesn't require a full roll. But the rest of the roll probably must be scrapped if the next story is under a different lighting condition.

There are two types of film sound tracks: optical and magnetic. With the optical method—when shooting single system—the sound is photographically recorded on the film at the same time that the picture is being recorded. The optical method was the only procedure used in the earlier days of black-and-white motion picture photography. It is still used to some extent.

However, in more recent years progressive news and photo departments have learned that the best way to get good single system sound on film is to record the sound magnetically. The superior quality of magnetic sound is even more noticeable with color film than it is with black-and-white. Among other advantages of magnetic sound tracks, they can be erased and re-dubbed at will, and they are entirely unaffected by the chemicals used in processing machines.

Film may be purchased with the magnetic stripe already on. Some news departments buy pre-striped film exclusively, even that intended for use in silent cameras. This done in the event of a later decision to put a sound track on the film.

Where optical sound is used on reversal color film, the deterioration of the sound quality can be prevented to some extent in two ways. One is to use a special applicator in the processor. The other and better way is to use a photoelectric cell in the projector that is not sensitive to the visible spectrum.

As news departments have converted their operations to color, they have usually turned to local laboratories for processing services. They are reluctant to face the headaches and high cost of installing and operating their own processing equipment.

Frequently, this has not been a satisfactory solution. Commercial labs usually have many customers and cannot always provide the fast service that is so essential to a fast-moving news operation. However, experienced laboratory supervisors counsel that unless a television station is prepared to invest a large sum of money in good color processing equipment and willing to provide the necessary trained personnel to run it, it is better to stay with a commercial lab and learn to endure irregular service.

A safe generalization is that color processing takes longer and costs about twice as much as black-and-white processing.

Those stations that decide to do their own color processing face a hard choice in determining the size of the processor they should purchase. A natural inclination is to buy a high speed machine that is large enough to handle future needs. Large processors are more costly, have higher processing costs and often require more maintenance than do medium-size and small machines.

Some experts contend that a news department of average size, shooting 2,000 or less feet of color film a day, and requiring two or three runs daily, should do nicely with a processor that operates efficiently at 30 feet per minute. Prices of such processors range upward from $10,000. To the base price must be added certain accessories and the cost of installation and floor space modification, if necessary.

There are several good processors on the market. Among the better known ones are those made by Hills, Houston Fearless, Filmlines, Allen, Treise and Pako. Regardless of make, a processor is a complicated piece of machinery that requires good maintenance and constant supervision.

It is imperative that a processor be operated by trained technicians who are capable of maintaining quality control. The importance of quality control is emphasized by Jett Jamison of WBAP-TV, Fort Worth-Dallas, Texas, in a paper delivered at a seminar sponsored by the Radio-Television News Directors Association and Time-Life Broadcast at Atlanta, Georgia in 1966.

> The time when a newsman could go into a lab and process his own film is a thing of the past. Color is too exacting, temperature and replenishment controls too important, to trust to luck.
>
> James A. Byron, the long-time news director of the WBAP Stations, realized lab operations and film production should be controlled by film technicians and not news personnel; so some nine years ago, these departments were made a separate operation from the news department. While the news cameramen are still in the newsroom, the lab technicians work under the supervision of the film service director.
>
> It would be natural to ask what all of this has to do with quality control. Actually, it has everything to do with quality control. It places the responsibility of processing squarely on the shoulders of the film

technicians. It requires the lab to be the one constant factor in the news-film operation.*

There is little excuse for a station to run a processing lab with untrained or poorly-trained personnel. The equipment manufacturers provide consultants for the installation and operation of their processors. Moreover, the major film manufacturers—Eastman and GAF—operate training schools or will teach their processing methods on location.

Mindful of the high cost of color film, not to mention the expense of processing it, station managers ask hopefully whether there may be some reduction in the quantity of film shot in the tint medium below that consumed in black-and-white. The answer is a conditional "no". The experience of most stations has been that the consumption of film increases as the change-over to color is made. This may be attributed to experimentation on the part of cameramen and a consequent increase in the amount of waste. It has been found, though, that after cameramen have become accustomed to color, the consumption levels off at a point near that which prevailed when the medium was black-and-white film.

Some news departments report that their film usage has declined with the conversion to color. One reason given is that cameramen have been impressed with the high cost of color film and the need to conserve it.

Color videotape is an important adjunct to television news, just as is black-and-white videotape. In the heat of the daily news battle, it is a great convenience to bring a newsmaker into the studio for a taped interview or to give comment on some significant issue. It is equally convenient to put on tape a film clip, adding at the same time the voice-over narrative.

There has been much speculation as to whether lightweight, highly-portable tape units would ever replace film. Surely the ability to bypass the time-consuming and costly operation of processing film would be a great advantage. Some of the networks and individual stations have experimented with black-and-white portable videotape machines. Thus far such devices have not won

---

*Jett Jamison, Director, Film Services Department, WBAP-TV, Fort Worth-Dallas, Texas, "Film Processing Calls for Specialists", *The Newsroom and the Newscast* published by Time-Life Broadcast, Inc., 1966, p. 88.

widespread acceptance. The chief reason is that they do not fully measure up to television engineering standards. Small, portable units capable of taping color are not yet available but they are expected on the market soon. Although it will be difficult to replace film, it is not beyond the realm of possibility that the day will come when portable tape machines may do just that.

Meanwhile, we may expect continued growth of the use of videotape machines in television studios and on remote assignments such as sporting events and other special events that are not strictly spot news in nature. The tape machines now employed for remotes are portable in a limited sense only. They are usually moved to location in a van and have none of the mobility of film cameras.

Some news directors have a policy against the use of still pictures in the news. They argue that television is based on movement and that viewers quickly lose interest unless the pictures wiggle. With them it is a matter of professional pride that they use motion picture film only in their news. This writer holds with many others that still pictures can be used to excellent advantage in television news and this is true in color television as well as black-and-white.

There are two common methods of projecting still pictures. One is to shoot them with a live studio camera. The other is to make slides and project them either directly or on a front or rear screen.

Front and rear screen projections have enjoyed great popularity in recent years. Such popularity is understandable as one observes the realism they give to the news.

Color stills that measure 5in. × 7in. and larger in size have the disadvantage of being considerably more expensive than black-and-white prints and therefore more difficult to obtain. As a means of supplying television stations with color pictures at the lowest possible cost, The Associated Press and United Press-International now sell 2in. × 2in. slide services to television stations. Although they serve a useful purpose, the slides are less effective than the larger stills which can be adapted through additional art work to apply to a given story and then projected either as a RP or shot with a live studio camera.

Regardless of their application in television news, it is safe to predict that still pictures will be used in television news for many years to come.

It is quite possible that we will see the transmission of color pictures by facsimile in the near future. Black-and-white pictures for TV news have been transmitted by facsimile for many years. The chief obstacle in transmitting color pictures by wire is one of economics rather than technique. When the cost drops to within the means of stations' budgets, the use of facsimile pictures probably will have wide acceptance.

Color adds a new dimension to studio sets and, if used wisely, can be particularly effective in news programs. Unfortunately, some news set designers have splashed color around with the abandon of those legendary alcoholic house painters of the vaudeville era. Riotous backgrounds may be suitable for—even an integral part of—certain entertainment programs, but they are quite out of place in a news setting. The best results are obtained when the colors are subdued and used sparingly. All colors are adaptable to news sets, just as they are to other types of sets. Blue is invariably cited as one of the most photogenic colors.

The news producer should remember that when a newscaster is on-camera, he is the most important element in the set. Other objects in the scene should be subordinated to him.

As long as black-and-white receivers remain in use in substantial numbers, set designers should be mindful of how their use of color will show up on monochrome. Color combinations that appear attractive on a color receiver may not have different gray-scale values, and therefore there will be no separation on black-and-white.

In the selection of wardrobe, the newscaster should avoid white shirts just as he has always done in black-and-white television. Pastel-tinted shirts are best. Gray is particularly good. Newscasters usually are permitted to follow their own tastes in the selection of suits and ties. Overall, the attire should be on the conservative side, in keeping with the dignity of the news. The use of make-up generally improves the appearance of both men and women on the screen and its use is recommended.

The utilization of graphics has become increasingly important in television news as a means of adding realism. Maps, charts, graphs, cartoons and sketches in color contribute greatly toward making the news more meaningful.

Looking into the future, one area in which we may expect further progress is that of live spot news remotes in color. In its brief history, television has achieved a brilliant record of reaching into difficult places. Witness the live coverage of such special events as political conventions and elections, and the unforgettable reporting of the events surrounding the assassination of John F. Kennedy. But television has not quite matched the speed and mobility of radio. The reasons are largely economic and technical. Inevitably those obstacles will be overcome. When that day arrives, the viewer will become eye-witness to the day's news almost as it happens.

In less than a quarter century, television—as revealed by the polling services—has become the No. 1 news medium. Almost certainly it will reach new heights in the years that lie ahead and color will aid in that advancement.

III

The Color Television Audience

9 The Impact of Color
A profile of color TV set owners: Television's "Class" Audience

THOMAS E. COFFIN
SAM TUCHMAN
National Broadcasting Company, New York

The pioneering position of the National Broadcasting Company in color telecasting has been acknowledged in many chapters of this text. The parallel research effort in recording the results of that programming has been documented, since 1949, by Dr. Thomas E. Coffin, vice president for Research; since 1964 has been aided by Coffin's associate, Dr. Sam Tuchman, manager for Marketing and Management Research.

There are four schools of higher learning and six degrees represented in the cumulative Coffin-Tuchman writing that follows. Coffin received his Ph.D. from Princeton in 1941, and was professor and chairman of the Psychology Department of Hofstra University before joining NBC. Tuchman, originally a Brooklyn College graduate, received his Ph.D. from New York University in 1963.

In another chapter, TvB's Pete Cash begs simplicity for the TV salesman who proffers the wares of colorcasting as an effective advertising medium. With missionary zeal, Drs. Coffin and Tuchman proceed to view color television in a score or so of "quality demographics" that—any way you look at it—may be combined with the Cash sentiment to total a convincing, almost unbeatable story on behalf of the values of color TV advertising . . .

FROM a marketing standpoint, one of the most intriguing aspects of color television is that it provides advertisers with the unusual opportunity to reach simultaneously both a "mass" audience and a "class" audience.

Until the advent of color television, there were basically two kinds of media: (1) "mass" audience media, such as prime-time television programs or *Life* magazine, and (2) "class" audience media, such as the *New Yorker* magazine. An advertiser wishing to reach both a "mass" and a "class" audience would have to buy both kinds of media.

Today, however, advertisers who place color commercials on color television programs can reach a "mass" and a "class" audience at the same time. The "mass" audience consists of homes with black-and-white sets only, who are of course viewing the program and commercials in black-and-white. Additionally, there is a "class" audience of color set homes, who can view the program and commercials in color.

How large is this "class" audience in relation to the "mass" audience? Nielsen Television Index ratings for October 1966 indicate that the average prime-time program reaches 1,600,000 color homes per minute, as against 8,443,000 black-and-white homes. These 1,600,000 color homes per minute exceed by a wide margin the total number of homes in the audiences for *entire issues* of such "class" magazines as *New Yorker* (494,000), *Saturday Review* (423,000), *Harper's* (294,000) and *Atlantic* (289,000).

The key point made here that color television owners represent a "class audience" stems from a special analysis of the characteristics of this audience. This chapter presents the major results from this study. It includes information on the usual demographic factors used to describe population groups, such as age, income and family size. However, the analysis goes beyond these demographic factors and by examining their product-usage patterns provides a new way of gaining insights into the kinds of people who buy color sets—their tastes, their interests, their values, their life styles. Together, the demographic and product-usage data furnish a profile-in-depth of the color audience.

As will be shown in detail in the following sections, color set owners are an especially affluent group. In addition, they tend to be "venturesome"—prone to buy new products; "convenience-oriented"—willing to pay a premium price to save their labor; and "status-minded"—consistently moving up-scale in their purchases.

The source of the information in this chapter is the 1966 Brand Rating Index Report (BRI), which is based on data secured by BRI from a representative national sample of the U.S. adult population. The sample consisted of 12,604 adults of 18 and over: 5,424 men and 7,180 women (of whom 6,525 were homemakers). A special tabulation of these data compares the demographic characteristics and product-usage patterns of those respondents living in color set homes, with the total population. Further information was supplied on the demographics of homemakers who said they planned to buy color sets within the next two years—a group indicative of "future" color owners. This makes it possible to compare the characteristics of "future" color owners with those of the current owners.*

1. *Demographic Characteristics of Current and "Future" Color Set Owners*

Who are the current owners of color TV sets? How well-to-do are they? How old? How large are their families? Where do they live?

These are important questions for advertisers who use color commercials to reach color homes, as well as for others interested in the characteristics of the color audience. Of at least equal importance is the question: How is the profile of the color audience apt to change in the next few years, as color set circulation continues to expand rapidly?

This section provides answers to these questions. The information on the characteristics of current color set owners is based on demographic data obtained by BRI on women living in color set homes. The profile data on "future" color set owners is based on the demographics of those homemakers who said they plan to buy color sets in the next two years.

(a) *Income.* The outstanding factor that distinguishes color set owners from the general population is *high income*. As Chart 1

---

*This is not to imply that buying intentions correlate perfectly with buying behavior—obviously they do not, on a *person-by-person* basis. However, it is likely that those population *groups* which have relatively high purchase intention levels for color sets will also furnish relatively large numbers of "future" color owners.

shows, only 21 percent of all women have household incomes of $10,000 and over ... but 43 percent of current color set owners are in this top income bracket—*twice* the national percentage. Conversely, while 38 percent of all women have household incomes under $5,000, a mere 12 percent of current color owners are found in these lower-income homes—only a third the national percentage.

It is of course reasonable that current color set owners are concentrated in higher-income homes, since it still costs a good many dollars to buy a color set. But how about the next generation ... the "future" color owners?

As might be expected, they will not have quite as high incomes as the current owners. However, their incomes will still remain well above the income level of the general population: 35 percent of "future" color owners versus only 21 percent of all women have household incomes of $10,000 and over. Relatively few "future" color owners will be drawn from lower-income homes: only 20 percent of "future" color owners versus 38 percent of all women are in the under-$5,000 income bracket.

Thus, the "future" color owners look much more like the current color owners than the general population in terms of income. The color audience will continue to be a high-quality market group for quite some time to come.

(b) *Age*. How old are current color set owners? As Chart 2 indicates, color set owners are quite evenly distributed across the population by age. (This is in marked contrast to the high concentration of color set owners in the upper-income brackets. Evidently, income is a far more important determinant than age level when a family buys a color TV set.)

There is some tendency for color set owners, though, to be centered in the 25-49 age group. This age bracket accounts for 48 percent of all women, but 53 percent of color set owners.

Future color owners will be even likelier than current owners to be drawn from the "young adult" 25-49 age group. Chart 3 reveals that this age group accounts for 63 percent of "future" color owners, as against only 53 percent of all homemakers.

It makes logical sense that color owners are being drawn in above-average numbers from the 25 to 49 age category. To coin a name, this is the "active and affluent" age group.

THE IMPACT OF COLOR   125

1. CURRENT & FUTURE COLOR SET OWNERS BY HOUSEHOLD INCOME

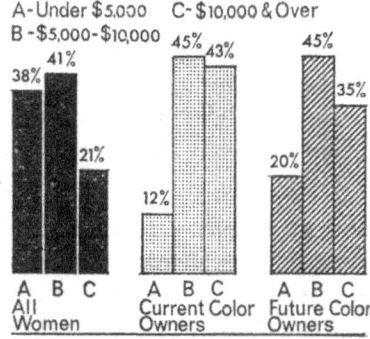

2. CURRENT COLOR SET OWNERS BY AGE

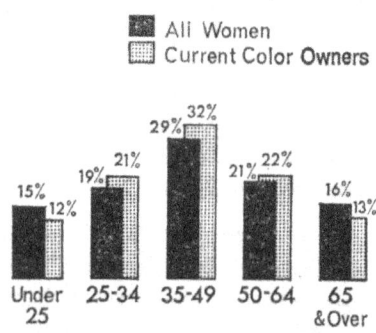

3. FUTURE COLOR SET OWNERS BY AGE

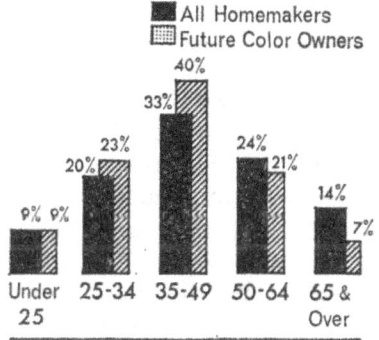

4. CURRENT COLOR SET OWNERS BY HOUSEHOLD SIZE

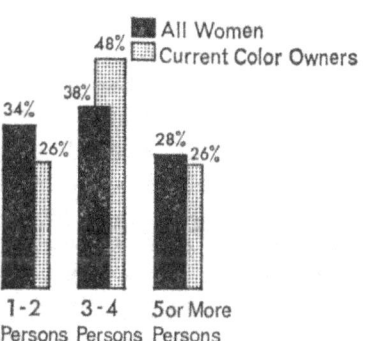

5. FUTURE COLOR SET OWNERS BY HOUSEHOLD SIZE

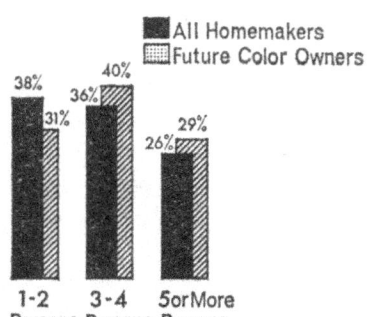

6. CURRENT & FUTURE COLOR SET OWNERS BY REGION

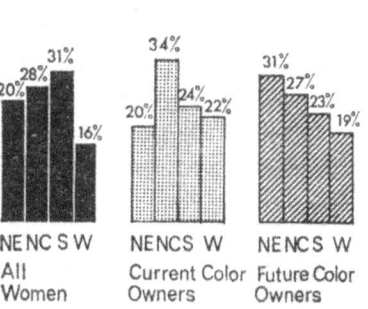

The very young people (under 25) are active but not affluent—they have not progressed far enough in their jobs to be making much money yet. Some of the older people (50 and over) have accumulated money, but they are not that interested in new things.

The people in the middle have it good *both ways*. They are far enough along to have built up to a good income—but they are young enough to be flexible, alert, interested in new ideas: . . . in short, they are both "active and affluent".

(c) *Household Size.* Today's color set owners are centered in medium-size families. As Chart 4 indicates, 48 percent of current color owners, compared with only 38 percent of all women, live in households with 3 or 4 members. The proportion of color owners in large families (five or more members) is slightly below the proportion of these families in the population. Relatively few color set owners are in small families (one or two members).

This finding is corroborated by information in the 1966 survey of television set ownership conducted by the United States Bureau of the Census and issued by the Advertising Research Foundation.* That study also indicated that color television ownership was relatively highest among three and four member households.

Increasingly, though, color set sales are apt to be made to large families (five or more members). Chart 5 indicates that a higher percentage of "future" color owners (29 percent) than of all homemakers (26 percent) live in large households. This contrasts with the preceding pattern for the current owners, who are found in below-average proportions in these five-or-more-member households.

(d) *Location.* Where do color owners live? Chart 6 shows the distribution of current and "future" color set owners by region of the country. There are three main points which emerge from the data:

First, the North Central and Western regions of the country account for a relatively high proportion of current color set owners (56 percent) as compared to the general population (44 percent).†

Second, indications are that the North-east region, which currently is a comparatively "weak" color market. will be the center

---

*Advertising Research Foundation, *National Survey of Television Sets in U.S. Households—August 1966.*

†This finding is also corroborated by the ARF/Census study of television ownership.

of considerable future color set sales growth. This region accounts for 25 percent of all women . . . only 20 percent of current color set owners . . . but 31 percent of "future" set owners.

Third, the South is currently a weak color TV market and does not show signs of improving its relative position. This region accounts for 31 percent of all women . . . only 24 percent of current color owners . . . and *only* 23 *percent* of "future" color owners.

(e) *Summary.* Current color set owners have much higher incomes than the general population. (Income is the key demographic factor associated with color set ownership.) Today's set owners are also found in above-average numbers in the 25-49 age group . . . in medium-size families (three or four members) . . . and in the North, Central and Western regions of the country.

How is the profile of color set owners apt to change in the next few years, as set circulation expands? Information on the characteristics of "future" set owners (i.e. prospective buyers in the next two years) furnishes a good indication. As might be expected, "future" set owners have somewhat lower incomes than the current owner group. But their income level is still substantially higher than that of the total population. Clearly, color set owners will continue to be an affluent audience for quite some time to come. Additional demographic information on "future" color owners indicates: the color audience will tend to become younger . . . have large families . . . and be located to a greater extent in the North-east.

This section of the chapter has described color set owners in terms of their demographic characteristics. The next section presents an additional and new approach to gain insights into the kinds of people who own color TV sets . . . through an analysis of their product usage patterns.

2. *Product Usage Patterns of Color Set Owners*

This section examines the buying habits of color set owners. It points up the fact that time after time color owners spend more freely. To take a very simple, but comprehensive, index: the amount spent per week in the grocery and supermarket. This is a good indicator of likelihood-of-purchase for a whole host of items.

Comparing color owners against all homemakers in Chart 7, fewer than normal of the color owners are in the low-spending category. Slightly more than normal fall in the medium-spending category. And lots more than normal fall in the high-spending category. In fact, 39 percent more than normal fall in this bracket.

Moving from supermarket items to the opposite end of the price scale, Chart 8 shows cars.

Again, color owners spend more freely. About 40 percent more of them plan to buy a new car soon . . . or own two or more cars. Color owners spend a lot more on travel, too, than most other people, as Chart 9 points up.

Over 50 percent more color owners than all men have taken trips to foreign countries. And about two-thirds more own travelers checks and have taken air trips in the past year. Not only do color owners spend more on current items, they also spend more on financial investments for the future.

As Chart 10 illustrates, 10 percent more color owners own life insurance and over 40 percent more own stocks and bonds.

Certainly, color owners are a choice market—and logically enough, in view of their age and income. They are "active and affluent" . . . and it shows in their buying. But lately we have been finding that we can learn a lot more about people than just their purchasing habits from studying their buying patterns. Reading between the lines, you can deduce a lot about their personalities. After all, if the psychologist finds that people are expressing their personalities in the books they choose to read and the friends they choose to make, why couldn't we discover that they are equally expressing their personalities in the products they choose to buy and the brands they choose to use?

If you look at the upcoming charts with this little twist, there is a lot of fascinating insight to be gained from this marketing information. A lot of useful marketing data, yes—about important target audiences and market segmentation. But much more—a lot of intriguing insight into *people*—in this case, the people who own color TV. Here, then, are some interesting "personality-test-scores", as it were, on these people:

(a) *"Venturesomeness"*. One of the outstanding personality characteristics of color set owners is "venturesomeness". Color

THE IMPACT OF COLOR

COLOR OWNERS...SPEND MORE
Amount spent per week in grocery/supermarket

	All Homemakers	Color Owners	%Diff	7
Low Spending (under $20)	42.6%	28.4%	−33%	
Medium " ($21-$30)	29.9	33.4	+12%	
High " (over $30)	27.5	38.3	+39%	

....SPEND MORE
CARS

	All Men	Color Owners	%Diff	8
Plan to buy new car	32.5%	44.9%	+38%	
Own 2 or more cars	33.3	47.7	+43%	

....SPEND MORE
TRAVEL

	All Men	Color Owners	%Diff	9
Trips to Foreign Countries	13.1%	20.1%	+53%	
Travelers Checks	17.1	28.0	+64%	
Air Trips	18.1	30.3	+67%	

....SPEND MORE
FINANCIAL

	All Men	Color Owners	%Diff	10
Own Life Insurance	71.5%	78.7%	+10%	
Own Stocks & Bonds	24.8	35.2	+42%	

COLOR SET OWNERS...ARE VENTURESOME
FURNITURE POLISH

	All Homemakers	Color Owners	%Diff	11
Liquid	27.6%	24.3%	−12%	
Spray	33.2	44.0	+33%	

....VENTURESOME
DISINFECTANT

	All Homemakers	Color Owners	%Diff	12
Liquid	41.1%	42.1%	+2%	
Spray	37.4	48.5	+30%	

owners tend to use newer, "modern" products. Indeed, the very fact they bought color sets before most other people is indicative of their "venturesomeness".

A comparison of the rates of usage of various products among color owners, as against the total population, draws an interesting picture of the color group. Here is a simple, ordinary household necessity: furniture polish. What kind do color owners buy?

As Chart 11 shows, color owners are below average in the standard variety, the liquid. But they are 33 percent above average in the newest type—spray-on polish.

And here is another product—disinfectant—which comes in both the standard liquid and the new spray varieties. What kind do color owners buy?

Chart 12 reveals that color owners are about average in the standard type. But they are a good 30 percent above average in the modern spray disinfectants.

Turning to another group of common household products, kitchen wraps, we find three major product types: wax paper, a product which has been on the market for a good many years . . . and aluminium foil and plastic wrap, relatively new wrapping materials. Again, which kinds do color owners buy?

Predictably, color owners are only about average users of wax paper, as indicated in Chart 13. By comparison, they are 18 percent above average in usage of aluminum foil and 28 percent higher than normal in usage of plastic food wrap—the modern ways to wrap foods.

In the soft drinks market there are two basic product types: the regular type containing sugar . . . and, much more recently, the diet, sugarless soft drinks. Given this choice, how do color owners behave in the marketplace?

Chart 14 shows that color owners are slightly above average in regular soft drinks. However, their leaning is even more strongly toward the newer product type—the diet soft drinks: 18 percent above average in usage.

All the preceding products were package goods—bought mainly by women. What about some other kinds of products—in particular, products bought largely by men? For example, what do men color owners do when they want to take pictures?

Color owners are well above average in taking still pictures, as

THE IMPACT OF COLOR

....VENTURESOME KITCHEN WRAPS

	All Homemakers	Color Owners	%Diff	
Wax Paper	37.7%	36.5%	-3%	13
Aluminum Foil	58.1	68.6	+18%	
Plastic Food Wrap	45.0	57.4	+28%	

....VENTURESOME SOFT DRINKS

	All Homemakers	Color Owners	%Diff	
Regular	37.4%	39.5%	+6%	14
Diet	38.6	45.5	+18%	

....VENTURESOME FILM

	All Men	Color Owners	%Diff	
Still Picture	23.8%	31.1%	+31%	15
Movie	16.3	28.1	+72%	

....VENTURESOME APPLIANCES

	All Homemakers Men	Color Owners	%Diff	
Elec: Toothbrushes (Purchase intentions among homemakers)	15.6%	19.6%	+26%	16
Elec: Shavers (Ownership among men)	39.4	51.4	+30%	
Tape Recorders (Purchases of tape recorder reels by men)	4.3	8.0	+86%	

....COLOR SET OWNERS ARE CONVENIENCE-ORIENTED

STARCH

	All Homemakers	Color Owners	%Diff	
Powder	26.0%	20.0%	-23%	17
Liquid	27.9	27.1	-3%	
Spray	33.6	41.5	+24%	

....CONVENIENCE-ORIENTED FOODS

	All Homemakers	Color Owners	%Diff	
Instant Potatoes	30.7%	36.6%	+19%	18
Frozen Cakes & Pies	37.4	44.5	+19%	
Frozen Vegetables	47.5	59.3	+25%	
Casserole Dinner Mixs	25.7	32.4	+26%	

Chart 15 points up. But most noticeably, they go for the new type of picture-taking: moving pictures. They are 72 percent above average in their usage of this type.

In the appliance field as well, color owners continue to display their preference for the more modern products.

As Chart 16 illustrates, color owners are 26 percent above average in purchase intentions for electric toothbrushes—a prime example of a product appealing to "venturesome" people. In ownership of electric shavers, 30 percent above average. And color owners have an especially high level of ownership of tape recorders, as indicated by their purchases of tape recorder reels. Their purchase rate is 86 percent higher than normal.

Are we not finding out something about people—not just statistics—by examining their product usage patterns? Here is more . . .

(b) *Convenience-orientation.* Color TV owners tend to buy "convenience" products and services, even though it means paying a premium price to save their labor. For example, take another simple, ordinary household product—starch. It comes in three types: the traditional, which is powder; the somewhat more convenient, which is liquid; and the newest and most convenient, the spray-on. How do color owners behave, facing this choice?

As Chart 17 indicates, color owners are below average in usage of powder starch . . . about average in usage of liquid starch . . . but are 24 percent above average in usage of the newest and most convenient type, the spray-on starch.

And color owners use easy-to-prepare "convenience" foods to a much greater extent than the average American housewife.

In illustration, Chart 18 reveals that color owners are 19 percent above average in usage of both instant potatoes and frozen cakes and pies. They are about 25 percent ahead of other housewives in usage of frozen vegetables and casserole dinner mixes. Similarly, color owners are well above average in usage of such convenience beverage products as frozen orange juice and instant tea.

Here are some household products heavily used by color owners which further illustrate their convenience-orientation:

Note in Chart 19 their high levels of usage of convenience-type paper products. Paper napkins: 22 percent above average. Paper

THE IMPACT OF COLOR

....CONVENIENCE-ORIENTED

HOUSEHOLD PRODUCTS	All Homemakers	Color Owners	%Diff	19
Paper Napkins	45.5%	55.6%	+22%	
Paper Towels	40.9	51.2	+25%	
Plastic Foodbags	38.4	49.0	+28%	
Automatic Dishwasher Soap	11.5	28.3	+146%	

....CONVENIENCE-ORIENTED

CREDIT CARDS	All Men	Color Owners	%Diff	20
Gasoline	33.4%	51.3%	+54%	
Entertainment & Travel	6.1	13.2	+116%	

COLOR SET OWNERS ARE STATUS-MINDED

WHISKEY	All Men	Color Owners	%Diff	21
Rye	24.4%	28.1%	+15%	
Scotch	19.6	30.4	+55%	

....STATUS-MINDED

WINE	All Men	Color Owners	%Diff	22
Domestic	24.3%	30.3%	+25%	
Imported	11.4	15.5	+36%	

....STATUS-MINDED

BOATS	All Men	Color Owners	%Diff	23
Outboard	8.5%	14.6%	+72%	
Inboard	2.1	6.4	+205%	

....STATUS-MINDED

CARS	All Men	Color Owners	%Diff	24
Own 2 cars	27.3%	36.7%	+34%	
Own 3 or more cars	5.9	11.0	+86%	

towels: 25 percent above average. And plastic food bags—the quick way to store foods: 28 percent above average. Most notably, color owners are going strongly for the convenience way to wash dishes—the automatic dishwasher. Nearly 150 percent above average.

Back to the men again—this next one had us puzzled at first. Why the exceptionally high level of ownership of credit cards by color owners?

As Chart 20 reveals, 54 percent more color owners own gasoline credit cards . . . and 116 percent more own entertainment and travel credit cards.

The significance of this? This is the *convenience* way to buy things. No need to carry lots of cash around. No need to keep records. Just "charge it", and at the end of the month receive an itemized statement of outlays. This is frozen pies, spray-on starch and automatic dishwashers—on the larger scale.

(c) *Status-consciousness*. Here is another facet of the picture which also jibes with the rest . . . In everything they do, color set owners move up-scale. (A color TV set itself is perhaps somewhat of a status symbol.) For instance, given the choice between drinking rye (blended whiskey) or Scotch, which type of whiskey do they choose?

Color owners are somewhat above average rye users, as Chart 21 shows. But their real preference is for Scotch: 55 percent above average. They are also above average for other "class" liquors, such as Bourbon and Canadian. And turning now from whiskey to wine. What kind of wine do color owners prefer?

Chart 22 reveals that they are, indeed, excellent marketing prospects for domestic wine: 25 percent above average. However, their edge is even greater on imported wine—the "class" wine. They are 36 percent above average in this category.

Color owners, an affluent group, also go in a big way for owning boats. Of interest, too, is the type of boat they tend to own.

Outboard motor boats are the most popular type. And color owners have a 72 percent higher-than-normal level of ownership of this type, as Chart 23 indicates. However, the real status comes from owning inboard motor boats. It is consistent, therefore, that color owners have *three times* the national level of ownership of inboard boats.

And here is one for the books. They say America is becoming a nation of two-car families.

Well, color owners are well in the lead on that score: 34 percent above average in owning two cars, as Chart 24 shows. But the real trend in color homes is not two cars—it is three cars. These active and affluent people are 86 percent above average in owning three or more cars. Here is the three-car family become reality!

3. *Summary*

In the introduction the point was made that color TV owners are a "class" audience, which can be reached simultaneously with television's "mass" audience of black-and-white set owners. The profile of color TV owners presented in this chapter, based on demographic and product usage information, provides detailed evidence of the high quality of the color audience.

In terms of demographic characteristics, the BRI data show that the color television audience has much higher incomes than the general population—is younger—and is found in above-average numbers in medium-size families. Moreover, the information on the characteristics of "future" color owners indicates that the high quality of the color audience is likely to be maintained for quite some time to come. While the "future" color owners have somewhat lower incomes than current owners, they still have much higher incomes than the general population. At the same time, the "future" owners tend to be younger and have larger families than the current owners.

The product usage data furnish additional insights into the kinds of people in the color TV audience. Not only are they heavy spenders, they are especially apt to be "venturesome", convenience-oriented and status-minded.

Together, the demographic and product usage information paint a consistent picture of the color TV audience. Color owners are the opinion-molders, the market-leaders, the vanguard who have the money and the turn of mind to catch an advertiser's new idea first, seize it and go out and spread it. They represent a true "class" audience—in a very real sense, a bonus audience reached along with television's general "mass" audience.

IV

Doing Business in Color

10 Selling Color Television

NORMAN E. CASH
President, Television Bureau of Advertising

In this essay on selling color, Pete Cash identifies himself as "a partisan advocate of television". Industry members will recognize this as one of the most self-effacing understatements made since the inception of the video tube. Cash, president of the Television Bureau of Advertising and industry veteran by dint of service with two networks (NBC, ABC) and the Crosley Broadcasting group, has been making forceful and convincing noises on behalf of the medium and its magic ever since TvB opened its doors on January 1, 1955.

Cash was head of station relations for the five-man TvB group at that time; became a vice president the same year, and in 1956 was elected to the presidency. Under his leadership TvB has grown to a staff of 50, with branch offices in Chicago, Los Angeles and Detroit. Bureau membership includes some 260 stations, the three networks, and 14 station representatives.

Dearie, Do You Remember When might well be the musical theme for Cash's exposition on selling the new, multi-hued medium . . .

As we look at television today and note the increasing number of commercials produced in color, we tend to assume that everyone knows the value and full measure of advertising via tint TV. Network, national spot, local commercial messages—from the most elaborate two-minute-or-more production epics in prime-time programs to simple slides—color is indeed with us in a wide variety of ways and on behalf of countless products and services.

But, if "everyone knows", then why this exposition on the selling of color? I believe it's because few in the industry have had time to close the door, prop their feet up on the desk and exercise their gray matter on the subject of selling color for its own sake. We've been too busy with the highly competitive business of selling *television*.

Our industry is more than ready for this cranial effort; has invested many millions in color production and transmission equipment, to the point where—at the start of 1966—97 percent of all network affiliates could transmit color programs in color. By September of the same year, 83 percent had the technical ability to *originate* color in some form—by film and slide chain and/or by videotape, if not by actual live camera equipment.

Large amounts of money have been spent on, and a great amount of creative effort devoted to, the promotion of color programming—both in other media and through our own. From double-truck, full-color ads showing that peacock in all his finery, to tint-dipped poodles and three-color skywriting and all of the countless promotional stunts in our facile industry's bag of tricks, pioneering color TV purveyors have thumped the drums in every conceivable way to call attention to video's new miracle.

With research, determination and major financial investment, the electronics industry worked to make color not only possible but readily available. People employed in television broadcasting must in turn develop the skills and techniques that will make color *profitable*—for the advertiser, his agency *and* the telecaster.

Most television salesmen have found it "easy as taking candy away from a baby" to switch an advertiser from black-and-white to color. Perhaps—and the pun is inevitable—the sponsors would rather switch than fight! But this, to me, isn't *selling* color television. Advertisers have switched to color in the most painless way possible— reversing the salesman's candy-and-baby simile, the clients have been handed multi-colored lollipops, almost without asking. It's been given away. Color has not brought *more* business in itself, nor has it led more and different advertisers to use more television. *Not yet.*

There is a way, however, and it isn't something we need to create or even to invent. For older members of the industry, the key word is *remember*; for newer members and fresh candidates in commercial videoland, it might be: *read, listen, pick the brains of those oldsters.*

Remember, those of us in the veteran category should say, the salesman's dream that some day he would be able to sell television without that inhibiting cost per thousand as his bible? That he'd be able to get signatures on contracts *without* those magic numbers? That maybe there wouldn't *be* ratings? That perhaps all he'd carry in his sales portfolio would be his circulation figure, even as his colleagues in space selling!

In this Utopian state, television advertising could then be sold as a sales medium rather than just another statistic. Then the salesman could talk about *impact* and *results* and not little fractions of people to be fed into the accommodating maw of a computer, to be compared with little fractions from other media. "Selling without numbers" has long been a telecaster's dream: even as he knows that every trend in his industry is to *more* numbers, *more* demographics, *more* fractionalizing of his audience and his market, he continues to dream.

But what's the first request when color becomes available? Make a study; come up with numbers; split the audience of television into fragments and run each minute particle through a full laboratory test; measure color's value compared with black-and-white; come up with a loading factor to add to the cost per thousand—above all, give us *numbers* to feed into a computer!

Even as with an expensive, pedigreed dog, so once you own a computer you want to keep it well fed. Giving evidence that there *is* something that abhors a vacuum more than nature, computer men like to imply that "there's nothing angrier than an empty computer!" Granting all manner of speed, efficiency and accuracy to the computer world, I'd still like to cry: *stop the machines*—if only for a minute—and to pose some questions. Do we need numbers? Is one more fraction going to help? Don't we really want to sell color television the way we *wanted* to sell black-and-white TV? Isn't it possible to sell color television *without* the numbers?

Yes, I will answer, and some veteran telecasters *know how.* They've already done it, with black-and-white television, without fragments and fractions, bits and pieces. Remember that, back in the early days of the medium, we didn't have numbers, except perhaps the number of television homes in a market (and in those days even a large market had a low number).

Because there were no numbers, black-and-white television had to be sold as a selective medium. There was no other way to sell it, because relatively few homes owned one of those magic watching boxes.

Early television was most certainly a *selective* medium, just as color television is today and will be in the next several years (granting larger numbers, *still* not in the truly mass saturation category of black-and-white TV and other mass media). The first black-and-white viewers were higher-income families, younger, more interested in new things. From the discretionary income point of view, television attracted the cream of the crop for TV's advertisers: those advertisers may have been small in number, but big in importance and remarkably successful in results.

Seldom in history does a medium get a second chance to do something. I believe the expansion of color television does provide a second chance—if the industry has the drive and determination to seize it. Here, in the immediate future, is the opportunity to get out from under the inhibiting numbers inundating the selling of most television advertising today, an opportunity created by one single factor of color television: at present, color TV has—on a regularly-reported, continuing basis—only *one* number, that of color television homes!

For the medium's newer salesmen, color is the answer to that envious dream of their print media sales rivals: a medium without limiting numbers, a sales vehicle for which they can, in the words of the oldtime traveling salesman, "paint sunsets on the mountains and rainbows in the skies".

For most of them it will take a new outlook on selling. What have they got for sale? *First*, color homes are higher-income homes (at the very least, with enough financial strength to afford the color set). *Second*, color set families not only have more money to spend—they spend it! (Note the purchase of the color set.) *Third*, these same families are interested in newer things (like color television).

Today's color audience (and tomorrow's, in terms of the next several years) may be targeted as a higher-income, larger spending, more willing-to-spend, selective audience.

With that audience in focus, the color salesman then has the challenge of matching it to those advertisers and potential advertisers most in need of selectivity in making sales. Particularly at the local level of selling, the salesman has opportunity to bring in new clients and new *types* of clients—investment houses, brokers, banks; the most expensive jeweler, the Cadillac dealer, the highest price department of the highest price department store, the most expensive restaurant—advertisers who aren't interested in reaching everyone but who want to go directly to *goal*: the color television household.

Selective audiences weren't the only things we talked about in the early days of black-and-white television. Before splinterization took over, we sold television as a dynamic means of moving products by moving people—a medium with *impact*. And that's what we sold: Impact.

What about the impact of color television? I don't think it will require a massive study with reams of those digits we don't need to prove that color—pure color, anywhere in what we see around us—has impact. Compare anything in color with the same thing without color and the value of color is obvious.

The difference between a black-and-white newspaper ad and one in color is also obvious. And as a partisan advocate of television, I will offer the reminder that this color costs extra—35 percent extra in newspapers. A black-and-white magazine advertisement is one thing, telling its story in variations of the gray-scale; for an additional 40 percent color can be added, and that ad is quite another vehicle for transporting an image and a message.

In television, we found that the best research into the value that color adds starts with a pair of shears. We took a black-and-white and a color print of the same commercial, snipped, pruned and spliced, and developed the most graphic demonstration possible of the additional values of color. From black-and-white to color, the girl went from "pretty" to "lovely", the product from "nice" to "startling—almost three-dimensional", the art work from "professional" to "wow"!

The most obvious way to utilize color in the video medium is to show things as they really are—a basket of apples, a grocery shelf stacked with packages, a bright red Mustang. Color is literal, but it's an emotional tool as well. It can create a warm, comfortable, quiet feeling of confidence, or it can convey an austere, dignified, or even uneasy sensation. All moods are possible.

So perhaps the color television salesman should use a color camera to replace his rating book. He can take pictures of his prospects, of their stores and their wares—first in black-and-white and then in color. And, unless he meets the insoluble problem of attempting that one color-blind prospect in a hundred, his snapshot sampling may very well do his selling for him.

The salesman should *look* for color. In that expensive section of the department store, is the wrapping paper colorful? Does the retailer already have a unique hue for his newspaper ads, flyers, shopping bags, delivery trucks, gift boxes, store windows? Color television, as the extension of this unique set of impressions, carries the store *to the viewer*, the product into the home of the potential buyer as it appears in the window or on the shelf.

At the risk of offending not one, but two, specialized areas in the advertising scheme, the color TV salesman must move out of the media department and its compilations of data and into the creative unit with its ideas!

Does that postman indeed ring twice? Color, I submit, is television's second chance to prove that it is a medium with values that range far beyond the fragmented statistics with qualitative impressions that can't be measured in cost per thousand.

Members of the television industry should be warned, however, that as color grows to be as universal as black-and-white television, the selective audience will be less selective—and the by-the-rulebook users of the medium will be after those numbers once again. Let's *not* reduce the medium to a statistic, the second time around!

Color can bring new advertisers, new strength, to television, if its representatives take color *to* them. Color can increase the television usage of current advertisers if they have demonstrated for them the power that color adds to television's impact.

In the industry, we have to remember the lesson of how television was sold when it was merely black-and-white. The clients must be reminded of why they bought television in the first place.

The Television Bureau of Advertising was in action for several years before its "E-Motion" study demonstrated that television is an *emotional* communications tool. Today, commercial production seldom shows products; rather demonstrates people's reactions to products. Commercials don't show action; they show *re*-action.

Color adds a significant flavoring to the emotional quality of television. It speaks out with a voice louder than the most screaming of headlines or the oldest of announcers. To the question: "What *is* color television?" the salesman might well reply: "It doesn't take numbers to show what it is. It's black-and-white television—brought to life!"

Let's sell color television for what it *is*: fast, exciting, valuable. All we've got to do is *remember* how to sell it.

11 Color Promotion

CHET CAMPBELL
Manager, Advertising, Promotion & Publicity,
WMAQ-TV, Chicago

With World War II, a journalism degree from the University of Illinois and credits as a newspaper sports writer behind him, Chet Campbell approached NBC-Chicago with an urge to join its news staff.

He was intercepted by the publicity department head: "You look like a press relations man to me." As writer, editor, assistant manager, then manager, Chet proved the man correct.

One of his earlier administrative decisions was the employment of this editor. While the relative wisdom of that decision has been debated since, it has served to put the editor in the position—an enviable one to many a journalist—of editing his ex-chief's writing!

In publicity, then in advertising, promotion and merchandising, Chet Campbell has been in the mainstream of NBC-Chicago's promotion effort for almost 20 years; was in early 1967 honored by the net with the title: "Showman of the Year". He worked with many of the venerable programs of the early "Chicago School" of television; has been an active supporter of the Broadcasters Promotion Association since its first days. For the 1966 "Color Conference" of the National Association of Broadcasters, he shared with this editor the duties of presenting BPA's definitive message on color promotion *before that group.*

In the following, Campbell both recalls early experiences in color promotion and defines day-by-day activities after *the color signal is put on the air* . . .

"COLOR? I'll tell you about color! The chief engineer says that the three primary colors are red, green and blue. And for a change, I agree with him. Red is for your eyeballs after 18 hours, weekdays *and* weekends, on the job; green is for the money we've been spending; and blue is for the boss's vocabulary if anything goes wrong with *this* promotion!"

Well, perhaps that's a bit strong. The speaker was a bone-tired promotion man on the eve of a major station promotion to introduce color to his market. To give the quote its most meaningful impact, it should be recorded that, even at his moment of maximum fatigue, he was thinking and responding *in color.* And well he should, having been living a rainbow existence for a period of several hectic months.

Promoting color television presents potentials which are almost numberless, from dipping of white poodles in red, green and blue vegetable dye to three-color skywriting . . . from hand delivery to agency executives of multi-hued Turkish cigarettes to the serving of red Manhattans, green-tinted martinis and blue (ugh) cocktails at a station reception. From installing a three-color telephone in the manager's office ("*I won't stand for it*") to painting the news department's mobile unit in rainbow stripes ("*I won't stand for it*").

All of this, and more, falls to the often over-burdened and understaffed promotion department; and it's only when it comes to the pleasant task of selecting three gorgeous damsels to parade the aforementioned red, green and blue poodles downtown that the station manager, news director and other assorted executives rally to the cause of color promotion.

This antic and fun-filled activity must, in all of its dimensions, be aimed in the general direction of one or perhaps several goals. As any broadcast promotion, if it is to be effective and purposeful, it must result in more *audience,* more *sales,* more *community stature.*

Overlapping all of this, even as these target areas are defined and listed, is a rainbow-tinted mystique that must pervade the TV station, from the management suite to the mailroom, from the sales bullpen to the business office. In another chapter of this text, WBAP-TV general manager Roy Bacus—"the man in the red coat"

—defines this *esprit de corps* when he writes of the "total involvement" of the staff so necessary to the successful launch of that color burst and to the station's image as *the color station*. As he says, "Staff enthusiasm will be the response to management enthusiasm."

What follows here proposes to examine in some detail several major target areas for station color promotion: (1) the viewing audience; (2) station advertisers and their agencies; (3) TV set retailers and their service departments; (4) the station's position of leadership in the community *and*, in a broader sense, in the industry.

Graphing the major color promotion target areas on a horizontal scale, there is a heavy line drawn through the middle. To the left, label it "before color"; to the right, color it bright and label it "so now color is here".

The two divergent sides of our graph are far from mutually exclusive, and much of what you do *before* and *after* is applicable to *both*. However, there are relative degrees of effort, in terms of time and money, to be applied against your targets at the various stages of the overall promotion.

Introducing Color—the before *stage*

The same case-hardened promotion man quoted earlier, but after he had replenished his verve and enthusiasm, puts it this way: "Were I promoting color on an NBC affiliate, even as the peacock unfolded his wings at the opening of a network show, I'd take the audio under and sneak in a local voice-over that said, 'I'll bet *that* looks beautiful in color!'"

This is a graphic way of delineating point number one: whetting the public's appetite for color. Which is to say that if 10 percent of the homes in a market have color, then an immense 90 percent do not—and the major project is to convert that 90 percent to the color camp.

Color-equipped homes are a measurable, reportable quality segment of your total audience even as you move into and expand station color programming. We speak of quality here because research studies have shown that the color homes predictably fall into the higher-income, better educated, bigger spending households. This is a market of prime interest to your advertisers. (For in-depth examination of this subject, note chapters in this text—*The Dimensions of Color* and *The Impact of Color;* also Nielsen Station Index *Color Set Penetration* in the Appendix.)

Let's document the steps in a major campaign to introduce color to a market and, more importantly, to sell those monochrome homes on color. This particular campaign was launched by NBC's Station WMAQ-TV (then WNBQ) in the Chicago market in 1956, when it became the "world's first all-color station" as a prototype for the industry.

It was a pioneering effort in many ways, and was calculated to appeal to all major target areas: to whet the home audience's appetite with a constant "color is here" theme; to excite retailers to the point of pushing color set sales through special displays and promotion; to acquaint advertisers and their agencies with the potential of color television advertising and to urge them to climb aboard the color bandwagon before the crowd; and, finally, to establish the station as a pacesetter and pioneer in the eyes of the community and the broadcasting industry.

1. *The Audience*—The word was implanted that "color is here". The first order of business was to select a Channel 5 spokesman who would shout the color story over the air; who would represent it graphically in newspaper ads, billboards, window displays and all the rest. This multi-purpose symbol of Channel 5's switch to all-color combined the voice of the penetrating and well-recalled "Mommy, I wanna Salerno Butter Cookie" kiddy image from radio with the precocious cartoon personality of Dennis the Menace (sans the menace). The station created an animated color spokesman—Tommy Tint—a bright and sparkling youngster with a shock of red hair, a green shirt and blue overalls.

On the air, using bright splashes of primary colors—Tommy Tint red, green and blue—he chanted that "Color is live on Channel 5" and "Hey look at me, I'm painting with color on NBC!" In his full color ensemble, including paint brush and pail, Tommy appeared everywhere—on mass transportation car cards, restaurant place mats, billboards; in regional magazines; in the windows of TV set retailers; in *TV Guide* and in the local newspapers (in the latter unfortunately *without* color).

A three-dimensional Tommy also appeared on the Chicago

scene, molded in plastic and hand-painted. As a measure of his success, no less than 20 of Tommy's plastic images were spirited away by guests at the top-level reception which introduced Channel 5's color promotion!

At the same time, the enormous effort behind the color changeover at the station was being documented in every detail for the trade and general press: the tearing apart and re-building of existing studios; the lessons being learned in lighting, painting, set design and make-up; the testing of advertisers' products before the color cameras.

Station personalities were used to help tell the color story. The Channel 5 weatherman lent his name to a feature article on the use of color in weather forecasting, and the glamorous redhead who conducted the women's program overnight became an authority on make-up and fashion for color television.

For the viewer at home, the station's color conversion was summed up and documented in a special half-hour program, *NBC and Color*, which took viewers on a behind-the-scenes tour of Channel 5 facilities and the frenetic activities leading up to "C-Day".

There was much more in terms of building the public's interest in color. Early in the promotion, color sets were installed in the Channel 5 reception lobby so that station visitors could watch available network and local programming in color. "Write-in" audience contests were held, with color TV sets as prizes. Group tours of the station were conducted for women's clubs, schools and touring groups, and a special animated display showing how color TV works was the high point of the tour.

Yes, there *really were* three-color telephones, especially assembled for Channel 5 by Illinois Bell and presented to the station manager with all attendant publicity fanfare. And there *were* those multi-hued cocktails, created in co-operation with the head bartender of the Merchants and Manufacturers Club in the station's headquarters building and served at client, agency and press receptions. In all candor it must be admitted that green "Tommy Tint" martinis *never* really did catch on.

2. *Retail Set Dealers*. This is an area of vital importance to any color promotion, and the one most likely to be misunderstood or overlooked. Normally, the station promotion manager does not maintain close liaison with retailers, especially in larger markets.

However, when introducing color to a market, TV receiver distributors and dealers become an integral part of the total promotion scheme, and you need them on your side.

It takes some romancing on the station's part and an effort to make the dealer feel that he's important to *you*. It's a much easier task if a dealer trade organization exists in the market, with mailing lists and perhaps regular meetings. If not, create your own mailing list from the local telephone book. In the case of Channel 5 in Chicago, such an organization did exist, and through it WMAQ-TV was able to reach hundreds of retailers with station promotion and to enlist the organization's help in making personal contact with major dealers.

Polk Brothers, one of the nation's most aggressive discount chains, was one of the first on the color bandwagon. Special displays of color receivers under controlled conditions, replete with Tommy Tints and other station promotion material, were set up in Polk stores. WMAQ-TV also won the co-operation of several color set manufacturers, who in turn urged the support of their own dealers. With the station sharing the expense, some manufacturers provided various types of promotional display material, including counter cards and window streamers.

Why so much emphasis on dealer relations? The facts of life in 1956 were that only a miniscule segment of the Chicago market had been exposed to color. And virtually the only places to see it were dealers' showrooms. If color circulation was to come at all, it had to be through the combined efforts of Channel 5 in providing the color program product, and the dealer in displaying that product on *his* product in *his* showroom. Ideally, this would move color sets (which then were quite expensive), the dealers would make a profit and be happy with Channel 5 for providing the programming, and Channel 5 would have the opportunity to sell the wonders of increasing color set circulation to its advertisers and potential advertisers.

Ideally—it didn't happen that way. At that time, many dealers lacked confidence in the quality of color. To some, color wasn't really "here" in 1956. Even as the station received pledges of full and complete co-operation from store management, the TV department manager or the salesman on the floor often didn't follow through, even to the point of talking a potential customer *away* from color to a black-and-white set.

WMAQ-TV found it expedient to spot-check major store displays of color sets. In too many cases the sets were being demonstrated under the worst of conditions—in rooms bright with fluorescent lights that distorted and weakened the best color picture, or by sales personnel who didn't know or didn't care enough about the careful tuning of receivers. In many cases this situation could be corrected by calling it to the attention of the store management or the manufacturer. Some set builders were concerned enough to conduct crash orientation programs for store personnel, and to offer advice on how best to display sets. In a smaller market, this is a function that could be taken over by the station even as it works to build dealer relationships.

3. *Agencies and Advertisers.* Channel 5 faced still another missionary challenge in 1956, this with advertisers and their agencies. While some forward-looking network advertisers had converted to color, on the local level advertisers and their agencies had little or no experience with the brand-new tint medium.

Channel 5 implemented their initiation into tint video by conducting a series of color clinics, with invitations to selected agencies to bring in clients' products for color television exposure. This was an excellent vehicle for displaying the station's stable of "color experts" in graphics, lighting, scenic effects and engineering, before a blue chip audience of top agency and client executives. Generally the agencies were delighted, and while only a little of the technical knowhow of color commercial production could rub off, the value in agency relations was immeasurable. This was another example of that involvement.

In addition to the color clinics, all agencies were bombarded with a constant stream of sales promotion material designed to acquaint them with every step of the colorization, its impact on the market and the prospects for a glowing, colorful future just ahead. Station salesmen, wearing three-color Channel 5 neckties and armed with "The World's First All-Color Station" gimmicks—from three-color ballpoint pens to handsome smoked-glass ash trays—left the Channel 5 imprint all up and down Michigan and Madison Avenues. On "C-Day" the invitation list for the big switch to *all-color* was replete with the major representatives of Chicago's advertising and business community.

4. *Community and Trade Relations.* Color coming to Chicago for the first time, and the fact that a Chicago station had been selected for a significant pioneering effort, with nationwide implications, created a burst of civic pride. The initial announcement—of a very well-kept corporate secret—came at a carefully staged closed-circuit television press conference, *in color*, and the local press pulled out all the stops. One unique touch was that Channel 5 provided "TV blue" shirts for all male reporters attending. (There was one heavyweight in attendance who caused a bit of frantic last minute shopping at a "big man's" store!)

Moreover, the station even had the audacity to "suggest" proper attire for woman reporters!

The two-way, New York-Chicago press conference included an announcement of the project by General David Sarnoff, then chairman of the board of RCA and NBC, with remarks by other NBC executives and by the head of the Chicago station operation. Charts and artists' concepts were used to detail the remodeling changes in studios and offices. The press conference was then opened to questions from the press in both Chicago and New York. The result was excellent coverage, even better than expected, including enthusiastic reactions from Chicago's mayor, the governor of Illinois, and other government and civic leaders.

The station leaned on the good offices of Chicago's mayor to proclaim "Color Television Week" in the city; in addition, when "C-Day" came about, the Mayor was on hand, blue shirt and all, to help pull the switch that converted Channel 5 to all-color. That opening ceremony was conducted on an NBC-TV network program, with Robert W. Sarnoff (then NBC president, now president of RCA) in the WMAQ-TV studios for the dedication. Over a thousand VIP guests viewed the ceremonies on color TV sets installed in the Merchants and Manufacturers Club.

Channel 5's "C-Day" was timed to coincide with the opening of the National Association of Broadcasters' annual convention in Chicago. This, too, was part of the overall promotion plan, and was designed to create maximum attention in the industry for the "first all-color operation" in the nation. Through trade advertising, convention posters and direct mail contact with every delegate, members of the industry attending the convention were invited to visit WMAQ-TV. Bus transportation was provided from the convention hotel. Scores of interested broadcasters welcomed this opportunity to see first-hand a pilot color operation. In addition, closed-circuit feeds were transmitted from Channel 5 studios to color receivers in exhibit areas at the convention. Reprints of trade advertising, trade press publicity and other promotional material were distributed at the convention.

Those Channel 5 activities attendant to the NAB convention closed out the book on the introductory phase for the "world's first all-color station". What came after that was necessarily anticlimax, and falls within the realm of continuing promotion. In many ways, the NBC Chicago color promotion was a one-in-a-million opportunity which probably could not be repeated a decade or more later. All of the elements fell into place in a neat pattern which spelled success in terms of *audience, community* and *industry*.

After "C-Day"—continuing promotion

As any good promotion and public relations practitioner knows, all the basic elements of a decade ago are present today in similar situations. The tools are basic, and can be used over and over again to achieve similar results—perhaps on a smaller but no less significant scale for the management of a television station turning to tint for the first time.

All the fanfare of the big color burst has faded into the background, and the press clips are turning yellow in the publicity scrapbook. You're back fighting for audience on a more or less even basis with everyone else. But *is it* an even basis? Not if you're *the* color station in town. If you can maintain that color image in the community, your station is going to enjoy a very distinct advantage over the competition.

1. *Maintaining Dominance.* First off, if you have the reputation as *the* color station, the growing number of color set owners in the market will turn to your channel for entertainment and information. As we have noted, studies have shown that color programs attract a larger audience in color television homes than in monochrome homes, and this advantage in color homes is often large enough to offset the lesser ratings of the monochrome audience. In other words,

the color advantage might put a color program in the top 20, even though with black-and-white viewers the program might not be in the top 20 running.

As more and more network programs—daytime as well as prime evening time—move into color, and with the saturation point close at hand, colorization and promotion of local programs assume new importance. Network notwithstanding, local color could provide the catalyst for boosting your station into market dominance. How do you meet the problem of promoting your color superiority at no sacrifice to your promotion thrust aimed at building *total* audience—color be damned?

2. *Color for Color.* Let's adopt the theme that nothing promotes color better than color. And, of course, there's no promotion tool better than your own television station. There should be total commitment to color in all station on-air material—promotions, public service announcements, station ID's—even in the face of a certain amount of black-and-white programming and commercials. For the bright, modern look in a station's image on the tube, there is no place for monochrome promotions, ID's, etc. In short: color *everything* COLOR! Color viewers will appreciate it and think color when they think of your channel. B & W viewers couldn't care less if you use color to promote black-and-white programs.

The keystone to success in colorizing a station's on-the-air appearance is a color-oriented graphic arts department. Graphic arts staff members have to live and breathe color even as everyone else concerned with station image. Modern equipment and graphic tools will enhance the quality of color on-air production. These are a must, and stations have learned the hard way that horse and buggy graphics just won't do in today's jet age of color.

Organizational setups vary from station to station, but generally the graphic artists work primarily for the program or production department. Usually they are overworked, with jobs coming in from all directions—promotion, news, program, sales, special "management projects", etc. This creates problems of job priorities, with promotion having to fight for its share of attention.

But this situation also gives the promotion manager an opportunity to co-ordinate and possibly to lend direction to his station's total on-the-air image. He should assume leadership in defining and creating a "family look" to everything the station does in terms of ID's, promos, title slides, flip cards, and the like. Everything—graphics, colors, patterns, layout—should enhance the continuity of that family look. Obviously, this must be applied as well to other areas in the station—letterheads, printed promotional materials, and *all* print advertising.

3. *Creativity in Color Promotion.* As in any other promotion activity, the ingredient of creativity is necessary to the development of effective, quality on-air materials. The most advanced graphics in the world can't put a spark in a soggy, limp idea. This is where experimentation comes into its own. In the privacy of our own studios we can experiment, try "far-out" ideas, even when the technical people may say they can't do it. While the complexity of the electronic system levels some limitations, it does at the same time open vistas for bold innovations.

But, whatever you do, check everything out on the system—especially if it's (as it should be) in color. Never trust your own color sense, the ordinary film or slide projection system, or the critical opinions of your colleagues. The television electronic system can raise havoc with graphics that look perfect to the naked eye. Whatever you *do*, don't be afraid to try something new. Your errors in the testing process are not inflicted on the audience, and mistakes pave the way for further creative development.

If your own graphics art staff is overburdened as a result of routine work, don't settle for an inferior or expedient-dictated promotion product. Seek help from the outside. It might appear that promotion budgets can't support the services of art studios, film producers and graphic experts, but these services may be more reasonable than expected. You'll find that some of these creative people will welcome an opportunity to work with color television, and will introduce innovations and ideas and be willing to share the cost of experimentation. Television holds a great attraction for the field of graphics, and promotion offers a chance to get a foot in the studio door.

4. *Color Promotion Costs.* While the facts of life of a promotion budget will encourage the use of your own facilities as much as possible as a means of keeping down costs, there are limitations in the production of a quality promotion product. Videotape, while a

great boon to television and a versatile and readily available tool for the promotion man, has its own artistic limitations. Film still offers superior advantages in terms of special effects, including animation, on-location shooting mobility, and color quality under all types of lighting conditions.

Production of color film promotions can be costly. But there are dollar-saving shortcuts available. The use of the Oxberry still camera technique can produce highly effective animation from still photos. The costs of a film sound track can be saved entirely by videotaping the color film promo and adding voice and music in your studios. Then all necessary extra copies can be dubbed on tape, eliminating the cost of additional color film prints. Good film producers, who value your business and the chance to work with television, can suggest many other steps to economy.

Dealing with an outside producer has other advantages. You can find relief from the pressures of trying to operate under the time, facilities and personnel limitations of your own TV studio operation. Necessarily, the program department has a top priority call on studios and personnel, and promotion may find itself waiting in line—at exactly the time that it can't afford to wait. It should be remembered that outside film production takes time, however: this is one place where videotape cannot be matched. The lesson in any event—give yourself plenty of time for the planning and production of on-the-air promotion!

5. *More Costs: Print Advertising.* The projection of a station's color status in print advertising poses its own problems. Cost is a major one, despite recent advances in newspaper color printing. There are newspaper-imposed limitations on production time required, positioning, and size of color newspaper ads. In most cases, an extensive four-color newspaper campaign is out of the question financially. Full color has to be utilized on a one shot basis: a special insert at the start of a season, or the occasional institutional ads designed to impress community and business leaders rather than build audiences.

Perhaps the growth of color in television and its increasing popularity with audiences and advertisers will spur print media to develop better and more economical methods of color printing, for purely competitive reasons. Until that time the television station, like most other local advertisers, will be relegated to the facility of black-and-white on the printed page. A sensible alternative would be to channel more newspaper advertising money into the production of better quality color on-air promotion material.

And why not? Our own television station is our most effective advertising tool.

6. *Promoting in Every Way.* Dozens of special promotion ideas will suggest themselves day-by-day. There is a wide variety of all-station promotion activity which must be color oriented. A strong, attractive and memorable color ID, signature or trade mark will make it easy to identify everything from the station's mobile units to its letterheads, from the newsmen's cameras to the display at the state fair and the bright blazers worn by station personnel (announcers *and* executives!).

The physical plant should not be overlooked, especially if your facilities are toured by studio visitors, VIP's, clients, etc. Many stations present a beautiful facade, with richly-appointed reception areas, executive offices and conference rooms—often with equally eye-catching receptionists and secretaries as well. But move behind the swinging doors that lead to the production area and see the dull decor of "Early Grand Rapids coffee ring" that most likely documents the station's years of growth!

Drab gray corridors can be livened with a coat of pastel paint and a colorful floor covering. And, while a brightly-lighted studio in which a program is being produced possesses a certain glamour, it more than likely has the appearance of a deserted warehouse when the overheads go down and the sets are put back in storage. A refurbishing, advocated to management with the same standards that you apply to your on-air promotion, can turn those warehouses into showrooms for your new color product.

In Summary. It's difficult to conclude a treatise on color promotion; even as the job itself, it has no end. Promotion should be, *must be*, a growing, expanding art, constantly reaching out in new directions, encompassing new areas of attention, developing new skills and techniques. You put to use—in every possible way—the same basic skills and tools used for any station promotion project, with the exception that the dimension of color must be exploited.

Whatever you do, color is FUN!

12 Advertising in Color

DONALD F. COLEMAN
Vice President, Interpublic GmbH. Frankfurt, Germany

Donald Coleman entered the world of professional communications at the age of eight, when he hand-set various items of neighborhood gossip in rubber type and peddled the Austin Flash *at two cents per copy. His older brother was the first subscriber. This heretofore-unpublished bit of trivia is made available years later only because this editor is the older brother—and still feels that he got a bargain at the price!*

Some years later, and with more advanced professional training, Don labored on the police beat with Chicago's City Press Bureau, later moved to the public relations department of the WGN stations. He was at one time advertising manager of the American Dairy Association, then moved to New York and ad agency work. For the Marschalk wing of the Interpublic group, he serviced accounts that included Speidel and Coca-Cola. His TV commercial production experiences, pleasures and problems have included duty in San Juan, Nice, and London—where he supervised the Speidel "Lady Godiva" color film commercials under the clamorous eye of Big Ben. Undaunted by the complexities of international advertising, he is currently on a major assignment in Frankfurt.

In the following pages, Don Coleman states the case for the advertiser and his agency as they view and work with color TV...

MAX BUCK, NBC vice president, tells the story: "Back in the first year of WNBC-TV local color work, we had a five-minute live insert in the network's *Home* show. A pitch gal did some sort of helpful-hints-for-the-homemaker feature, along with a straight, stand-up commercial for the client.

"We weren't selling women's clothing, but had a deal with a fashion outfit, so that the girl had a fresh, different and colorful costume each day. On about the fourth day, she wore a wide, shiny, bright red belt over a blue dress. When we had six phone calls in less than five minutes, asking where you could buy a *bright red belt* like that, we knew that we were—ready for it or not—in the business of selling color advertising on TV!"

Red belts or red Stingrays, one of the dynamic forces behind the pressure toward color telecasting—especially in the early days of the 1960s—was the demand for color *programming* exerted upon stations and networks by advertisers. The advertiser—justifiably proud of his *avant garde* position in the use of color TV materials—needed a suitable showcase for those color commercials he had made, tested and found highly rewarding. "Color attracts and enhances color," was the reasoning. "You wouldn't put a new car in a print ad—a $5,000 hunk of Detroit iron, all red and gleaming and with black leather seats and whitewalls—in a drab, black-and-white setting. Too stark. Contrast too great. Too much like that Bob Newhart downbeat parody of *Julius Caesar:* 'Friends, Romans, countrymen—*I got sumpthin' I wanna tell yuh.*' "

So, for a variety of reasons, it was and is apparent that the red belt must be encircled by an even wider and infinitely longer red, green and blue belt of color programming.

The quick switch from black-and-white to color commercial production came almost as fast as the response to that red belt. Some advertisers, notably those who sponsored NBC's early color programming, have made *no* B & W commercials since 1956. Reasoning for the changeover: the sales power of color commercials in the transition period from black-and-white to color has proven more than worth the additional cost of color commercial production.

Specific and detailed documentary research on this subject is available in other chapters of this text. However, one method used by this writer—*Total Prime Time* audience recall, as reported by

Gallup and Robinson* has been particularly valuable in making judgments on the use of color TV materials.

Among the conclusions reached: color commercials viewed by people viewing on color TV sets delivered their messages *twice as effectively* as did the identical commercials—viewed the same night within the same program and at the same time—by people watching black-and-white sets!

One of the commercials singled out in the G & R report was that of a new men's after-shave and cologne, *British Sterling.* According to the data, 18 percent of the audience in the B & W homes recalled correctly the message of the commercial, while 35 percent of the people who viewed the identical commercial in color-equipped homes responded to the sponsor's message at the same level of effectiveness.

Important to the advertiser? Obviously—this either (*a*) *doubles* the efficiency, or (*b*) *halves* the cost-per-thousand, in that segment of the total audience viewing in color!

Earlier research data had brought out the point that people in color set homes experienced a "second childhood" of TV viewing, and became heavier viewing units simply because of the new impact of color transmissions.

The advertising agency, faced with backing up its recommendations to clients for the automatic use of TV color, finds increasing demand for documentation. In an earlier era of color as a selective device for reaching those "quality" homes, agency executives borrowed from print media research to cite Starch: "50 to 75 percent jump in the recall of a full color ad" ... from Crosley: "A 34 percent advantage in color recall" ... from Schwerin: "An increased preference average score (for color) of 151 against a black-and-white norm of 100" ... from the ANA: "A 55 percent advantage for color commercials."

The raven (jet black) may well be crying "Nevermore". The concept of color as a compensation factor—compensating for a nondescript product, a fuzzy concept, an absence of that "unique

---

*Gallup and Robinson Research Co., Princeton, N.J., has conducted a continuing research study since 1963 in the Philadelphia, Pa., market, where interviewers call homes 24 hours after the broadcast of a program and probe to find out how much the respondent can recall about the commercials—first on an unaided, then an aided basis. These studies, called *Total Prime Time* audience recall, have been used by many leading advertisers to measure commercial effectiveness.

selling proposition"—is of little value; may actually be a disadvantage in putting the product in a setting so low-keyed that it is less than real, or so unrealistically bright that it may be subject to ridicule.

All of which is to say that, whenever that magic "added dimension" of color TV is contemplated, it must be carried from original concept and planning conference through to production as one of the most important elements of the successful commercial—and sale.

To echo the sentiment expressed by Pete Cash in his chapter on *Selling Color Television*, advertisers saw the *kind* of household owning the color set as possibly the most important value of the new medium: higher-income group, younger segment of that group, larger families—in short, as the *Saturday Evening Post* once stratified this same potential audience, these are the "influentials" of the American consumer economy.

The advertising force generated by these realizations was felt throughout the TV industry, as the scramble for more and more color programming began at local station as well as network levels. By 1966 the fact became obvious that, as that magic "added attraction" for the viewers *and* the advertisers, the program had best be marked with a "C" in the *TV Guide* and newspaper listings.

Color Commercial Production

The first and most significant thing that advertisers realized about the color commercials themselves was that the cost of production went up—and up and up. *How much* those costs increased solely because of color is difficult to pinpoint, but most advertisers reported increases of from 20 to 60 percent in production costs because of color.

The reasons for the increased cost are of interest, because of the theoretical point that the only physical elemental cost that should have changed was the price of film and processing. Film and processing, however, are the least expensive ingredients in cost, and the actual difference of an estimated 2,000 feet of 35mm.* film shot to

---

*Almost all commercial films are produced on 35mm. film because of the added quality advantages and ease of handling vs. 16mm. stock. The networks use 35mm. film for transmission, whereas the agencies must make 16mm. reduction prints for local station use.

make the typical 60-second commercial* was about $175 over black-and-white, including processing and based on 1966 New York charges.

Studio lighting costs skyrocketed, however, because of the need for much more light in color photography. Costumes, make-up, set designs, all became more colorful, complicated and costly.

One of the major cost increases to accommodate color advertising, however, was in the very nature of the *type* of commercials executed in color versus B & W. All hands in advertising will endorse the truism that, as costs increase in media and production, the net result to the advertiser rarely is *arithmetic*, but much more likely *geometric*.

The kinds of commercials many advertisers were accepting in the "only B & W" days simply did not live up to their expectations when literally done over in color footage—and at the higher price tag. The size of the cast increased, outdoor scenes encompassed broader views, sets and props increased in number and complexity—as the desire to *use* color developed.

Commercial costs went up, but so did—in the eyes of many critical observers—commercial quality. Of course the whole art of making TV commercials was advancing because it was growing older, but the new influence of color seemed to have accelerated many artistic developments. The new element—*color*—was used splashily, and, like any new toy, perhaps too much of it was used in early work.

However, the vital need to have color commercials transmit well to the majority of homes still using B & W sets† provided a healthy brake to color excesses.

The production of color TV commercials also accomplished an important plus factor for all advertisers: they had brilliant, exciting films to show for the advertising portion of sales meetings, trade shows and dealer conventions. (One advertiser, who had best remain nameless, made a full season's worth of television commercials—circa 1957—in full color, for use *only* at his annual convention, when he didn't have a single media buy to be transmitted in color. The management felt that the emotional response of the delegates, and

---

*A 60-second commercial in finished form actually requires only 90 feet of 35mm. film, but experience has shown that most productions require about 2,000 feet of shooting film. Most commercials are produced in a basic 60-second length, with edited versions made of 20-second (30 feet) and 10-second (15 feet) lengths.

†See Appendix for Nielsen Station Index *Market-by-Market Color TV Set Penetration*.

the increased budget they authorized, more than offset the cost. It was, after all, an interesting experiment for the future!)

The actual cost of producing any commercial is governed entirely by its content; thus any attempt even to commit to form generalizations on production costs could be misleading. But to give some guide to the realities of the matter, a hypothetical commercial has been costed-out by Jacques Lemoine of the TVA Groups, Inc., a world-wide production company with offices in New York and London. (Jacques Lemoine has produced commercials in the U.S.A. and around the world for such leading TV clients as General Motors, Coca-Cola, Pan American Airways, and scores more.)

The mythical commercial is conceived to include the following elements: 40 percent of the filming would be in a studio "kitchen set", 60 percent would be outdoors, adjacent to a lake. The scene is summer. Two adult players, a "mother" and a "father", plus their two "children" of 7 and 12 years, are used.

The commercial is 60 seconds long; no music or sound effects; all commentary done by an off-camera narrator.

Element	Estimated Color Cost	Estimated B & W cost
Cast—Four principals, two days; one announcer for one session (includes payroll taxes)	$1,291.00	$1,291.00
Set Construction (kitchen)	2,300.00	2,300.00
Studio Time—one day building, one day shoot, one day strike	900.00	900.00
Lighting	500.00 (2 hrs.)	300,00 (1½ hrs.)
Film Stock (4,000 feet)	725.00	340.00
Developing and Printing	365.00	170.00
Sound (recording session)	200.00	200.00
Optical Negative	800.00	500.00
Fifteen 35mm. prints	355.00	150.00
Fifty 16mm. prints	600.00	250.00
Editing, including mix, etc.	1,200.00	1,200.00
Crew—Two days (one studio, one day location)	6,244.00	6,244.00
Location costs, incl. per diem	500.00	500.00
	$15,980.00	$14,345.00

(To the above would normally be added 17.65 percent agency commission.)

Opposite is a detailed cost sheet of the estimated budget required for the various elements of the proposed commercial, both for black-and-white and color production.

One of the facts of the business that the above table cannot cope with, however, is that of possible additional charges in working toward a color film print that is completely satisfactory. Color film is more difficult to control in the processing lab than in B & W; with this reality, extra print costs often are experienced.

The usual problem is one of faithful reproduction of the color quality of the product and/or its package; two, three or more answer prints,* or even new negative printing materials,† are sometimes required to achieve the precise color reproduction desired.

Based on the above costs, one additional color printing negative and three additional answer prints could raise the total color cost by an additional $950.00 net.

Happily, black-and-white productions seldom require additional negative or answer print work.

Color TV Media Costs

The switchover to colorcasting obviously had some bearing on the costs of the medium in that many of the same factors that influence commercial production also influence the programs, i.e., film and processing costs, extra lighting needs, more elaborate sets, costume details, make-up, etc. The increases were not as sharp as might be expected, from a percentage view at least, in that almost all of the film shows in production were shot in color from the beginning, for the secondary international theatrical market.

Those live shows switched to color, such as the early *Perry Como Show, Garry Moore, Ed Sullivan*, and others, ran into the same extra set and lighting costs, but overhead charges were such a small portion of the total show price (with talent and crew costs ranging

---

Answer print is a term used to define the first print where picture and sound are married into one unit. Until the answer print is correct, additional quantities of prints are not ordered.

†In all TV (and movie) work, the original negative is rarely used to make prints. A duplicate negative is produced for printing purposes; in color work sometimes must be made more than once to capture the colors of the original.

from 75 to 90 percent of production charges) that these increases were absorbed within the upward spiral of *all* costs.

The cost of doing business in color, in terms of the placement of color commercials on a market-by-market national spot basis, can most charitably be described as in a state of flux: in the decade before color becomes an all-encompassing entity, virtually synonymous with the reach of TV, pricing must of necessity range as far as the color spectrum itself.

Why? One area is that of *program source to the station*. The cost of reproducing a color print of a feature movie is a constant, regardless of whether that print is intended for play at the $25,000 rate in a top market or the $25.00 rate in Open Switch. The color film labs are limited, specialized, and "cost is cost".

This cost must be passed on to the local station buyer, and wrapped up in the contract that includes the size of market, reach of the station, rate card, by the *seller*—the distributor of the program product, be it feature film or off-network program feature.

And the station, in constructing its rate system, must take into account this added cost: for the very large market areas, this may be so small on a percentage basis as to be absorbed without mention; in the *bottom* 50-or-so markets it might double the cost of the film.

What color costs the advertiser, as far as putting it on the air at the local level, evidently depends on where you are and which trade paper you read. In January of 1966, Station WFGA-TV (Jacksonville) put a bright red roof on its trade advertisement house to illustrate that "Color is on the house", pointing out that "it doesn't cost you a cent extra to present your advertising in full color . . . because we are a COLOR station."

By contrast, just one year later Station WHEN-TV (Syracuse) laid a 5 percent increase on its rate card for the transmission of advertising in color—*not* based on production costs, as some earlier charges had been, but on the intrinsic value of the medium. The WHEN rate structure was championed by its sales representative, the Katz Agency (a longtime representative of newspapers in all of their infinite variety of color costs).

New York trade editor Lionel Kaufman (*The Promotion Brain-Storming Sheet*) observed: "True, the station has to tool up for color programming—*but so does the viewer!* But the extra cost of color in the commercial is paid by the advertiser who produces it himself."

Back in its red roof ad, WFGA-TV said: "Of course we'll welcome your black-and-white commercials if that's all you have, but remember color costs no more."

WHEN-TV was in truth *more* generous—allowing black-and-white commercials a 5 percent discount from its new (5 percent increase) rate. And, as Kaufman deduced, if you don't think that's being generous, then *add* 5 percent to $100—and then take 5 percent away from that figure, (Shortly after its original announcement, WHEN-TV rescinded its special color charge!)

Color TV and Creative Departments

A veteran producer of TV commercials recalls with glee that bygone era of the 1950s when many commercials (all B & W) were produced largely by the "seat-of-the-pants" school of instant creativity: "Standard procedure then in a good many agencies was to write a script of sorts, cut out a nice picture from a magazine that showed some people doing something close to what might happen, convince the client you had some idea of what you were doing, and then turn the whole sorry mess over to a TV producer—who would do what he felt like doing, and maybe make the agency account man a hero in the process!"

Color, with its increased costs, has helped change much of this. Most major agencies now have standing policies: all commercials must be fully storyboarded*, the script must be approved by the client *and* his attorneys *and* the agency attorneys, and the script and storyboard must be reviewed *prior* to production by the NAB Code Office and the continuity acceptance departments of the networks (or stations if a local campaign) for suitability wherever the commercial might appear.

Most one-minute commercials in storyboard form have at least 15 frames—a creative activity which often becomes an agency

---

*A storyboard is a series of 15 to 30 pictures in miniature, usually hand-drawn, indicating the action of the commercial. Under each picture, the copywriter adds appropriate dialogue. Camera movements also are indicated.

out-of-pocket expense. Since storyboard artists charge from $10 to $25 a frame (depending on completeness or reputation), and agencies are seldom noted for their willingness to spend *their* money, it is easily apparent why the creative process for TV commercials has become more businesslike. Although the changes may have happened without color and its higher costs, color commercials have required greater care since their inception.

An interesting sidelight to the advent of color commercials is the history of "color corrections"*—an artistic piece of detailing that occupied much time and demanded additional money in the early days of television. "Color-corrected" packages—detergents and cereals and beer six-packs, for example—were handled with great care. Still today, agency storerooms are cluttered with hundreds of real live pieces of black, gray and white "pop" art.

Today the actual color packages (sometimes redesigned for color TV) are used for commercials—which means that the majority of homes still using B & W sets are subject to seeing products in un-color-corrected glory.

Oddly enough, this "problem" doesn't seem to be one any more!

Color Videotape Commercials

Little commercial work has yet been done in color videotape (exception: some local stations, for local clients) because of the technical difficulties present in the editing and duplicating procedures.

There is bright promise for the future, however, since color videotape offers agencies and advertisers opportunities to secure the color balances they require *as the production is going on*, rather than later in the laboratory. Color videotape also will make it possible to assure compatibility of color and black-and-white transmission instantly. This problem can be particularly acute with metallic colors, which can be beautiful in color but virtually *full black* on B & W TV sets.

---

*Color correction is simply the pictorial translation from the natural colors in the design of a product or package into tones of gray for what was felt to be better transmission on television (black-and-white only), that is. Because of the exacting nature of the work, photo retouchers (among the commercial art world's highest-paid members) were used for these special assignments.

The Future of Color TV Advertising

My sister-in-law and brother have a continuing argument over what is *blue* and what is *green*—an internal squabble only decided when the object of the debate is placed next to a "pure" blue or green, or in contrast to a bright red or brilliant yellow. After a moment's readjustment to the newly-introduced interloper in the spectrum, there is usually some—albeit grudging—agreement reached.

This would be their very own unpublished vendetta, if it didn't serve so well to demonstrate a problem in color TV advertising—one that goes beyond the controlling abilities of the network, the station, even the film laboratory. This has been described as "the tendency of the human eye to make an involuntary adaptation to large differences in brightness and color values—and in so doing allowing the predominant hue and brightness of one impression to have major bearing on the following impression".

In TV viewing terms, this means that the watcher of a scene of 30 seconds or so in predominant bright reds will, in turn, *not* be able to receive properly a following scene in blue.

The conscientious and worrying TV commercial producer can surmount part of this problem—plotting the color content and relationship of art work and scenes, indoor or outdoor, within his own filmed or taped product. But he quite obviously has no control over the placement of that perfectly-matched, painstakingly produced gem of a message in juxtaposition to fluttering peacocks, spinning discs, station promotion slides or *pow*, *bam* and *zap* program content aired fore and aft!

Despite this occasional problem, the three-colored handwriting on the wall would indicate that nearly all commercials on U.S. television will be in color by 1968. The projections of a 25 percent, or greater, color set penetration in U.S. households will all but require the advertiser's total involvement with color. Color in TV advertising probably will be used in about the same ratio as color printing is used by advertisers in magazines. For food and clothing, for automobiles, for beverages, for almost all products, color adds a definite appeal when photographed.

For shock value, however, when everything else is in color, there is no doubt that some advertisers will use the *lack* of color as a stark difference to attract attention.

The projections of the 1967-1970 period for color set sales indicate that the benefits of greater viewing because of the new ownership of a color set, and the greater penetration of color sets into the mass market of the middle and lower income households, still hold much on the horizon of a still-blooming color factor in TV advertising.

The building of new laboratories for the quicker, and hopefully less expensive, processing of higher speed films which will require less extra studio time and lighting, plus greater human experience with color materials, should combine to have a major bearing on the holding down of continued escalation in the physical costs of color TV production—perhaps will even lead to reductions in this cost area.

The comparison was made that, while something less than 50 percent of the entries in the 1966 competition among TV commercials were in color, over 75 percent would be fully tinted by the following year's event.

If true, this rapid advance places demands not only on investment and desire to produce materials in color, but on the mechanical facilities that process those (by-and-large) films. The July, 1966, issue of Eastman Kodak's *TV Film Trends*, discussing the tremendous pressures on color film laboratories to "get it out yesterday", and the growing bottleneck in processing of color film prints, cited some estimates of needs in expansion:

"To build a brand-new color motion picture lab in New York, nerve center of the commercials industry, veterans agree that you need—
about 50,000 square feet of midtown loft space,
financial backing of $500,000 or more,
a reservoir of trained personnel and technicians,
ready delivery (virtually impossible) on new processing and printing equipment.

And even then, you're still about a year and a half away from large scale operations."

Which is to note, realistically, that those hoped-for cost reductions are something more remote than just around the corner of 49th and Madison!

If you remove the factors of production and media costs and new set ownership from a look at the future, a major influence in focusing on the color horizon comes from the continuing research work done by Schwerin*. In brief, after the audience becomes familiar with color TV and its offerings, and the novelty factor diminishes, its response to color TV advertising moves much closer to the response of people to black-and-white advertising.

A note of interest: in 1966, Speidel (a division of Textron, Inc.) made a television commercial that was a combination of B & W and color—for what they hoped would be greater impact on viewers in color set homes.

Thus the wheel of color for TV advertising may have taken a full turn, if you please. By the early 1970s, the world of color TV advertising—as we know it, examine it, measure it—may well be considered one for historical review only. By then, it is more than likely that some way of transmitting taste or aroma will be devised— a new "breakthrough" which will revolutionize television advertising in the same manner as *did* color!

---

*The Schwerin Research Corp., New York, N.Y., released a report in March, 1966, which, on the basis of Schwerin Competitive Preference Scores, showed that audience reaction to the same commercial shown in black-and-white versus color had declined from a color advantage of 51 percent in 1957 to 12 percent in 1965. On a basis of brand identification, however, the color advantage in 1965 was but 1 percent.

13 The Local Station and Color

ROY BACUS
General Manager, WBAP AM-FM-TV

The position of NBC affiliate WBAP-TV in pioneering color television programming for the Dallas-Fort Worth market is well described in its advertising slogan: "Our peacock has whiskers." (Whiskers *because WBAP-TV, one of the nation's earliest color outlets, took to the rainbow May 15, 1954!)*

General manager Roy Bacus has pushed the station vigorously along the tint trail. Today he and his staff think total color. *When Bacus took a thoughtful view of the signal on the TV receiver, he saw too much clutter—"The result of television's inheritance from radio, the stage and the movie screen." He commissioned industrial designer Crawford Dunn to create a tough, disciplined "ikonogenic" image-control design philosophy for the station. On October 15, 1963, the new WBAP-TV look was introduced: viewers, admiring the striking simplicity, wrote that "You've had a bath!"*

Bacus is a recipient of the Printers' Ink *silver medal for service to advertising, a former vice president of the Advertising Federation of America, and a journalism graduate of Texas Christian University. In this chapter he writes that "The local station is the final link in the chain." Engineering, promotion, sales; employee orientation and morale and the aggressiveness of TV set retailers; cost and concept and function and responsibility to the community—all are parts of the Roy Bacus documentation of that* final link *in action ...*

THE spectacular dimension of color in television, it is interesting to note, arrived on the scene after the video communication was definitively established as one with which all other media would be in contention. It is not surprising, therefore, that many knowledgeable broadcasters a decade ago—operating with a high degree of efficiency in news, sports, and network identification, and boasting a commendable record of community service—saw no great need to race into color just because it was available.

At that time color TV had neither commercial sponsors standing in the wings nor audience chafing for the rainbow *extra*; it was something in the distance.

The importance of color to the local station today is direct. Color has audience. Color can build audience, hold audience, switch viewers, switch advertisers; can be the difference between first and second in ratings. The dollar sign is unmistakably at the end of the rainbow, both in terms of sponsors wanting total dimension and viewers quickly finding new interest in the station doing the best job in the color arena.

A handful of station operators *did* calculate a spreading of the spectrum through the megacycle band. They *did* foresee a tremendous sales promotion advantage as an important pillar in their future image.

Robert Louis Stevenson was one of the earlier exponents of color! Traveling with that donkey, Stevenson mused: "If landscapes were sold, like the sheets of characters of my boyhood, one penny plain, and twopence coloured, I should go the length of twopence every day of my life." Another way of citing that, while gray is relatively noncommittal, colors stimulate the emotions.

Today late but aspiring station operators, with color gear on order, find themselves yearning to move at flank speed—only to chafe because the sudden color "burst" piled up an enormous backlog of equipment demands. So, many progress at snail's pace.

It is *not* rule-of-thumb that all broadcasters automatically take to new ideas with built-in enthusiasm. When television first came into being a broadcaster remarked: "This has to happen, just as we get radio under control." Six years later the broadcaster—if he took the TV dip—was lamenting that "Color has to happen just as we get black-and-white under control." But I hope he took the color plunge as well.

Even as the buggy manufacturer who chose not to see the horseless carriage as a dramatic extension of transportation, our era of 20th century technology is chronicled with stories of companies who thought they were in one kind of business only to discover one day they were in something else—or out.

For the local television station, color is simply an extension of the eye toward total electronic dimension. It is an important extension in communications. An interesting sidelight: some of the nation's most respected publishers realized a long time ago that they were in the communications business and not just newspaper or magazine publishing. As a result many of them pioneered radio, then television, and frequency modulation and FM stereo radio. And these same pioneers were quick to act when the news came that color was a reality, capable of taking its rightful place in the total electronic communication.

Today color pioneering has been accomplished. Now the question: What does one do to become known as "*the* local color station"? What are one's needs? Motivations? If one is behind—how far? How does one play catch up? Certainly the color step today is "catch up", compared to the infinitesimal interest shown by stations 10 years ago.

The attitude of the local station toward color starts with the motivation of the men who authorize the checks. No such drama separates black-and-white television from color television to those who retort that 80 percent, or even 90 percent, of the home receivers are still black-and-white. Certainly the difference is not that which separated television from radio. In fact, too cautious a pencil put to the color proposition may discourage the owners, the profit-makers, and all who examine the financial outlay or scan the horizons for a sure sign of sudden gold.

Someone other than the writer would have to write the chapter on *Immediate Profit in the Color Plunge*.

Nevertheless, conscientious managers desiring to be progressive and contributive are likely to push for a total color capability, rather than hedge the bet. Color television is more exciting, more powerful, and dimensional enough in its own right to attract a lengthening parade of stations anxious to ride the tint bandwagon. As earlier mentioned, let the manager who doubts that the parade has formed see where *he* lands in a line awaiting color gear!

The station manager contemplating color for the first time is already enmeshed in one color problem. What do you tell all of those advertisers who are sending their commercials in full color, only to have them telecast in black-and-white on your station? "Someday we'll have color" is now a tardy answer.

For the color pioneer that problem vanished long ago. He persuaded all local advertisers to use color because it was available. He dismissed the questions about tiny percentages of color set owners by saying: "Put your message in color and you'll get a color response."

In the area of color, newspapers, magazines and network television are far ahead of those stations not yet in the hue parade. Spot announcement orders can be "switched" because one station has a color capability greater than another. Farsighted local advertisers have also increased the pressure on local stations for color, by demanding broadcast facilities to include the dimension of color in their commercials.

More advertisers and agencies than ever before push color film commercials through the existing production channels. With increased production, and ever greater demands for speed, processing houses are literally swamped with color. The local station is the final link in the chain.

In one way, the early color station manager was "damned if he did; damned if he didn't". If he did *not* commit himself to as near total local color as possible, he faced the dilemma of firing up both color and black-and-white gear, or deciding the times of day he would stay black-and-white or venture into color. It is scarcely practical to keep both fired up simply to operate at the whim of the buyer, who can be encouraged to take the color route if the station leads him in this direction through various kinds of persuasion.

Color Equipment: Step-by-Step

In discussing the electronic portion of the move into color it appears that a chronological listing of equipment might be of interest, as one man's opinion in evaluating the position of each piece of gear in the color system. The first item, of course, would be the adaptation of the antenna and transmission system for adding hue to network programs or anything else which might come down the line in color. A station limited to this capacity would hardly be considered a color station.

If one additional piece of equipment were added at this point it would preferably be a film chain. While some might speak on behalf of a live camera chain, the projector and film chain would accommodate color from outside sources, such as movies, travelogues, film shows, as well as film commercials, slides, and public service announcements created and shipped in.

The third item would be a color camera—and here the engineering, production and creative staff begin to apply all of their color knowledge to the color challenge (except recording!). With the live color camera, studio news, weather, sports and other locally originated studio programs take on hue. Plus, of course, local live commercials.

Next on the list is the videotape machine, for the purpose of recording commercials and programs and for airing tape commercials.

Thus the minimum equipment requirement for a "working" color station would be telecasting and transmission facilities, a film chain, a studio camera, and a videotape recorder. After each item is a cut-off point if the station investors must go no further. A ten-to-one zoom lens is also a need, to allow flexibility in a one-camera operation. A tape editor is valuable.

If the enthusiasm of owners and staff tends to build as color is given its rightful recognition, it becomes obvious immediately that another film chain and another videotape recorder are sorely needed. This adds much flexibility in film programming and in tape recording and playback. It is also a hedge against equipment failure.

Finally comes the second studio camera, and the system is complete, with switching and transmitting gear, two film chains, two studio cameras with zoom lenses, two videotape machines, and a tape editor.

With ingenuity in planning and scheduling, that equipment roster can provide many color hours. It can provide the momentum for any imaginative promotion department to lay claim to being the "number one station" and back it up with performance, *even if* not the most facilities. This excludes, naturally, those stations doing remote telecasting.

One word of caution for those stations not yet heavily involved in tape commercials. As this "Topsy" grows it requires storage space, the same as film, and a checking system whereby a videotape playback unit must be at the command of the commercial standards supervisor in the same manner that the film projector is used. This seems superfluous, but as more equipment is added and more tapes arrive and are held for varied lengths of time, the space-eaters suddenly outgrow their nest!

Somewhere the ultimate goal of total color should be inscribed as a long-range objective of the station.

Present WBAP-TV color gear includes three studio cameras, two film chains, zoom lenses, tape editors, seven videotape machines —with additional remote equipment due for "soonest" delivery, plus a 16mm. newsfilm color processor.

Once the station manager has completed his technical (and financial) chores of lining up equipment, he turns inward to examine his staff and see how much color penetration he can accomplish in the shortest possible time, once the gear is operative.

Engineers must of course know the equipment, and well: this calls for selected individuals to visit manufacturing plants and attend seminars. Hopefully a few of the better qualified will relish the color challenge. On the production side the personnel not only must relate the color dimension to sets, space and lighting, they must restrain themselves to keep the color dimension from overpowering the message and becoming a projection simply to show off color. The station that is cramped in its quarters while operating in black-and-white will find the pinch more severe in color.

A reasonable "lash-up" for that lucky station that has everything would include two color-equipped studios, four studio cameras, three film chains, six tape machines—with two of the tape units mounted in a van along with four additional cameras for the taping of commercials and special events on location, plus other necessary portable gear for remote telecasting. Zoom lenses and tape editors are assumed. A color film processor for news, and equipment for processing color slides, complete the inventory for total color. As previously reflected, the long range goal of the progressive station which moves scientifically into color is *all color, total color.*

Color in the News Operation

Some reactions to the idea of news in color may be less than enthusiastic. "New is news—black-and-white or color, makes no difference." But it *does* make a difference. Color again adds a dramatic extension and has a marked effect on viewer and newsmen.

For the television station manager who is satisfied with nothing less than the ultimate, he no sooner gets his transmitter, switchers, film machines, tape units and staging in color than the subject of news in color moves forward on the "things to do" agenda as a natural follow-up.

With some enthusiastic coaching on the part of a progressive news director, and some equally enthusiastic claims of capability on the part of the station film laboratory chief, a scholarly analysis of equipment available and operating costs can be made and the news plunged into the spectrum. The processing gear chosen should provide the necessary speed. Station newsmen are eager to listen to the need for changes necessary for shooting in color. Laboratory control is precise to the point that any weakness in the trip from news camera to home receiver can be pinpointed, and corrective measures can be taken.

After watching news in color for a few weeks, a switch to black-and-white gives one a feeling of drabness—news *lacking* a dimension. And color news presents no problems that an alert news department, including a film laboratory supervisor, cannot solve.

Operating the Station in Color

Generally speaking, no more personnel are needed to extend station operations into color, but more is required of all operating personnel. This may mean more personnel in the electronic maintenance area. The ratio of potential trouble is three times greater—namely red, green and blue! Color tubes cost more and, in a manner of speaking, three times as much electronic gear is involved. Then there's studio color, tape color, old film color, new film color, slide color, outdoor color in the sun—and outdoor color in the shade!

Solid state components have lessened space requirements, but color calls for stricter engineering standards. Transmitters, cameras and videotape machines require more attention. Color is a meticulous business compared to black-and-white.

In the area of lighting, more illumination is required and more careful illumination. Tubes made for color are more closely matched, more sensitive. Where greater depth of focus is sought, lighting is increased. Some stations manage on 350 to 500 foot candles at 3,200° Kelvin with "F" stop of eight. Others use more.

And of course another item costlier than black-and-white is *any* kind of a color print.

More time is required to line up color cameras; and when the lights are increased the air conditioning system asks for more muscle. The production director takes another look at the floor, to see if a lighter material will provide more desirable reflection. Sets, too, break away from shades of gray and contribute to the color scheme.

If one knowledgeable station employee in any area is given the job of color co-ordinator, and a color philosophy is set forth by management, the total color image presented can be one of harmony and attraction. A new station is likely to go through a "gaudy" stage before settling back to let each color assume its usual role in a natural setting.

From the first, the WBAP-TV production staff has not made rigid rules for color presentations. A man in a white shirt has been projected in a white shirt, and *not* advised to rush out and buy a blue one even though blue is preferable. Except on promotional occasions the production has not been "gimmicked" up to accent color.

Max Factor make-up has been used from the first, but sparingly. This make-up ranges in shade from light TV-4 through dark TV-8 for both men and women, with Pan Cake as well as Pan Stick being used.

News, weather and studio sports programs are usually the first to sprout color when the live studio cameras are fired up. These simple programs can be artfully designed and projected attractively with one camera and a zoom lens. This is not to say that a second camera is not desirable, but if one camera is on the premises there is no sense in postponing "C-Day" for the arrival of a second.

After the standard "bread and butter" shows and the public affairs panels, an ideal vehicle to carry your initial color programs is "music, motion and merriment".

You will recall that the early *Arthur Murray Show* had all of these—handsome men, beautiful women, music, party gowns, and swirling, colorful dancers—and was an early color favorite.

One finds similar opportunities in robed choirs, ballet (with recorded accompaniment), drama teams from local universities, square dance clubs, jazz bands, barn dances, teen-age "down beats", talent shows and talent competitions. Color also gives a fresh sparkle to home shows featuring the kitchen and fashions. But color does not alter the fact that only a small audience patronizes these types of presentations. The *play* ultimately emerges as *the thing*—in color *or* black-and-white.

Creative people who populate television stations for the most part should be eager for color. In our own station all sets were painted in color from the very first—1948!

Certainly the absorption of color whetted the appetites of video artists, engineers, production crews, and talent, for the great step from shades of gray to the rainbow of live colorcasting.

The Station Color Philosophy

To be known as a color station it is necessary that the manager of that aspiring outlet respond enthusiastically to color. Staff enthusiasm will be the response to management enthusiasm. Such total involvement is no different from that required to be highly identified with other facets of broadcasting—stations known as the "sports station" or the "news station", or the "station with personalities". Dreaming, planning, involvement and execution make these things come true.

After a production staff is geared to handle color from a technical point of view, it is likewise helpful that they be alerted to handle color from a conversational point of view. Engineers and producers can have much to do with the attitude of station salesmen, talent, clients and agencies toward color. Even in jest, a derision of color can fall on willing ears and cause a potential buyer to decide it isn't worth the effort.

The addition of color opens a new world to a group of potential advertisers who may or may not have found promotion effectiveness in television. A few of these are food manufacturers, food stores, and home furnishings establishments. Color moves fast when the president of a company or the ad buyer buys a color receiver and sees his black-and-white commercials surrounded by the gorgeous hues of the rainbow. An invitation to these clients, along with their advertising agency people, to join in color experimentation with their products—at station expense—can create enough excitement to cause all of the principals to purchase color receivers for their homes, and lead them to a regular color advertising schedule.

Certainly color receivers pushed into the home of station department heads, client principals, opinion leaders and amusement writers, can cause the wheel of fortune to spin more rapidly in attracting audience and commercial support to the station to help increase sales. Ironically, a station can scarcely afford to provide each of its staff members with a color set, so 90 percent of your effective, loyal employees working in color are viewing at home in B & W—completely in the dark as to what the picture they have labored on all day looks like in color.

Building Awareness: We ARE in Color

Several things take place, or *should* take place, in connection with making clients, agencies and viewers aware that the station is now in color.

First, the on-the-air identifications of color programs should be as readily recognized by the black-and-white viewer as the NBC peacock—which incidentally on an NBC program has no duty other than to join its musical audio for heralding color.

Secondly, all station advertising and printed promotion should have at least one color added to the basic color. Generally this means a print job in black and red, red and blue, or green and red, etc., if not full color. But to identify your station effectively with color, remember that color speaks for itself.

Thirdly, the station itself must look color-*full*. When a client or advertising agent or program producer or "visiting fireman" walks into your studio, he must be made aware visually that he is in a color operation. This can be accomplished by painting light scoops in various hues, hanging color draperies, painting sets and the like. Color harmony should prevail in this situation.

There should be at least one red coat in the house, and preferably this coat should be on the station manager at any time he is making an appearance on behalf of color. The enthusiasm of a manager for color can kindle fires in every department of his station. To make a negative point, a manager who is color blind would likely approach the subject with no communication of the believeability of color's charm. But the odds are that the manager does have this color interpretation. And he should have more. He should seek a knowledge of the power of each basic color, its personality characteristics, plus a knowledge of the blends and harmonic combinations. He should talk color in color terms to his employees, his golf buddies, his service club associates, and his audience at large. At this stage of the game he is certain to have to discuss color in self-defence everywhere he goes.

Corny as it may sound, a station person sitting on a panel discussing television color should use colorful attire for instant relation to his subject. A trail-blazing manager working with color is certain to be asked on many black-and-white occasions: "Where is the red coat?"

A station image can be gaudy, or it can simply reflect a natural use of color, no different from that of a newspaper or a magazine. Twelve years ago the art director of a large agency exclaimed, upon seeing his first color television commercial: "Color is still color, no matter where."

The temptation to be lavish with color is strong; perhaps it's good for both the production staff and the viewers to realize that the rainbow has become an exciting addition to the station's image. But fundamentally red coats and blue trousers are *not* part of the message, and should be reserved for special occasions and promotions.

Color and the Advertising Dollar

The financial aspects of the color investment have been discussed pro and con for over 10 years. Print color—newspaper, magazine, direct mail—costs more than black-and-white. It follows that color television should cost more.

But the major difference is that the print color has a 100 percent circulation, while video color is a small part of the total circulation in the average market, with the result that 80 to 90 percent of the viewers are "black-and-white circulation".

A theoretical proposal then is that the same extra percentage should be charged as is the proportion of color to black-and-white. In other words, in a market where the color penetration is 15 percent, charge 15 percent extra!

But suppose your penurious buyer says he'll settle for the black-and-white circulation only? Since the color circulation accumulation has been slow and deliberate in our experience, it has been more important to promote the *use* of color rather than begin a commercial conversation with the pronouncement: "This is going to cost you 15 percent extra." The enthusiastic client, pleased with his color messages, is likely not only to be a missionary for color but a champion of television in general, and to place added emphasis on his television advertising—even to use more television as a result!

Also, color can have a unique appeal to food manufacturers, supermarkets, home furnishing shops and other retailers. Thus rate increases and new business gains are practical possibilities for those station operators with the dominant color franchises. And color at this stage is just about the best sales promotion feature that has come along since television itself became a commercial reality.

Sometimes it is difficult to pinpoint that dollar gain as reflected in ratings, shares of audience, and commercial patronage, but seldom has anything created the television interest at all levels—viewers, clients, agencies, opinion leaders—as has color. And one color receiver in the home of an enthusiastic executive can ensure a color schedule of many thousands of dollars a year.

Actually, the biggest payoff for our color pioneering was that our station was established as the *first* and *only* local color television outlet. This was a substantial though delayed harvest that may have cost no more than it would cost a station to introduce an equally ambitious sports and news program.

As color was promoted and as the audience warmed to it we were, in reality, engaging in a switch-pitch for the viewers' favor. As has been statistically reported elsewhere, the viewer's new color receiver marks one time in his video life that he re-examines what is on channels *other than* his favorite.

While there was no increase in time charges for our color advertisers when our station plunged into a professionally-designed program, there were of course additional costs for the advertising materials used. We did provide free design and color art for a few of our more prominent clients—this because they sponsored color programs in areas where the station wished to assume a professional control over all introductions and closes for an across-the-board, well-designed common denominator. Clients, however, show no hesitancy in paying extra color production charges once they have cultivated an enthusiasm for using color.

Foot Dragging in Color

Two "before the buy" situations have had influence on the acceptance of color by the contented, black-and-white viewing public. In promotion, many set sales have been stillborn in appliance stores and appliance departments because the color receiver was given no special consideration on the display floor.

A color receiver plunked down among a bevy of B & W receivers usually shows a poor picture when all the sets are turned on for demonstration purposes. The public has come to accept light reflections in a black-and-white picture tube; knows that with a bit of living room furniture-shifting he can correct this situation.

But not so with color. When an ordinary citizen—happy with his black-and-white world—sees a color picture struggling against its unwanted reflective lights and washed-out picture, he simply says silently (or sometimes aloud!): "If that's color, I'll take black-and-white."

Yet if that same color viewer (and potential color set buyer), visiting in a color home, sees a scene from *Bonanza* he will remark: "Gosh, that's beautiful. I never knew color television looked like that."

Appliance dealers have learned—in some cases by prodding—that a color receiver, if placed for immediate comparison with a single black-and-white unit and with proper attention to possible reflections and to shading of the screen, will give many prospective purchasers their first real experience with the rainbow picture. And they'll buy!

Second is the nagging (but fortunately decreasing) problem of the technician foot-draggers. For years some television repair men, who probably dreaded the indoctrination necessary to "get with" color servicing, would slyly tell a housewife, even as they patched up the old B & W set, that if she bought color: "Get an engineer along with it."

Color station operators have heard these old wives' tales at service clubs and luncheon meetings so often that many have abandoned any desire to retort.

Color is also an opinion. Staff personnel *and* viewers all have different ideas, different mental images of how the picture should look. For that reason, *two* receivers in operation have two different pictures for anyone who is looking.

Finally, color is a two-way street, and some individuals gain little or no stimulus from, generate no response for, color television. While these people may be few in number, it is important that the manager, the salesman, the staff artist, probe cautiously when discussing color with a potential color client or color viewer, to sense *how* this person relates to color. He *may* even be color blind!

Pioneering the Second Time

Once all stations in a market are reasonably equal in color equipment, the color pioneer has no special advantage except his experience. Where all channels are color, once again "the play's the thing". It is easily possible that the last station in the market to board the tint bandwagon may wind up doing the most attractive job of color programming and production.

Thus the addition of the color dimension gives the station manager a new opportunity to pioneer—to take a long, hard, objective look at his community image as the viewer sees him. Research advisers and other consultants may tell him that his station is highly identified with news, sports, network, kiddy programs, feature films, or color. He may learn that viewers describe the station as old and conservative or lively and exciting. The image of a station should be progressive but authoritative, colorful yet communicative, controversial but compassionate.

The remaining "secret" ingredient in the solid television dimension is in truth no secret at all, but has been recognized by only a fraction of stations and advertisers. That element is professional communications design. When an intended television communication cannot be comprehended in the time and space allotted, the viewer has little opportunity and even less inclination to decipher what you are trying to tell him or show him. Television is fabulously successful —yet often is but radio with pictures, a cluttered mimic of the legitimate stage, or a squeezed-down version of big screen movies.

Color will have a tendency to add to that clutter, unless a bold manager wipes clean the screen and takes a painstaking inventory of his communicative intentions. The command is simple: Place only on the screen that which you intend to communicate. Remove from the screen anything that is distracting and irrelevant.

Once an *image objective* is established, the station's staff should become totally involved in projecting that image through every activity and particle of material in the station—audio, video, promotion pieces, rate cards, program schedules, coverage maps, sales presentations; station vehicles and equipment, studios, building appearance—and word-of-mouth!

The arrival of color gives a station manager opportunity to have a *total revival*, and move *out* of a heterogeneous collection of loosely related items which diffuse into a confused image, *to* a boldly projected homogeneous profile which speaks plainly the goals of management.

Once a station has decided what it wishes to be and plans and designs accordingly, color and design become friends and allies.

14 Color it Local
A Sampling of Local Station Color Activity

KENNETH A. MILLS
Associate Director, Research-Promotion,
The Katz Agency, Inc.

In the previous chapter, Roy Bacus made the point that the "local station is the final link". In the vernacular of the mid-sixties, Here's What's Happening at the Link, Baby, *might well be the sub-title of Ken Mills' exploration of local TV station color activity—from his era of the "reckless pioneers" to the local color explosion of 1964-66.*

Mills came to his present work via an avid interest in sports, an undergraduate career (Princeton) that included disc-jockeying, live sports announcing and numerous forays into print journalism. With a background of professional broadcast activity, including air work, publicity and promotion, he joined The Katz Agency in 1948. Among his many outside functions in broadcasting, he is editor of "Sound Off", a provocative column of opinion and occasional hyperbole in Big Ideas, *the monthly publication of the Broadcasters Promotion Association—of which he is in turn an active and supporting senior member.*

In late 1966, The Katz Agency (pioneer advertising media sales representation firm, with three generations of experience in newspaper, radio and now TV selling) surveyed a selected list of its represented stations on the subject of color—and what are you doing?

In the following report, Mills delineates the results—and the lessons to be learned—from that survey . . .

Coloring a Station

At the end of 1953 the FCC adopted the current standards for compatible color telecasting. Color, we were told, was "here". It may have been, but neither broadcaster, advertiser nor, most important, consumer, was ready to recognize the fact.

In the decade that followed, color TV, with a few exceptions, treaded water. Only one network (and that because of an obvious vested interest) made a serious attempt to program in color. The price tag on color sets kept them well beyond the reach of the average buyer. Advertisers, aware of the lack of color penetration, were unwilling to invest the dollars needed to produce their commercials in color. And stations, with the exception of a few reckless pioneers, were content to equip themselves to transmit network programs in color or, perhaps, to originate slide and film material.

Somewhere between 1964 and 1966, however, the breakthrough took place. Prices on receivers came down drastically. Network programming in color became the norm, not the exception. Stations began to gear up for the transmission of more and more color on the local level. And advertisers sensed that the added impact of color was going to hit enough potential customers to make it worth the investment.

Whether the chicken came first or the egg is immaterial. By Fall 1966 color at the local station level was indeed "here". Because Katz Television represents a cross-section of stations, in terms of market size and geographic distribution, we considered ourselves in a unique position to report to the advertiser on station color activity. We had been keeping tabs, on a continuing basis, on the color equipment status of our station clients: how many could transmit film and slides, how many could handle color tape, how many could put on a live performance.

A Few Pertinent Questions

We needed information, however: hours of color program origination, amount of advertising carried in color, increased operating expenses because of color.

So we did the obvious: we asked. We circulated a questionnaire

COLOR IT LOCAL 189

STATIONS PARTICIPATING IN KATZ COLOR SURVEY

		Market Color Penetration (*NSI*, 11/66)
		%
WRGB	Albany-Schenectady-Troy, N.Y.	13
WMAR-TV	Baltimore, Md.	15
WBRC-TV	Birmingham, Ala.	14
WMT-TV	Cedar Rapids-Waterloo, Iowa	14
WSAZ-TV	Charleston-Huntington, W. Va.	14
WKRC-TV	Cincinnati, Ohio	21
WTVN-TV	Columbus, Ohio	24
KTVT	Dallas-Ft. Worth, Tex.	14
KLZ-TV	Denver, Colo.	18
KRNT-TV	Des Moines, Iowa	14
WFIE-TV	Evansville, Ind.	17
KMJ-TV	Fresno, Calif.	23
WOOD-TV	Grand Rapids, Mich.	17
WFRV	Green Bay, Wisc.	18
WFBM-TV	Indianapolis, Ind.	19
WJTV	Jackson, Miss.	14
WAVE-TV	Louisville, Ky.	12
WREC-TV	Memphis, Tenn.	12
WTCN-TV	Minneapolis, Minn.	11
WLAC-TV	Nashville, Tenn.	13
WWL-TV	New Orleans, La.	17
WVEC-TV	Norfolk-Hampton, Va.	12
WKY-TV	Oklahoma City, Okla.	15
WEEK-TV	Peoria, Ill.	19
KPHO-TV	Phoenix, Ariz.	12
WCSH-TV	Portland, Me.	15
WSLS-TV	Roanoke, Va.	10
KCPX-TV*	Salt Lake City-Ogden-Provo, Utah	16
KONO-TV	San Antonio, Tex.	13
KOGO-TV	San Diego, Calif.	22
KOMO-TV	Seattle, Wash.	17
KTBS-TV	Shreveport, La.	13
WHEN-TV	Syracuse, N.Y.	14
WTVT	Tampa-St. Petersburg, Fla.	16
KAKE-TV	Wichita, Kans.	16

*No longer represented by Katz Television.

among Katz-represented stations. The thirty-five who completed it represent, in our opinion, a good sampling of U.S. TV stations. They range in market size from Dallas-Ft. Worth, No. 12, to Evansville, No. 92*. And, significantly, the list does not include the New Yorks, Chicagos, LA's, where the pace of gearing up for color might have been atypically accelerated.

To what we already knew about station color status, coupled with the published price tags for equipment, we added further information. The result, which was circulated to stations, agencies and advertisers, and also published in broadcasting trade magazines, represents a fair estimate of the dimensions of the "color explosion" at the station level between Fall 1964 and Fall 1966.

The Dimensions of the "Explosion"

In 1964 fewer than half the stations were even equipped to put color film on the air. Less than 10 percent had tape, and only 25 percent were set up for live. Two years later they could *all* transmit film; only four respondents were tapeless; and nearly three-fourths of the sample were "live".

GROWTH OF STATION COLOR CAPABILITY
(Fall, 1964 *vs.* Fall, 1966)
(*Selected Katz-represented Stations*)

	Fall 1964		Fall 1966	
	No. Stations	% Total	No. Stations	% Total
Film equipment	15	43	35	100
Tape equipment	3	9	31	88
Live equipment	7	20	25	71

Source: Katz Agency Research Department.

In dollars and cents the average station of this group has put $293,000 on the line, approximately 70 percent of that total since Fall 1964.

---

*Based on ARB "primary" ranking as reported in its 1966 Market Analysis.

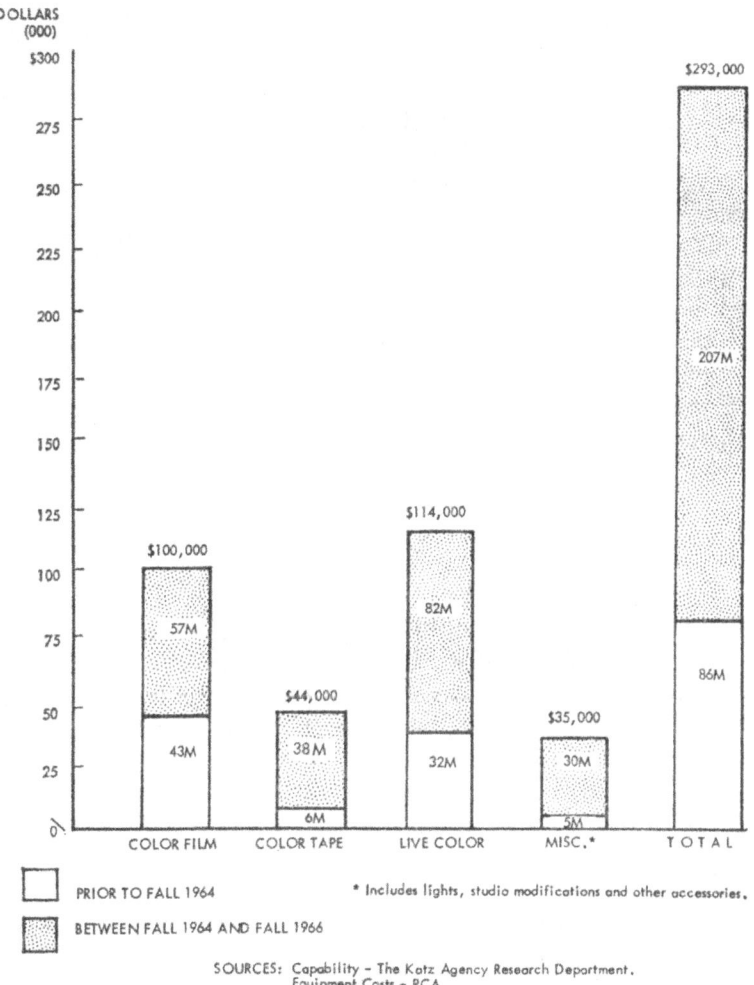

Average color investment equipment per station.
(Selected Katz-represented stations.)

The total investment range runs from a low of $100,000 to almost $1,000,000. The variable exists principally among those who have chosen to go "full color". Film chains and tape recorders are, after all, self-contained pieces of equipment. They occupy slightly more space than their black-and-white counterparts. But that's it.

Live color requires studio modifications, entirely new lighting requirements, etc. The cost is totally dependent on the imagination and resources of the individual station operator. One respondent, for example, had budgeted $250,000 for a new studio alone.

Expenditures for color equipment during the two-year period averaged about 12 percent of national spot revenue, ranging all the way from 3 percent to 87 percent. The reason for this spread represents another of the frustrations of coloring a TV station: equipment costs make no distinction between rich and poor. The operator in Evansville pays as much for a color film chain as his counterpart in Dallas. The same goes for tape recorders and cameras. Tough as it may be on the little guy, he has no choice. If he's going to keep up with electronic progress, he has to put the dollars down. The alternative is stagnation.

The Unavoidable Recurring Costs

Substantial as the outlay for equipment may be to a station manager already weighed down with problems, it is still just a one-time shot, amortizable over a longer or shorter period of time, depending on his accounting procedures. But operating costs are a continuing expense. And there's no question that color pushes them in only one direction: up. Lighting for color kicks up your electricity bill. Maintenance of equipment is substantially more complicated. Art work in full color is more demanding, and more expensive. Scenery, make-up and wardrobe costs follow the upward trend. Color tape costs more. So does color film—not to mention its processing. For the average station the cost came to an additional $40 per hour of locally-originated programming, when telecast in color as opposed to black-and-white. The bill over a year added up to well over $30,000, and one operator reported an increase of $94,000.

Filling the Air with Color

In spite of this costly prognosis, stations are programming more and more hours in color. It's the price not only of leadership but even of survival. As of Fall 1966, network affiliates among the station respondents indicated that about a quarter of all locally-originated programming was in color. In terms of hours this represented 15 a week, with one adventurous broadcaster hitting as many as five hours a day.

LOCAL COLOR PROGRAMMING HOURS PER WEEK
(Fall, 1966)

(*On selected Katz-represented Stations**)

	Per Station Estimates		
	High	Low	Avge.
No. locally programmed hours per week	71	22	56
No. local color hours per week	35	2	15
No. local live color hours per week	22	0†	5

*Does not include independent stations in survey.
†For those stations producing live color the low was three hours per week.
Source: Katz Agency Color Survey.

As more and more stations become full-color operations, the percent of color hours can only increase. And there's still another trend, one that has become more pronounced since the questionnaire results were released: color news. Many of the more enterprising among stations have installed color film processing units and are producing most, in some cases all, of their news footage in full color.

Anticipating Consumer Demand

And what about color commercials? The replies indicated that more than half (57 percent) of the average station's commercial minutes are in color. This total includes, incidentally, network as well as spot and local advertising. (Parenthetically, industry estimates indicate that, at the start of 1967, 70-80 percent of the commercials being produced by national advertisers are in color, a development that should quickly obsolesce the station figure reported here.)

There was no correlation between the amount of color commercial time and market color penetration. Advertisers still seem to be choosing their markets on the basis of more overriding marketing considerations.

But among station respondents there appeared to be a tendency (logical enough) for those carrying the largest amount of locally-originated color programming to profit thereby in terms of color advertising.

Not only is there little correlation between market color penetration and the amount of color advertising carried by a station; there is also little between the degree of station color commitment and the market penetration figures. With nearly three-fourths of the stations prepared to originate live color, and with more than half of the commercial minutes in color, at a time when the average penetration for the 35 markets involved hovers around 16 percent (NSI 11/66), you have to conclude that both advertisers and stations are waist-deep in color long before the consumer. But the breakthrough has been made, and stations, large and small, are responding. It won't be long before set population catches up ... and black-and-white TV is as anachronistic as silent movies.

V

The Sum of the Parts

15 It's in Color—so what?

HOWARD W. COLEMAN
Press Relations Director, A. C. Nielsen Company

A publisher's note:
Color Television *editor Howard Coleman first came to our attention in 1964, when he contributed the chapter "Advertising, Promotion, Publicity" to our* Television Station Management, *which we published that year under the editorship of Yale Roe.*

From his writing and biography, we learned that he had pioneered in the promotion of color television in 1956, as ad-promotion manager of Chicago's WNBQ (now WMAQ-TV) when the NBC-owned TV outlet became the "world's first all-in-color station"—a date and year that coincided with the Chicago convention of the NAB.

Ten years later, Coleman joined ex-boss and fellow NBCite Chet Campbell to produce How to Promote Color, *a Broadcasters Promotion Association-sponsored presentation offered before the first Color Conference of that same NAB assembly—also in Chicago. (From that Conference came five of the authors and much of the thought offered in this text.)*

In the years between, Coleman has been a frequent contributor of articles in the broadcast trade press, a lecturer before groups with a wide variety of broadcast interests, and an archivist of the TV industry. In this chapter, he maintains, in spite of the title of his article, that "for better or worse", television "will be in color and will . . . demand a new level of knowledge and skill in criticism" . . .

EARLY in the red-, green- and blue-sky promotional days of color television, before 1960, a critic of the medium unconsciously coined the title for this chapter with a diatribe under the copy editor's head: "It's in Color—So What!"

The theme of the anti-tint essay had some merit: Vintage programs from video's infant years (he cited *Boston Blackie*, the *Jerry Lester Show*, *The Cisco Kid*, as prime examples) would never, *never* have been enhanced by splashes of any hue; might even have had shorter, more deserved destinies had they been seen all over in color from their beginnings! (The continued residual income of two of these B & W programs, from international sales, might prove to be embarrassing, but that's another part of the story of TV.)

The scribe did admit to added color values with Mary Martin's *Peter Pan*, with *Amahl and the Night Visitors*, with Burr Tillstrom's KFO puppet production of *St. George and the Dragon*. But these, he concluded, were special programs of merit in monochrome, and color was but a bit of icing on the cake.

That icing was of no worth whatsoever, he continued, in such outdoor events as the coverage of a presidential inauguration. "Dignitaries in black dress suits and striped pants, riding in black Cadillacs (he even had the brand wrong!) are scarcely made exciting by a color camera." (It can only be concluded that the West Point Corps of Cadets, gray-and-white with red sashes and multi-hued flags; the Navy blue WAVES; the grass green-and-scarlet Green Mountain Boy pipers—all moved down Pennsylvania Avenue while the writer was contemplating the ghost of Boston Blackie.)

"Color is here" is the motif of virtually every forward-looking broadcast operation, from NBC headquarters at "30 Rock" in New York to the smallest TV teapot in Open Switch, U.S.A.

At any given moment in the past several years, *First in Color* is or has been the promotional slogan of at least 30 stations across the country, as transmitters are re-tuned for the relay of network tint offerings, color film projection chains are added to the equipment list, and a "real live camera" is delivered, uncrated and hitched to the system.

The electronics industry's data wing reports continually-accelerating statistics to document the sale and delivery of color TV sets: what portion of these shipments goes to non-ratable installations—private clubs, cocktail lounges, quality hotel and motel suites and rooms—is difficult to ascertain. As a result, the "color set penetration" data in circulation swings on a pendulum with an uncomfortably wide arc that depends from—at one time of the month or another—a number of mechanisms, each wound to and geared to a different rate of speed.

From the commercial approach, color means *dollars*. We have seen ample evidence that it costs the broadcaster more to originate his offerings in color. Should the advertiser share in this added cost? Answer: a very conditional and diagonal *Maybe; maybe not*.

When touting its jitney-painted color vehicle for advertisers, television crunches head-on against a veteran front line of competitors for the advertising budget, ranging from billboards and car cards to the heavyweights—magazines and newspapers.

The magazine publisher puts together a product that is a combination of words, pictures and overall design, under an umbrella of editorial concept. This design-concept pattern uses color in many ways—single lines, splashes, full-color delights; tables of epicurean goodies and illustrations teasing the reader to the feature fiction that follows.

The publisher's overall product combination of cover and content is calculated to give forth an appeal that is readily measured in subscriber circulation and news-stand sales. Presumably, in relation to this measurable worth in terms of circulation, the advertiser is indeed paying for the editor's and the designer's use of color to enhance the quality and appeal of the magazine—as a part of his advertising fee.

But this has been a static circumstance, never spelled out as such, and the advertiser doesn't think of color versus black-and-white—other than in the easily-identified advertising costs o presenting his own materials in the many possible color sizes and forms.

In magazine advertising, be the vehicle weekly or quarterly, *time* in production and placement is the only real problem: quality is production-controllable, and the size of the budget is the chief factor in opting for a slim treatment of red with basic black or full process color in all of its glowing tones. Even *Variety*, that venerable show biz bible, offers a spot color advertising possibility to bring the message out of its otherwise drab gray-black-and-newsprint facade.

(To soften the comparison, it must be admitted that the weekly identifies itself as a newspaper.)

Time one week in late 1966 cut back from its generations of phizes (mostly singular, sometimes plural) of the world's newsmakers, to headline "Is God Dead?" in fire red on flat black. There is no evidence that advertisers received a rebate because of this economy in cover production; to the contrary, it was to be assumed that they received a bonus in circulation, due to the attraction of that controversial cover story!

To turn to the other major part of print media advertising—newspapers—and to examine color advertising potentials and realities in some relation to editorial color—the picture (no pun intended) is somewhat different.

Basically, editorial color (fashions, feature photos, news) is a "few-and-far-between" item, limited to a scattering of major markets, and then mostly in Sunday feature sections illustrating socialite Bibsi von Snodgrass in the apparel she intends to wear in the Easter parade.

In advertising color, the range of choices is as wide as the ensuing problems are long.

The first step in the advertising color offering for a newspaper is the familiar R.O.P. (run of paper) color, printed (if the newspaper owns the equipment) during the regular press run and, because of speed in production, most often adding but one color to the regular black-and-newsprint potential. While *not* quality printing, the tint splashes make effective eye-catchers for many products. It should be noted that, while the technique of R.O.P. color has been with us for 60 years or more, its availability is offered in the rate cards of about 1,100 daily newspapers in the U.S. out of approximately 1,750.

R.O.P. has difficulties in living up to its name, in that most papers make it available only on certain days; continue to find problems in print registration and in control of the added color. (Of those 1,750 or so dailies, around 560 are identified as being equipped to print full, halftone-screen process color.)

One of the newsprint medium's answers to the need for color advertising exposure is the Hi-Fi process—the preprinting of rolls of paper from specially prepared cylinders similar to the technique of regular rotogravure printing. The full-color quality is obvious; the problems enormous. These rolls are treated as normal blank newsprint on their reverse side, and have printed on them whatever advertising and/or editorial copy falls on that page.

But, due to a lack of uniform page size among newspapers, plus the tendency of the paper to stretch during the press run, it simply isn't possible to standardize the size and format of the preprinted advertising message. This has led to the "wallpaper" concept—the advertising has to be designed to accommodate a random cut-off and still make sense. Plainly, this would never work in any attempt to emulate the *Playboy* center-spread technique—the staple just wouldn't hit in its accustomed spot!

Hi-Fi is listed as available in over 800 newspapers; a fact that should have maximum appeal to advertisers of wallpaper.

Another high quality color print technique, SpectaColor, has the promise of solving the rolls-of-wallpaper problems of Hi-Fi. This is, as Hi-Fi, a preprint process, but brings its advertising message into registration with the other pages of the newspaper. As with so many good things, the price is the problem here: with the newspaper's investment estimated as between 15 and 20 thousand dollars, the roster of SpectaColor-equipped papers approximates 250.

It must be added that, as with Hi-Fi, SpectaColor can be overprinted with special black imprints.

The production problems in any of the above newspaper-offered color advertising possibilities are obvious: they interfere with the basic job of the paper—to turn out daily (and most often in several editions, demanding fresh make-up) *news*, on a schedule where every minute is golden and a lost hour may cost a return of 25 percent of the news-stand runs.

The major color opportunities in newspaper advertising—the color comics, the Sunday supplements, the local Sunday magazines—just as obviously do not suffer from the "stop the presses" timeliness of daily press operation; as such, offer quality and placement on a level with their magazine competitors.

And, to return to our basic subject, many of those color comics now race across the color TV screen in animated form—and TV stars and their personal lives would seem to be a favorite theme in the cover story features of the Sunday "Supps"!

Color is on the Horizon; is Coming; is   ?
(Or, Veni, Vidi,   ?)

General Sarnoff pre-acknowledged the RCA-NBC "vested interest" in color described by one of our writers when he stated, in 1954, that "color will speed the day when the volume of RCA business will reach and exceed a billion dollars a year."

The corporation's $1·7 billion 1962 volume was reputed to have realized close to half of a $15 million profit increase from color.

Reporting to its stockholders in that same year (1962), the rival CBS network—without a set manufacturing facility—defended a "let's wait a while" policy regarding color with the conclusion that there was no profit to be made in colorcasting.

During the same season, ABC-TV offered a 20-gauge scatter pattern of color programs, even though its owned stations were almost as far behind as those of CBS in gearing for local, live color.

Somewhere in the hot-and-cold internecine warfare of the TV industry, Robert Sarnoff threw a verbal sidetrack signal at ABC with a reference to the "junior" network operation as a "narrow-gauge network". Some years later, a more informal (and anonymous) spokesman added insult to injury: "You want to know how to end the Viet Nam war? Just book it on ABC, and they'll cancel it after 13 weeks!"

But as we know from the record, those imbalances of color operation are in the musty past, along with the remains of a score or so of programs from each year of television's brief history—titles that can't even be brought to mind in a post-midnight Trivia game.

Just to keep the undertowing pull of "Color is here" from becoming too acceptable a shibboleth for members of the advertising profession, *Time* felt compelled to state—in 1966—that "Given the errant ways of all flesh, a listener who wants realistic color can hardly afford to take his hands off the controls." (Surely they meant *viewer!*)

In the commercial minds of TV network salesmen, the message contained overtones played by *two* hands, all-stops-out on the mighty Wurlitzer, and aimed toward the big-money advertiser: "You can hardly afford to take your hand out of your wallet pocket and extend it in the direction of color TV!"

By contrast, one advertising agency president raised *both* hands—possibly permitting *Time's* flesh to run its errant course—to exclaim: "The really perfect advertising medium—sight, sound, circulation, demonstration, and color!"

From an approach almost diametrically opposed to that of the "perfect advertising medium", National Educational Television (NET) revealed a chain of 25 non-profit affiliates in 14 states plus Puerto Rico, with color-capable transmitters and signed to air a minimum of one NET hour in color per month, beginning in the fall of 1966.

At the same time, it was announced that NET's New York City affiliate, WNDT-Channel 13, had received a $729,122 grant from the U.S. Department of Health, Education and Welfare, for the adding-on of color production facilities and for other technical expansion.

Noting an earlier report of the average cost for a commercial station to "go color"—approximating $350 thousand—it would seem safe to assume that WNDT would be able to raise the NET color list to 26.

Whether tint video will make educational programs on the order of *Know Your Vivaldi* and *Successful Tulip Bulb Storage* more acceptable to the general public remains to be seen: it must be concluded that the addition of color will enhance and make more effective the use of ETV in its primary educational function.

From Rorschach, We look To The Future

It has been reported that color is *naturally* desired by humans: that a tint versus B & W analysis of Rorschach "ink blot" tests has indicated that black-and-white patterns are more prone to excite those test-takers with mental aberrations; that multi-hued blots drew favorable reactions from people with normal responses.

The information is offered without any particular moral to be drawn—unless it be conceived as a sales promotion point in furthering the cause of color set sales and program tune-in! Thus, if the headline "Be the first in your block to have color" fails to stimulate purchasing, the amended slogan: "Be thought of as the most normal person in your block—buy color TV!" might do the trick—depending, of course, on the social structure of the neighborhood.

That analysis of the Rorschach respondents must have *some* validity! Other than to members of the Horseless Carriage Club of America, the very thought of Henry Ford's basic black *Tin Lizzy* is repugnant: even granting the slight setback in concept when Lucky Strike Green went to war, color has become increasingly important in the appurtenances of everyday living, be it Mondrian dresses as a fleeting fashion of the moment, bronze refrigerators or pastel sheets. Pioneers in packaging have known this, and stayed with such instant-recall images in color as the Kodak film box and the Hershey wrapper. "Why did Philip Morris ever give up its color?" some veterans still wonder, even as more than one oldtimer in the General Mills' organization secretly deplores the abandonment of *Jack Armstrong, the All-American Boy*.

Color Over the Waves

Color on an international basis has so far been integrated only in the gossip columnists'-delight Jet Set—at least in the interpretation of the actions of the major and minor European nations.

Germany's misnamed PAL system of colorcasting has been adopted by Britain, promptly rejected by France in favor of its own SECAM III system—with Russia siding with France, since it has an improved and compatible SECAM IV system of its own anyway.

The International Radio Consultive Committee (CCIR), sitting in Oslo in 1966 to resolve the incompatibility of the different systems (the U.S.'s NTSC system was entered in the lists as well), met with the success of a marriage counselor during the second act of *The Taming of the Shrew*. After 20-odd days of tint video poker, the result was: 30 countries for French SECAM III, 15 for German PAL, nine for U.S. NTSC.

"Anyway," concluded an international film salesman for a major U.S. producer, "they can all use our color film."

In Summary

In his *Letter from the Publisher, Television Age's* Sol Paul did a realistic summing up of "That Color Cliché" at the end of 1966:

"The plain fact of the matter is that color television still has a long way to go. Technically, color is here. But it is not here in 85 percent of the television homes. And among the advertisers missing, there are still several categories—soft goods, housewares, department stores—which have yet to include color television in any appreciable allocation of their advertising budgets."

Paul pointed up the many predictions made over the years concerning the potential of the color medium, and said: "When the prediction becomes a reality, it appears as if it's been with us all the time. Take, for example, package design. The designers have been working for several years on packages with shelf eye-appeal. Recently several packages have been redesigned specifically for color television. Miss Midge Wilson, executive director of the Color Association of the U.S., points out that color TV *generates* public taste in color as well as *displaying* it. For example, the mood of the times dictates the use of pastel colors in both men's and women's fashions for the fall season. Color TV will give these shades almost immediate public acceptance, as they appear in backdrops, set designs and clothes worn before the cameras."

If those predictions that become realities continue, there is much in store for the viewer of color video: the *mirror screen*, large, flat, mounted on the living room wall, with tint images larger than life ... the pocket-sized *transistor TV set*, with color on the beach to compete with striped bikinis, bronzed forms and pastel surfboards ... *stereophonic* color TV, rivaling Cinerama in the living room ... and *home movie color sets*, making the household's tint screen doubly or trebly useful by the ability to project 35mm. slides, also 8mm. home movies, through the picture tube!

With continued expansion in color telecasting at all levels, with continuing development in color production and transmission and viewing components, with the promise of color micro-viewing under the beach umbrella and macro-viewing on the living room wall, the textbook producer is hard pressed to set a cut-off date for any planned "up-to-date" broad scale examination of the "world of color".

Certain truths, however, should come through to the reader, be he or she embryonic broadcaster, advertiser, critic. Color television is television with more than one added ingredient: there is need for additional vocabulary, for better skills and techniques, even for that subjective thing called *taste*. The rapidly-developing technology brings with it more problems, but also more opportunities. Be it commercial, be it educational; be it advertising via the display of package goods or cultural programming illustrating art masterpieces; a murder mystery that is resolved by the *color* of the strangler's scarf, or the instructional map that shows the tinted mountains and valleys of a distant land—color television promises to be with us in many shapes and forms, possibly even in a dimension that will refute the cries of TV's "mediocrity—chewing gum for the eyes" school of print media critics.

In any event, it can't help but answer the antagonistic lament that titled this chapter: "It's in color—so what?" For better or worse, it *will* be in color—and will, along with everything else that has been said, demand a new level of knowledge and skill in criticism!

16 Colour Television Systems

A. V. LORD
Head of Physics Group, Research Department,
British Broadcasting Corporation

In the preface of this text, reference was made to the many and varied, real and attributed quotes of Hollywood's legendary Sam Goldwyn. In a slightly different milieu, American expatriate Gertrude Stein's "A rose is a rose is a rose" must rank among the most-cited single utterances of the century.

The wandering point comes a bit closer: in the following, writer A. V. Lord extracts the essence if not the thorns to show that—Miss Stein's rosy tints to the contrary—colour is not colour is not colour!

Which is to say that colour, universal in itself, has differing video era interpretations due to the divergent transmission and reception technologies of the various systems extant—the PAL and SECAM of Europe as well as America's NTSC.

A comparison of these major colour systems is the purpose of Mr. Lord's chapter. As Head of the Physics Group, British Broadcasting Corporation Research Department, he presents pre-eminent qualifications for the task. A graduate of the University of Manchester, he began his career in 1941 as a research physicist with Pye Ltd., Cambridge; joined the BBC in 1948 as an engineer in the Television Section of the Research Department. Since that time he has served in the Research Department continuously, as Head of the Video-Frequency Section, then as Assistant Head of the

Television Group, and since 1966 as Head of the Physics Group. Our British technical editor comments: "Here is a key article; long it is true, but not too difficult to understand, and authoritative."

To which might be added the thought that, if anyone can bring the light of compatible understanding to an incompatible technical situation, Lord is that man . . .

1. *Primary Colours and Additive Colour Mixing*

Colour television is only possible because the effect on the human eye of any spectral distribution of light energy can be simulated by the addition of three monochromatic light radiations. These radiations must be situated at the long-wavelength end of the visible spectrum (red), in the centre of the spectrum (green) and at the short-wavelength end of the spectrum (blue). The mechanism of the human eye enables an addition of radiation at three discrete wavelengths to be observed as having a particular colour.

Suppose there are three sources of light: red, green and blue, and that these sources are all projected simultaneously on to the same white screen. First, it must be noted that the brightness of light (the brightness assessed by an average observer, irrespective of colour) is measured in lumens. Suppose now that the brightness of light reflected from the screen from the three sources when used independently is R, G and B lumens of red, green and blue light respectively. The brightness of the reflected light of the combined sources will be:
$$L = R+G+B$$
where L is in lumens and will have, in general, a particular hue.

Suppose now that the sources are adjusted in brightness to give one lumen of white light so that L equals 1, and we can write:
$$1 = r+g+b$$
where r, g and b are the quantities of red, green and blue in lumens required to give 1 lumen of white light.

There are three primary colours in the first example quoted, so that there must be a proportion of white light. Suppose, for example, that the amounts of red and green light are both greater than those

required to be added to the blue light to produce white. Then we may write:
$$L = R' + G' + W$$
where R', G' and W represent the brightness in lumens of the red, green and white light comprising the total.

This shows that the light from any illuminated coloured area of a scene can be split into two components:

First—The amount of white light present.
Second—The amount of pure coloured light present which must comprise one or two primaries.

We can therefore define coloured light by three parameters:

(a) The luminance.
(b) The extent to which the light is coloured which is called the saturation. Completely saturated light contains no white light and completely desaturated light is composed entirely of white light.
(c) The hue of the light which is determined by the ratio of the primaries left after the deduction of the white light.

The representation of coloured light by the parameters luminance, saturation and hue, may at first sight seem more complicated than a simple statement of the luminances of the three primaries. It is, however, essential to the operation of colour television systems.

2. *The Three-colour Simultaneous System*

Since the light from any part of a scene can be synthesized by the addition of three primary colours, a colour television system may use three separate cameras to generate electrical signals corresponding to the quantities of red, green and blue light required. The cameras (actually three tubes in one camera assembly) will produce electrical signals corresponding to amounts of the required primaries and these can then be transmitted to three display tubes, each of which is arranged to give light of the hue of one of the three primaries. The red, green and blue light thus obtained can be superimposed by an optical system on a common screen and the original coloured scene re-constituted.

A three-channel R, G, B system of this type would be unsuitable for broadcast purposes because three separate transmission channels would need to be provided. However, the arrangement is of interest because the three-tube camera arrangement is typical of that required in modern broadcast systems of colour television. The essential feature of the camera is that each tube should be equipped with an appropriate optical filter. The optical filters have characteristics which ensure that the brightness of the light reaching each camera tube corresponds to the relative brightness required for the appropriate primary in the display system. Thus the characteristics required for the optical filters in the cameras cannot be calculated without a knowledge of the precise hues of the display primaries. Finally, it should be noted that such a system could use the modern three-gun shadow-mask display tube which is in effect three tubes with red, green and blue phosphors superimposed.

3. *Sequential Colour Television Systems*

Before discussing the currently-proposed systems, it is interesting to consider the simplest practical method of achieving colour television using only a single transmission channel. As early as 1928, J. L. Baird demonstrated that colour television could be achieved by using sequential colour analysis and synthesis and more recently a workable system was developed in America by CBS. A sequential system comprises a rotating disk of red, green and blue analysis filters placed in front of a single camera so as to intercept, field by field, the light reflected from the scene to be televised. The received picture is displayed on a monochrome tube and the light is fed through a similar disk comprising the corresponding colour synthesis filters. Thus providing that the rotation of the two disks is synchronized, a coloured version of the original scene will result. It will be seen that for the period of time during which light from the scene is intercepted by one of the analysis filters, the camera output signal will be describing the variations of the quantity of that primary required for the synthesis. During the same period, the image reproduced by the receiving tube will be presented to the viewer via the colour synthesis filter of the same primary so that the viewer's eye will be receiving the appropriate proportion of the primary required in the coloured reproduction. The three versions of the scene corresponding to the three primaries thus occur sequentially and because of the persistence of human vision, the successive images combine to produce the required result. Amongst other disadvantages, however, it is necessary that the cycle be completed in about one twenty-fifth of a second if flicker is not to occur. This means that three times the bandwidth is required, as compared with that necessary for a normal monochrome transmission. The system cannot therefore be regarded as a practical solution to the problem of broadcast colour television.

4. *Compatible Colour Television Systems*

Two possible colour television systems have been briefly discussed but neither of these is suitable for practical application since neither system produces a "compatible" signal. Compatibility means that:

(a) The signal radiated must give a satisfactory black-and-white picture when received on a conventional monochrome receiver.
(b) It must be possible to radiate the signal within the bandwidth occupied by a normal monochrome transmission.

Since a colour picture source (camera, telecine, etc.) produces three electrical signals corresponding to the red, green and blue primaries, the requirements of compatibility can be stated in another way:

(a) A signal corresponding to the brightness of the scene must be transmitted which will provide the signal for a monochrome receiver.
(b) A signal or signals must be transmitted corresponding to the colour of the scene.

4.1 *Mixed-Highs and the Constant-luminance Principle.* Fig. 1 shows a basic three-colour simultaneous colour system as outlined in Section 2. Three camera tubes sensitive to red, green and blue light respectively provide three colour-separation signals which are conveyed to the three guns of a three-colour display tube, the signal from the red camera tube producing a picture consisting of the red component of the scene and the green and blue camera tubes producing signals which similarly cause the green and blue components to be displayed; the composite display then consists of a substantially faithful reproduction of the original scene. However, in order to provide a sharp picture each of the three component signals must have the full bandwidth (i.e. the bandwidth required for a black-and-white transmission); thus such a basic system would be too extravagant in bandwidth. Further, none of the three component signals would be fully satisfactory for use by a black-and-white receiver. Two properties of the human eye may, however, be exploited to permit the three signals to be coded in such a manner that the requirements of compatibility may be fulfilled.

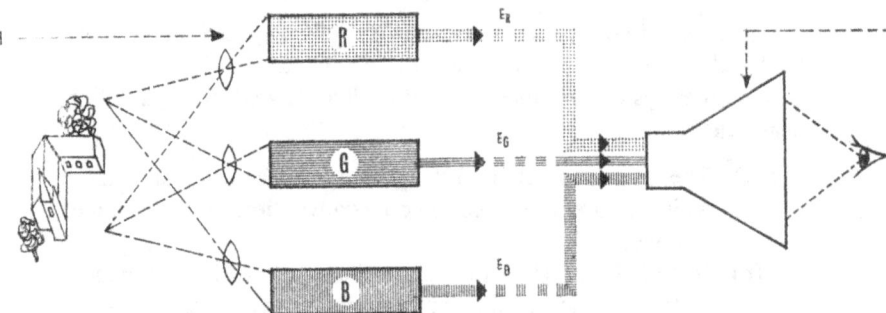

Fig. 1. Basic 3-colour simultaneous system. 1: Camera tubes. 2: 3-Gun display tube.

The first of these properties is that the eye does not perceive colour in fine detail; it is only aware of brightness changes in such areas. If an observer is asked to name the individual colours in extremely fine patterns he is unable to do so. As the coarseness of the patterns is increased he first begins to distinguish between orange and cyan patterns and then, as the pattern grows even coarser, he begins to appreciate all colours within the colour triangle.

The second of these properties is that the human eye is more sensitive to disturbance of brightness than of colour. Thus, if a colour television signal is subject to interference, it is more important to ensure that the interference has less effect upon the instantaneous brightness of the displayed picture than on the instantaneous hue or saturation.

In modern colour television systems advantage is taken of the first of these properties by employing what has been termed the "mixed-highs" principle. As the human eye can only perceive brightness differences in fine detail it is necessary to transmit only one wideband signal which describes the instantaneous brightness of the scene being scanned. As the observer can perceive colour in only the coarser patterns of the picture, a signal (or signals) representing colour information can be transmitted in reduced bandwidth. The second property of the eye may be exploited if the signal used for conveying information about brightness is made appreciably greater in amplitude than the signal (or signals) used for conveying the colour information.

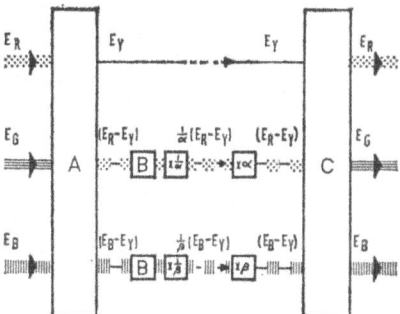

Fig. 2. Constant luminance system using "mixed highs". A: Matrix M_1. B: Low-pass filter. C: Matrix M_2.

One way in which the three colour-separation signals may be re-arranged so as to take advantage of these factors is illustrated in Fig. 2. In this arrangement the three colour-separation signals are combined in a precise manner to produce three other independent signals. The process is one of linear transformation and is performed by a device conveniently termed a matrix (M_1). The three new signals E_Y, (E_R-E_Y) and (E_B-E_Y) are derived as follows:

$$E_Y = lE_R + mE_G + nE_B$$
$$(E_R-E_Y) = (1-l)E_R - mE_G - nE_B$$
$$(E_B-E_Y) = -lE_R - mE_G + (1-n)E_B$$

Considering first the luminance signal E_Y, the coefficient l, m and n are the relative luminances of the three primary colours used in the colour display tube and correspond respectively to r, g and b of Section 1.

$$\text{thus } l+m+n = 1$$

and one lumen of white light is produced by l lumens of red, m lumens of green and n lumens of blue light. Assuming that white light is displayed by the three-gun tube when

$$E_R = E_G = E_B = 1:$$

Then the luminance of any area of the displayed picture (whether coloured or not) is

$$Y = lE_R + mE_G + nE_B = E_Y$$

The E_Y signal carries the information concerning the instantaneous brightness (or luminance) and is termed the luminance signal. Thus, this signal is suitable for use by a conventional black-and-white display. It will be seen that for greys and white

$$E_R = E_G = E_B$$

and $(E_R - E_Y)$ and $(E_B - E_Y)$ are both zero. Thus, the colour-difference signals carry information about colour only. The mixed-highs principle thus permits them to be limited in bandwidth.

At the colour receiver the luminance and colour-difference signals may be applied to a matrix (M_2) which is the inverse of that used at the transmitter, thus

$$E_R = E_Y + (E_R - E_Y)$$
$$E_B = E_Y + (E_B - E_Y)$$

and E_G may be derived from E_Y and $(E_G - E_Y)$, which is obtained from:

$$(E_G - E_Y) = -\left[\frac{l}{m}(E_R - E_Y) + \frac{n}{m}(E_B - E_Y)\right]$$

The effect of adding interference or noise to the colour-difference signals may now be investigated.

The red colour-separation signal fed to the display is

$$E_Y + (E_R - E_Y + \Delta_1) = E_R + \Delta_1$$

The blue colour-separation signal is

$$E_Y+(E_B-E_Y+\Delta_2) = E_B+\Delta_2$$

where Δ_1 and Δ_2 represent independent noise voltages and the green colour-separation signal is

$$E_Y - \left[\frac{l}{m}(E_R-E_Y+\Delta_1)+\frac{n}{m}(E_B-E_Y+\Delta_2)\right]$$

$$= E_G - \frac{l}{m}\Delta_1 - \frac{n}{m}\Delta_2$$

Therefore, the displayed luminance is

$$Y = l(E_R+\Delta_1)+m(E_G-\frac{l}{m}\Delta_1-\frac{n}{m}\Delta_2)+n(E_B+\Delta_2)$$

$$= lE_R+mE_G+nE_B+l\Delta_1-l\Delta_1-n\Delta_2+n\Delta_2$$

$$= E_Y$$

Hence the interference or noise accompanying the colour-difference signals does not contribute to the displayed luminance. This principle by which the primary signals are coded is known as the "constant-luminance" principle.

As they are less susceptible to interference than the luminance signal, the colour-difference signals may be attenuated somewhat before transmission and restored in level by amplification in the receiver, as shown in Fig. 2.

As yet, no values for l, m and n have been given. The three display-tube primary colours have been specified in terms of co-ordinates on the C.I.E. diagram.

	x	y	Y (*relative*)
Red	0·67	0·33	0·30
Green	0·21	0·71	0·59
Blue	0·14	0·08	0·11

The standard white is C.I.E. Illuminant C (average daylight).

	x	y	Y (*relative*)
Illum C	0·310	0·316	1·00

It will be seen that the luminosities of the red, green and blue primaries, when producing a white corresponding to Illuminant C, are in the ratio $0{\cdot}3 : 0{\cdot}59 : 0{\cdot}11$.

Hence,
$$l = 0{\cdot}3$$
$$m = 0{\cdot}59$$
$$\text{and } n = 0{\cdot}11$$
$$E_Y = 0{\cdot}3E_R + 0{\cdot}59E_G + 0{\cdot}11E_B$$

In order to obtain correct colour reproduction using these display-tube primaries it is necessary to use correct colour-analysis characteristics at the camera. When ideal analysis characteristics are added in the ratio of 30 percent red, 59 percent green and 11 percent blue the resultant curve has the same shape as the luminosity curve (sensitivity of the eye versus wavelength). This ensures that the luminance signal conveys information about brightness only.

The following table gives the values of E_R, E_G, E_B, E_Y, $(E_R - E_Y)$ and $(E_B - E_Y)$ for various colours each having maximum brightness.

Colour	E_R	E_G	E_B	E_Y	$(E_R - E_Y)$	$(E_B - E_Y)$
White	1·0	1·0	1·0	1·0	0	0
Red	1·0	0	0	0·3	0·70	−0·30
Green	0	1·0	0	0·59	−0·59	−0·59
Blue	0	0	1·0	0·11	−0·11	0·89
Yellow	1·0	1·0	0	0·89	0·11	−0·89
Magenta	1·0	0	1·0	0·41	0·59	0·59
Cyan	0	1·0	1·0	0·70	−0·70	0·30

4.2 *The effect of gamma.* Hitherto, it has been assumed that all the processes outlined in Figs. 1 and 2, and described in the text, are linear. In practice, however, the law connecting scanning-beam current and video drive voltage in display cathode-ray tubes is non-linear.* The brightness of a displayed picture point, B_D, is related to the corresponding video drive voltage by

$$B_D = E_s^\gamma$$

where γ has a value of approximately 2·2 in three-gun colour tubes and approximately 2·5 in conventional black-and-white tubes.

---

*Correction for this in the receiver is impracticable.

In order to ensure correct reproduction it is necessary that a compensating characteristic be applied to the signal before transmission. Thus a signal from a camera tube must be corrected to the form

$$E'_s = B_s$$

where B_s is the scene brightness of the point under consideration.

Thus, in Fig. 1, the colour-separation signals require gamma correction and now become

$$E'_R, E'_G, \text{ and } E'_B.$$

In Fig. 2 the luminance signal now becomes

$$E'_Y = 0{\cdot}3E'_R + 0{\cdot}59E'_G + 0{\cdot}11E'_B$$

and the colour-difference signals are

$$(E'_R - E'_Y) \text{ and } (E'_B - E'_Y)$$

The effects of these changes upon the colour and compatible-monochrome pictures will now be considered.

In the colour receiver the three colour-separation signals may be derived as follows:

$$E'_R = (E'_R - E'_Y) + E'_Y$$
$$E'_B = (E'_B - E'_Y) + E'_Y$$
$$\text{and } E'_G = E'_Y - 0{\cdot}51(E'_R - E'_Y) - 0{\cdot}19(E'_B - E'_Y)$$

When the luminance signal E'_Y is applied to a conventional black-and-white tube, the displayed luminance is

$$Y' = \left(0{\cdot}3E'_R + 0{\cdot}59E'_G + 0{\cdot}11E'_B\right)^\gamma$$

Correct reproduction is obtained when luminance is related to E_R, E_G and E_B by the equation:

$$Y = 0{\cdot}3E_R + 0{\cdot}59E_G + 0{\cdot}11E_B$$

In general $Y' \neq Y$ but for grey and white areas of the scene we have

$$E_R = E_G = E_B$$

i.e. $Y' = \left[E'_R(0.3+0.59+0.11)\right]^\gamma$

$= E_R$

$= 0.3E_R + 0.59E_G + 0.11E_B$

$= Y$

For, say, a saturated red of maximum brightness

$E_R = 1.0$ and $E_G = E_B = 0$

Therefore, $Y' = (0.3E'_R)^8$

$= 0.3^8$

However, the correct luminance is

$Y = 0.3$

For a black-and-white tube $\gamma = 2.5$ (say)

$$\frac{Y'}{Y} = 0.3^{1.5}$$

$= 0.163$

A black-and-white display is thus somewhat distorted, in that saturated colours in the scene, particularly red and blue, are reproduced as greys that are too dark.

In the colour display the luminance of large areas is correct (colour-separation signals are formed correctly at the receiver). However, contributions to the displayed luminance are made by both the luminance and colour-difference signals (except for greys and white) and in saturated coloured areas (particularly red and blue) the major contribution to luminance is made by the colour-difference signals which are restricted in bandwidth. Thus definition is lost in such areas and noise in the colour difference channels can contribute to display luminance.

4.3 *The elements of modern colour systems.* The modern compatible colour systems NTSC, PAL and SECAM, utilize the fundamental principles outlined in Sections 4.1 and 4.2. They are all based upon the use of a luminance signal, having a bandwidth equal to that required by the corresponding monochrome system, together with two colour-difference signals providing information about colour. It will be appreciated that if the luminance signal occupies the whole of the available bandwidth then the colour-difference signals must be located within the luminance-signal band and each system must be so devised that all three signals interfere with one another to the minimum extent. Such an arrangement is known as "band sharing".

In all three systems, the two colour-difference signals are effectively combined so as to form a single signal which is known as the "chrominance" signal; in fact, the systems differ mainly only in the ways in which they form their chrominance signals.

As compatibility is a prime requirement of a colour system, a complete colour signal must be of a form that is acceptable to receivers, designed for the corresponding monochrome system, which may already be in the hands of the public when the colour system is introduced. The colour signal must, therefore, contain all the conventional synchronizing and blanking pulses, and the chrominance signal must be of a form such as not to interfere with the operation of the monochrome receivers.

In order to satisfy the foregoing requirements the chrominance signal is transmitted to the colour receiver as the modulation of a suitable subcarrier whose frequency lies within the luminance band. However, it will be appreciated that the presence of the subcarrier will result in an interfering pattern on the screen of the monochrome receiver and, in all three systems, measures are taken to minimize the visibility of this interference. These measures include the use of as high a subcarrier frequency as possible, thus ensuring that the interfering pattern has a fine structure. Further measures include (for NTSC and PAL) the use of specially chosen frequencies bearing particular relationships with the scanning frequencies; in the case of SECAM, the polarity of the subcarrier is reversed during certain lines and fields.

As already pointed out, the main differences between the three systems lie in the formation of the chrominance signal (i.e. in the modulation of the subcarrier).

NTSC and PAL utilize amplitude modulation of the subcarrier. In both cases, however, the suppressed-carrier method is used rather than the more conventional form. This ensures that the chrominance-signal amplitude is directly dependent upon the amplitudes of the colour-difference signals; it is zero for all picture areas lying on the grey-scale and is only high for picture areas of bright saturated colour. A further advantage of suppressed-carrier a.m. is that, for a given chrominance signal amplitude, it is more resistant to noise than is conventional a.m.

Normal forms of amplitude modulation (both suppressed carrier and conventional) are used for the transmission of only one modulating signal. As has already been pointed out, the colour systems require that two independent colour-difference signals be transmitted. In order to satisfy this NTSC and PAL utilize what is termed "quadrature" suppressed-carrier a.m.

Quadrature a.m. may be regarded as the separate modulation of two subcarriers, of precisely the same frequency, which bear a quadrature phase relationship one with the other. If one recalls that the peaks of a sine wave coincide with the zero-crossings of a cosine wave having the same frequency, and vice versa, it will be appreciated that the two waves may be separately modulated, in amplitude, by two signals; the two modulated waves may then be added together to form a single resultant wave which is modulated in both amplitude and phase. The separate modulating signals may be derived from the resultant wave by examining its amplitude, first at the instants corresponding to the peaks of the sine wave and, secondly, at those corresponding to the peaks of the cosine wave. In NTSC and PAL coders the quadrature modulation of the subcarrier by the two colour-difference signals results in the chrominance signal which, in turn, is added to the luminance and synchronizing signals to form the composite colour signal.

In an NTSC or PAL colour receiver the chrominance and luminance signals are first separated by means of filters and the two colour-difference signals are then derived from the chrominance signal by means of two demodulating waves, representing the sine and cosine components, which are obtained from a local subcarrier oscillator in the receiver; this oscillator is maintained in synchronism with the master subcarrier source at the coder by means of a special synchronizing signal consisting of a short "burst" of subcarrier located in each post-synchronizing line-blanking interval (except for a few lines during the field-blanking interval). The two colour-difference signals and the luminance signal are then used to form the colour-separation signals required by the display.

If, at the colour receiver, the phase relationship between the demodulating waves and the chrominance signal is incorrect, say, due to phase distortion of the chrominance signal during transmission or to distortion of the burst, the colour-difference signals obtained may be erroneous; instead of the two original colour-difference signals, two mixtures of them are obtained.

The NTSC system does not incorporate any measures to prevent this form of distortion causing errors in the colour picture. However, in PAL, one of the two colour-difference signals used to modulate the subcarrier at the coder is reversed in polarity during alternate lines; a special form of burst is also used which indicates, to the colour receiver, whether the colour-difference signal of a particular line has been reversed or not. This periodic polarity reversal of one colour-difference signal enables the PAL system to minimize the effects of distortion.

In a simple form of PAL receiver the polarity reversals of one colour-difference signal are compensated by a further reversal effected by a simple switch. In such circumstances the effects of chrominance-signal phase distortion cause colour errors of opposite sign during successive lines, as displayed on the colour-receiver screen. Provided that the errors are not large, the viewer's eye performs an averaging process and the correct colour is seen. However, a PAL receiver may include an ultrasonic delay which permits the chrominance signal to be delayed by one line period; this arrangement allows the chrominance signal of one line to be combined with the chrominance signal from the previous line. In this way an average chrominance signal may be derived electrically and large phase errors substantially corrected; in addition, the action of the delay enables the two colour-difference signals to be separated, one from the other, more easily.

The SECAM system differs rather radically from NTSC and PAL. The system does not attempt to transmit both colour-difference signals along with the luminance signal; it transmits them sequentially so that one colour-difference signal is transmitted during one line and the other during the succeeding line. Further, instead of amplitude-modulating the subcarrier, each colour-difference signal deviates the subcarrier frequency by an amount which is proportional to the colour-difference signal amplitude; when the colour-difference signal is zero (grey-scale) the subcarrier frequency has its normal value. Thus the SECAM chrominance signal consists of a frequency modulated subcarrier whose amplitude is not zero in grey-scale picture areas. Various forms of pre-emphasis are used to modify the colour-difference signals prior to modulation and to vary the amplitude of the chrominance signal so as to increase its resistance to noise. As with NTSC and PAL, the SECAM chrominance signal is combined with the luminance signal to form the complete colour signal. As the colour-difference signals are transmitted sequentially, it is necessary for a special signal to be included in the complete colour signal indicating the colour-difference signal sequence.

At the SECAM receiver the chrominance and luminance signals are again separated by suitable filters. However, as only one colour-difference signal is transmitted during any one line, the SECAM receiver must contain a one-line delay which enables the chrominance signal from one line to be available while the chrominance signal corresponding to the other colour-difference signal is received during the succeeding line. In this way both colour-difference signals may be derived simultaneously although only one of them is directly associated with the luminance signal being received at any one time.

The chrominance signals, obtained directly and via the one-line delay, are then passed to an electronic double-pole, double-throw switch which is actuated so as to result in two further chrominance signals that correspond to two continuous and separate colour-difference signals.

After amplitude limiting, the two colour-difference signals are recovered by frequency discriminators; suitable de-emphasis of the signals is also carried out. Finally, the recovered and corrected colour-difference signals are combined as in NTSC and PAL, with the luminance signal to form the colour-separation signal.

The foregoing account of the three modern colour systems has merely outlined their operation. Sections 5, 6 and 7 describe the three systems in more detail, and Section 8 compares some of their properties.

5. The NTSC System*

The NTSC system was devised by the U.S. National Television Systems Committee in the early 1950s and was adopted as the standard system for use in the U.S.A. at the end of 1953 and since then an increasing amount of colour transmission has taken place in that country. At the present time a very significant proportion of all television programmes broadcast in the U.S.A. are radiated in this form. Japan and Canada have also adopted this system of colour television as standard.

As described in Section 4, three independent signals E'_Y, $(E'_R - E'_Y)$ and $(E'_B - E'_Y)$ are required by the colour receiver. E'_Y occupies the full video bandwidth available (being suitable for a black-and-white receiver) and each colour-difference signal occupies a fraction (say, one-fifth to one-third) the luminance-signal bandwidth.

In order to combine these three signals into a composite signal occupying only the luminance-signal bandwidth the NTSC system utilizes, for the colour-difference signals, the suppressed-carrier amplitude modulation of, in effect, two subcarriers having the same frequency but a quadrature relationship.

Ordinary amplitude modulation may be expressed as:

$$F(t) = \left[1 + f(t)\right] \cdot \cos \omega_s t$$

where $f(t)$ represents the modulating wave (with maximum and minimum values of $+1$ and -1) and $\frac{\omega_s}{2\pi}$ is the carrier frequency.

Suppressed-carrier amplitude modulation by a function $f_1(t)$ is then

$$S_1(t) = f_1(t) \cdot \cos \omega_s t$$

Another suppressed-carrier amplitude modulation signal having the same carrier frequency but a quadrature relationship is

$$S_2(t) = f_2(t) \cdot \sin \omega_s t$$

---

*In the interests of clarity, only a simplified version of the system is described prior to Section 5.2.

If we add these two signals together we have

$$S_1(t)+S_2(t) = f_1(t) \cdot \cos \omega_s t + f_2(t) \cdot \sin \omega_s t$$

Multiplying this sum first by $\cos \omega_s t$ gives

$$\left[S_1(t)+S_2(t)\right] \cdot \cos \omega_s t = \tfrac{1}{2} f_1(t)\left[1+\cos 2\omega_s t\right] + \tfrac{1}{2} \cdot f_2(t) \cdot \sin 2\omega_s t$$

If the twice-carrier-frequency components are removed by filtering, we have

$$\left[S_1(t)+S_2(t)\right] \cdot \cos \omega_s t = \tfrac{1}{2} \cdot f_1(t)$$

Similarly,
$$\left[S_1(t)+S_2(t)\right] \cdot \sin \omega_s t = \tfrac{1}{2} \cdot f_2(t)$$

and, in the more general case of multiplication by $\cos(\omega_s t+\theta)$,

$$\left[S_1(t)+S_2(t)\right] \cdot \cos(\omega_s t+\theta) = \tfrac{1}{2} f_1(t) \cos \theta - \tfrac{1}{2} f_2(t) \sin \theta$$

The two modulating signals, $f_1(t)$ and $f_2(t)$ may thus be obtained, separately or added in any desired ratio, by multiplicative demodulation using a suitably phased subcarrier.

The two modulating signals, $f_1(t)$ and $f_2(t)$ may thus be separately obtained. In the NTSC system:

$$f_1(t) = k_1(E'_R - E'_Y) \text{ and } f_2(t) = k_1 k_2(E'_B - E'_Y)$$

The composite colour signal (excepting synchronizing signals) is

$$E'_M = E'_Y + S_1(t) + S_2(t)$$
$$= E'_Y + k_1\left[(E'_R - E'_Y) \cdot \cos \omega_s t + k_2(E'_B - E'_Y) \cdot \sin \omega_s t\right]$$

where $k_1 = \dfrac{1}{1 \cdot 14}$ and $k_2 = \dfrac{1}{1 \cdot 78}$.

k_1 and k_2 are so chosen that the excursions of the composite signal do not extend too far into the region normally occupied by synchronizing signals nor too far beyond white signal level. The coding of the three colour-separation signals to form a composite colour signal is illustrated in Fig. 3. The colour-difference signals are

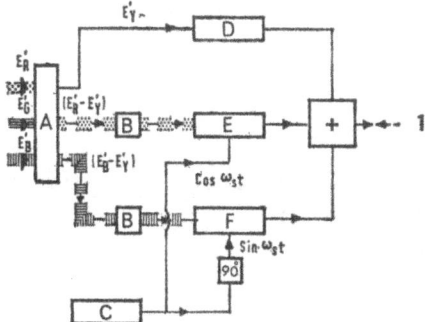

Fig. 3. NTSC coding (simplified). A: Matrix M_1. B: Low-pass filter. C: Sub-carrier generator. D: E'_Y delay. E: $(E'_R - E'_Y)$ balanced modulator. F: $(E'_B - E'_Y)$ balanced modulator. 1: Composite output signal.

limited in bandwidth and fed to balanced modulators where they modulate (in a suppressed-carrier manner) the two quadrature-related subcarrier components. The resulting signals are added to the luminance signal (which has been delayed in order to compensate for the band-limiting and modulation processes) to form the composite colour signal. Fig. 4 shows one line of a composite signal known as "colour bars" in which signals corresponding to white, black, the saturated primaries (at maximum brightness) and their complementaries (at maximum brightness) are transmitted.

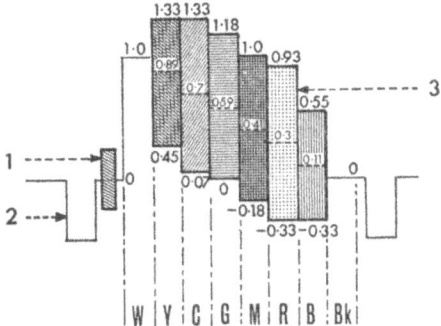

Fig. 4. Video signal corresponding to one line of colour bars. W: White. Y: Yellow. C: Cyan. G: Green. M: Magenta. R: Red. B: Blue. Bk: Black. 1: Burst. 2: Line-synchronizing pulse. 3: Subcarrier.

The addition of the two subcarrier components

$$k_1(E'_R - E'_Y) \cdot \cos \omega_s t \text{ and}$$

$$k_1 k_2(E'_B - E'_Y) \cdot \sin \omega_s t$$

results in the chrominance signal. This consists of a subcarrier signal whose phase and amplitude are functions of the amplitudes of the colour-difference signals. Fig. 5 shows a vector diagram describing the chrominance signal E_c' where

$$E'_c = k_1 \left[(E'_R - E'_Y) \cos \omega_s t + k_2 (E'_B - E'_Y) \sin \omega_s t \right]$$

As can be seen, the amplitude of E'_c is the vector sum of the amplitudes of the two colour-difference components. Further, the phase ϕ of E'_c is determined by the ratio of their amplitudes.

If now a subcarrier used for demodulation is represented by a further vector on this diagram, its projections on the $(E'_R - E'_Y)$ and $(E'_B - E'_Y)$ axes give the respective proportions of these signals in the output of the demodulator.

$$E'_c = k_1 \left[(E'_R - E'_Y)^2 + k_2^2 (E'_B - E'_Y)^2 \right]^{\frac{1}{2}}$$

$$\angle \tan^{-1} \cdot \left\{ k_2 \frac{(E'_R - E'_Y)}{(E'_B - E'_Y)} \right\}$$

As the colour-difference signals describe colour it is worthwhile considering the relationships between the amplitude and phase of E'_c and certain colour parameters. As the amplitude of both colour-

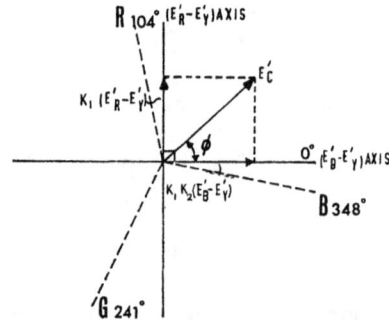

Fig. 5. Chrominance signal vector diagram. R: Red. G: Green. B: Blue.

difference signals depends upon the degree to which the colour is diluted by white (i.e. desaturation), it is to be expected that the amplitude of E'_c is related to colour saturation. Further, as a given hue of colour will result from colour-separation signals having amplitudes in a unique ratio, it is to be expected that the same hue will be described by a unique ratio of colour-difference signals. From this it may be concluded that the phase of E'_c is closely related to hue. Fig. 5 shows the phase angles for the three colours red, green and blue.

5.1 *Choice of subcarrier frequency.* It will be appreciated that, as the chrominance signal is added to the luminance signal E'_Y to form the composite colour signal, it should interfere with the luminance signal as little as possible. As both colour-difference

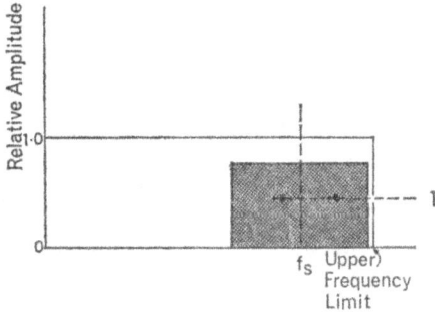

Fig. 6. Composite signal spectrum. 1: Chrominance signal sidebands.

signals are zero for all points on the grey-scale, the chrominance signal vanishes in all black, grey and white picture areas. In the coloured areas of the picture, however, the chrominance signal is present and appears as a pattern on the screen of the black-and-white receiver. Raising the subcarrier frequency reduces its visibility. However, in order to avoid cross-talk between the two colour-difference signals it is necessary that at least one of them be transmitted in a double-sideband manner. Hence, the subcarrier frequency must be chosen so that there is sufficient space in the signal spectrum for the upper sideband of the chrominance signal. Fig. 6 illustrates a typical composite-signal spectrum.

The visibility of the chrominance-signal pattern on the black-and-white display and the interference between the luminance and chrominance signals are minimized by utilizing the "frequency-interleaving" principle. This is based upon the fact that the spectrum of a normal television signal, such as a luminance signal, consists of a series of harmonics of line frequency; associated with each line harmonic there is a set of symmetrical sidebands corresponding to field frequency and harmonics of field frequency. If the subcarrier frequency is chosen to be an odd multiple of half the line frequency, its position in the spectrum lies midway between two line harmonics and mutual interference is reduced to a minimum. The principal sidebands of the subcarrier are spaced symmetrically from it by multiples of line frequency so that they, in turn, lie between the line harmonics of the luminance signal; the secondary sidebands of each principal subcarrier sideband (corresponding to field frequency and its harmonics) interleave the corresponding sidebands of the luminance-signal line harmonics.

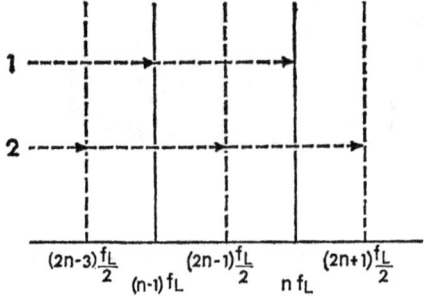

Fig. 7. Simplified diagram of "frequency interleaving". 1: Components corresponding to luminance signal. 2: Components corresponding to chrominance signal.

Fig. 7 shows, in simplified form, the interleaving of luminance and chrominance spectrum components.

The effect of using a subcarrier frequency which is an odd multiple of half the line frequency minimizes the visibility of the chrominance signal at the screen of the black-and-white receiver. This is illustrated in Fig. 8 in terms of a five-line raster and a subcarrier frequency which is 2·5 times the line frequency. As will be

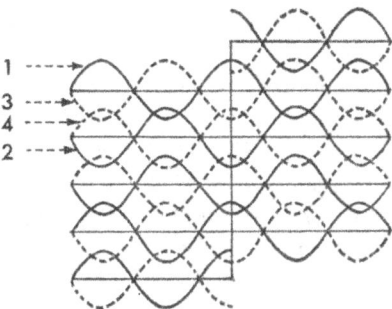

Fig. 8. Five-line raster with subcarrier at 2·5 times line frequency. 1: Field one. 2: Field two. 3: Field three. 4: Field four.

seen, the alternations of brightness are in antiphase on successive lines of the same field and are also in antiphase on successive scans of the same line. The pattern is repetitive in a period of four fields. The pattern appears as a fine dot pattern which, due to stroboscopic action, appears to "crawl" in several directions.

5.2 E_I' and E_Q' signals. In the foregoing outline only the colour-difference signals $(E'_R - E'_Y)$ and $(E'_B - E'_Y)$ have been considered. However, it was pointed out earlier that the two colours which are first distinguished one from the other, as the coarseness of colour patterns is increased, are orange and cyan. Hence, it would be

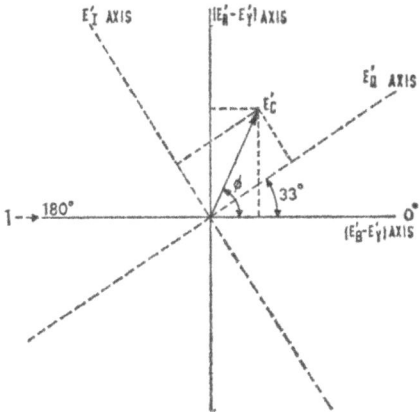

Fig. 9. The E'_I and E'_Q chrominance axes. 1: Burst phase.

reasonable to design the system so that, given an ideal receiver, the highest colour resolution occurred for these two colours. Further, it has been pointed out that in choosing as high a subcarrier frequency as possible it is necessary to ensure that at least one colour-difference signal is transmitted in a double sideband-manner. In the NTSC system these considerations have been taken into account.

The two colour-difference signals actually used in forming the chrominance signal are known as the E_I' signal and the E_Q' signal. These two signals can be formed either by direct matrix operation from E_R', E_G', and E_B' or can be derived from $(E_R'-E_Y')$ and $(E_B'-E_Y')$. They can be represented on the chrominance phase diagram, Fig. 5, by two orthogonal axes rotated with respect to the $(E_R'-E_Y')$ and $(E_B'-E_Y')$ axes by 33°. The E_I' axis then describes the colours orange and cyan, the E_Q' axis describes the colours green and magenta. This is illustrated in Fig. 9. The matrix operations deriving E_I' and E_Q' also incorporate the coefficients k_1 and k_2 so that the chrominance signal E_C' can now be written

$$E_C' = E_I' \cdot \cos(\omega_s t + 33°) + E_Q' \cdot \sin(\omega_s t + 33°)$$

where $\quad E_I' = k_1(E_R'-E_Y') \cos 33° - k_1 k_2 (E_B'-E_Y') \sin 33°$

and $\quad E_Q' = k_1(E_R'-E_Y') \sin 33° + k_1 k_2 (E_B'-E_Y') \cos 33°$

In forming the chrominance signal the E_Q' component modulates a suitable subcarrier component in a double-sideband manner, each sideband having a width equal to the spacing between subcarrier frequency and the upper video-frequency limit. The E_I' component modulates the quadrature subcarrier component in an asymmetric manner; the upper sideband is equal in bandwidth to the upper E_Q' sideband but its lower sideband is wider. This arrangement permits the subcarrier frequency to be as high as possible and also permits the lower sideband of the E_I' component to carry medium-resolution information about orange-cyan detail.

The spectrum of a signal using the E_I' and E_Q' chrominance signals is shown in Fig. 10. It will be appreciated that such a composite signal may be used in either of two ways by the colour receiver decoder:

(a) The decoder may only accept that portion of the chrominance signal spectrum which is double-sideband. This then enables the colour-difference signals $(E_R'-E_Y')$ and

COLOUR TELEVISION SYSTEMS

($E'_B - E'_Y$) to be demodulated directly, by means of subcarriers whose phases lie along the respective axes of these signals.

(b) The E'_I and E'_Q components may be demodulated in the colour receiver, by means of subcarriers whose phases lie along the "I" and "Q" axes. In this case the output of the E_I signal demodulator will be attenuated by 6 dB for all modulation frequencies that are not transmitted in a double-sideband manner. Further, the output of the E'_Q demodulator will contain cross-talk from the E'_I signal for all modulation frequencies that are not transmitted double-sideband. These must be removed by filtering.

5.3 *Colour synchronizing*. As was indicated in Section 5, the NTSC decoding process in the colour receiver requires the provision of two subcarriers of precisely the same frequency but having a quadrature relationship. These c.w. subcarriers are required in order to demodulate the chrominance signal so as to provide the separate modulating components, for example ($E'_R - E'_Y$) and ($E'_B - E'_Y$). It is, therefore, necessary to provide a synchronizing signal in the transmitted waveform which controls, very precisely, an oscillator in the receiver; this oscillator then provides the two demodulating subcarriers. The synchronizing signal consists of a "burst" of subcarrier which is transmitted during the back porch of the composite signal, as shown in Fig. 4. In the proposed standards for a 525-line NTSC colour system for use in the U.S.A., the burst consists of eight to eleven cycles of subcarrier.

In a typical NTSC decoder the phase of the burst is compared at the beginning of every line with the phase of the receiver subcarrier oscillator and any phase error is then corrected by a suitable reactance control operating on the oscillator. The transmitted burst in the composite video waveform has a phase of 180° with respect of the ($E'_B - E'_Y$) axis. This is illustrated in Fig. 9.

5.4 *NTSC decoding*. The essential principles of NTSC decoding have been outlined in previous sections. A block diagram describing a high-quality NTSC decoder is shown in Fig. 11. This decoder utilizes the E'_I and E'_Q chrominance signals and can make use of the orange/cyan axis for medium-resolution colour detail. In the decoder

232   THE SUM OF THE PARTS

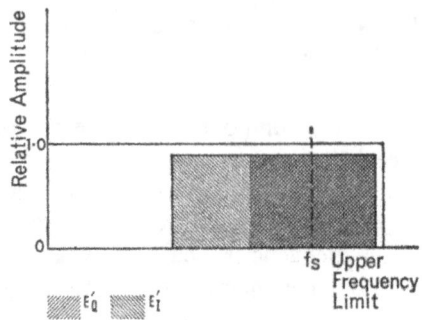

Fig. 10. Composite signal spectrum using E'_I and E'_Q.

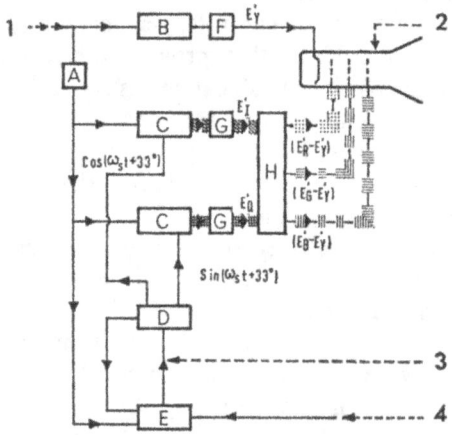

Fig. 11. NTSC decoder using E'_I and E'_Q. A: Band-pass filter. B: Band-stop filter. C: Synchronous demodulator. D: Subcarrier oscillator. E: Subcarrier locking circuits. F: E'_Y delay. G: Low-pass filter. H: Matrix. 1: Composite video from detector. 2: 3-Gun display tube. 3: Control signal. 4: Pulses from line-deflection circuit.

of Fig. 11 the composite video signal, from the detector in the radio frequency portion of the receiver, is divided between two paths.

In the first path, a band-stop filter attenuates frequencies close to subcarrier frequency (in order to remove dots in large areas of the displayed picture) and the signal is then delayed to compensate for delays in the chrominance circuits. The signal is now fed to the cathode of the three-gun display tube as the luminance signal E'_Y.

The second part of the output from the radio frequency detector is fed to a band-pass filter which accepts the whole of the chrominance-signal band but rejects that part of the luminance-signal spectrum falling outside the chrominance band. The output of the band-pass filter is fed to two synchronous detectors which are similar to balanced modulators. The first synchronous detector is supplied with continuous subcarrier having a phase lying along the E'_I axis which results in a synchronous-detector output consisting of the E'_I signal; this is passed to a suitable low-pass filter and correction for the 6 dB attenuation of upper frequencies may be applied. The E'_I signal is then fed to the matrix. Similarly, the second synchronous detector is supplied with continuous subcarrier having a phase lying along the E'_Q axis which results in an output of E'_Q which is then correspondingly passed through a low-pass filter to the matrix. In the matrix the E'_I and E'_Q signals are combined in various proportions to produce $(E'_R - E'_Y)$, $(E'_G - E'_Y)$ and $(E'_B - E'_Y)$ which are then passed to the three grids of the three-gun display tube; the resulting grid-cathode potentials are then E'_R, E'_G and E'_B respectively. The two supplies of continuous subcarrier are provided by an oscillator which, as already mentioned, is controlled by the burst signal in the composite video waveform. The burst is separated from all other signal components by means of a keying-pulse derived from the line-deflection circuit of the receiver and is compared in phase with an output from the oscillator and a control voltage used to maintain phase lock of the oscillator. Such a decoder, however, is usually found only in a professional monitoring receiver; at the present time most NTSC colour receivers effectively decode using the $(E'_R - E'_Y)$ and $(E'_B - E'_Y)$ axes and do not take advantage of the potentially higher colour resolution along the orange/cyan axis. In such receivers the continuous subcarrier feeds are phased to lie along the $(E'_R - E'_Y)$ and $(E'_B - E'_Y)$ axes. In some forms of receiver decoder three synchronous detectors are used with demodulating subcarriers lying along the $(E'_R-E'_Y)$, $(E'_G-E'_Y)$ and $(E'_B-E'_Y)$ axes. Even other variants are possible.

5.5. Summary of the NTSC system as used with the U.S. 525-line, 60 field system*

$$E'_Y = 0\cdot30E'_R+0\cdot59E'_G+0\cdot11E'_B$$

where $\gamma = 2\cdot2$

$$E'_I = 0\cdot60E'_R-0\cdot28E'_G-0\cdot32E'_B$$
$$= 0\cdot74(E'_R-E'_Y)-0\cdot27(E'_B-E'_Y)$$
$$E'_Q = 0\cdot21E'_R-0\cdot52E'_G+0\cdot31E'_B$$
$$= 0\cdot48(E'_R-E'_Y)+0\cdot41(E'_B-E'_Y)$$

The luminance signal carries information describing brightness, while the colour-difference signals describe colouring. The luminance signal E'_Y is transmitted with the full system bandwidth of 4·2 Mc/s while E'_I and E'_Q are bandwidth-limited to approximately 1·5 Mc/s and 0·5 Mc/s respectively.

E'_I and E'_Q are then used to "quadrature modulate" a subcarrier of frequency $\frac{\omega_s}{2\pi} = 3\cdot579545$ Mc/s. This frequency is an odd multiple of half the line frequency in order to cause the minimum interference to the picture when the signal is displayed by a black-and-white receiver.

The composite signal (excluding sync pulses and burst) is:

$$E'_M = E'_Y + \left\{ E'_I \cos(\omega_s t+33°)+E'_Q \sin(\omega_s t+33°) \right\}$$

and, for colour-difference frequencies below 500 kc/s, may be expressed as:

$$E'_M = E'_Y+\frac{1}{1\cdot14}\left\{ (E'_R-E'_Y)\cos\omega_s t+\frac{1}{1\cdot78}(E'_B-E'_Y)\sin\omega_s t \right\}$$

---

*Full details have been published in Doc. X1/128 (U.S.A.) of the CCIR, Oslo 1966.

In another form:

$$E'_M = E'_Y + \left\{ E'^2_I + E'^2_Q \right\}^{\frac{1}{2}} \cdot \angle \tan^{-1} \cdot \frac{E'_I}{E'_Q} + 33°$$

This is the sum of a luminance signal E'_Y and a chrominance signal whose amplitude is $\{E'^2_I + E'^2_Q\}^{\frac{1}{2}}$ and whose phase angle, with reference to the $(E'_B - E'_Y)$ axis is

$$\phi = \tan^{-1} \frac{E'_I}{E'_Q} + 33°$$

The amplitude of the chrominance signal represents saturation (depth of colour) and the angle ϕ describes hue.

In the colour receiver, either the colour-difference signals E'_I and E'_Q, or $(E'_R - E'_Y)$ and $(E'_B - E'_Y)$, are extracted by synchronous detection and are combined with E'_Y to form E'_R, E'_G and E'_B.

The synchronous detectors require a supply of continuous subcarrier. This is generated by an oscillator locked in frequency and phase to the subcarrier generator at the signal source by means of a burst of approximately 10 cycles of subcarrier located within the back-porch interval of line-blanking.

5.6 *A weakness of the NTSC system.* The NTSC system has many good features. These include good compatibility, good utilization of the available bandwidth, the fact that no difficult problems are posed in receiver design, good signal-to-noise performance, etc. However, the fact that the hue of a picture area is described by chrominance phase angle means that any distortion in which the relative phase between the chrominance signal and the burst is altered causes errors of hue in the displayed picture; in practice, errors of 5° are perceptible and errors greater than 20° are obvious.

This characteristic of the NTSC system renders it vulnerable to a form of distortion which can arise in long links and is known as "differential-phase" distortion. This is probably the most serious weakness of the NTSC system; the distortion takes the form of a variation of chrominance phase angle as a function of luminance-signal magnitude and can cause a change in flesh colour as an artist moves from a bright area of the scene into the shadow. The principal technical reason why the PAL and SECAM systems were proposed is the vulnerability of the NTSC system to this form of distortion.

6. *The PAL System*

The PAL system was devised and developed in the Federal Republic of Germany by Dr. W. Bruch of Telefunken A.G. His first proposals were published in 1963.

The main modifications to the NTSC system, which result in the PAL system, consist of reversing the phase of the $(E'_R - E'_Y)$ chrominance component on successive lines and transmitting bursts which alternately lag and lead the NTSC burst phase by 45° on successive lines.* This is illustrated in the phase diagram shown in Fig. 12.

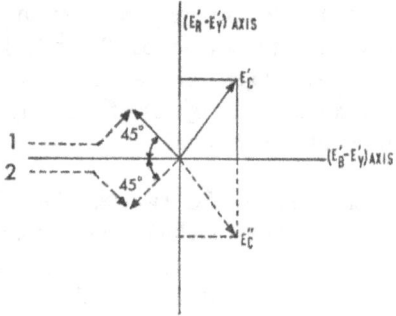

Fig. 12. Phase alternation of the $(E'_R - E'_Y)$ components of chrominance and burst. 1: Burst for E'_C. 2: Burst for E''_C.

Thus, during one line, the chrominance phase is identical to that obtained with the NTSC system; the burst phase, however, lags by 45°. Let E'_C represent the chrominance vector during this line. During the succeeding line the $(E'_R - E'_Y)$ chrominance component is reversed, the $(E'_B - E'_Y)$ component remaining unaltered and the chrominance vector is now E''_C; the burst phase, during this line leads by 45°. By means of a further process at the decoder, in which

---

*The reason for the alternation of burst phase is given in Section 6.1.

the $(E'_R - E'_Y)$ component of E''_C is again reversed, the vector E''_C is, ideally, made to coincide with E'_C. However, should a phase error between chrominance and burst be introduced in the path from coder to decoder, the hue error introduced during one line is followed by an equal and opposite hue error on the succeeding line. This is illustrated in Fig. 13.

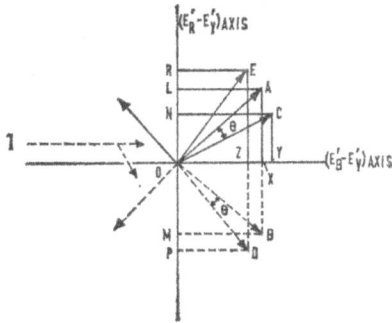

Fig. 13. The effect of a chrominance phase error in PAL. 1: Bursts.

In the figure, OA is the chrominance vector during one line (i.e. E'_C); this vector has an $(E'_R - E'_Y)$ component OL and an $(E'_B - E'_Y)$ component OX. OB is the chrominance vector during the succeeding line (i.e. E''_C); OM is the $(E'_R - E_Y)$ component and OX is again the $(E'_B - E'_Y)$ component. It is obvious that reversing the $(E'_R - E'_Y)$ component of OB in the decoder results in the vector OA (since OM = OL).

When distortion causes a chrominance relative phase shift θ the vector during the first line is OC and during the second line is OD. The $(E'_R - E'_Y)$ component of OC is ON and that of OD is OP; the $(E'_B - E'_Y)$ components are OY and OZ respectively. Reversing the $(E'_R - E'_Y)$ component of OD at the receiver gives the component OR; together with the $(E'_B - E'_Y)$ component OZ, this results in the vector OE. Thus it will be seen that the hue distortion on succeeding lines is in equal, but opposite, directions. Therefore, if means are provided in the decoder for obtaining the average of the chrominance phases on successive lines, the effect of chrominance phase errors will be substantially zero.

It will be seen that, although the NTSC system utilizes the E'_I

and E'_Q colour difference signals to form the coded signal, the PAL signal is formed using $(E'_R - E'_Y)$ and $(E'_B - E'_Y)$. The chrominance signals corresponding to $(E'_R - E'_Y)$ and $(E'_B - E'_Y)$ are weighted in amplitude by the coefficients k_1 and k_2, as in NTSC. This is permissible for PAL, because cross-talk from one colour-difference signal to the other during one line is exactly opposed by the corresponding cross-talk during the succeeding line. Thus an averaging process in the decoder can eliminate the effect of such cross-talk and, in principle, both colour-difference signals may be transmitted using asymmetric-sideband modulation the of subcarrier and both may describe medium-fine colour detail.

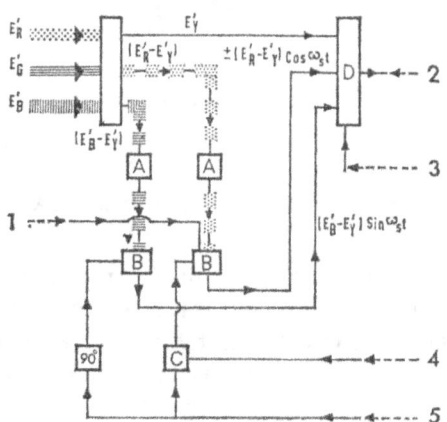

Fig. 14. PAL coding. A: Low-pass filters. B: Balanced modulators. C: Phase-reversing switch. D: Adder. 1: Burst-keying pulses. 2: Composite colour signal. 3: Sync. 4: Line pulses. 5: Subcarrier.

6.1 *PAL Coding and Decoding.* Fig. 14 shows a PAL coder. It is very similar to the NTSC form of coder. However, it includes a switch that reverses the phase of the subcarrier fed to the $(E'_R - E'_Y)$ balanced modulator and arrangements for adding to the inputs of both balanced modulators, burst-keying pulses of equal amplitude; thus the $(E'_R - E'_Y)$ chrominance component is reversed in phase during successive lines and the burst phase alternately lags and leads the phase of $-(E'_B - E'_Y)$ by 45°.

A decoder for the PAL system can have two main forms. The

first, illustrated in Fig. 15, is very similar to an NTSC decoder. However, it includes a phase-reversing switch, in the circuit supplying subcarrier to the $(E'_R-E'_Y)$ synchronous detector, which corrects for the phase reversals in the received $(E'_R-E'_Y)$ chrominance component.

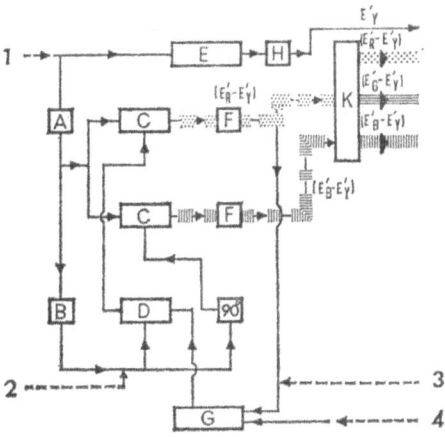

Fig. 15. Simple decoding for PAL. A: Band-pass filter. B: Burst-locked oscillator. C: Synchronous detector. D: Phase-reversing switch. E: Band-attenuating filter. F: Low-pass filter. G: Switch operating circuit. H: Delay. 1: Composite signal. 2: Subcarrier. 3: Burst pulses. 4: Line pulses.

As in a NTSC coder, a source of demodulating subcarrier is provided by a burst-locked oscillator. However, although the burst phase alternately lags and leads the $-(E'_B-E'_Y)$ axis by 45°, the speed of response of the oscillator control servo is such as to adjust the oscillator phase according to the average burst phase, i.e. the $-(E'_B-E'_Y)$ axis. Thus during the burst, the output of the $(E'_B-E'_Y)$ detector consists of identical negative pulses, once per line. If the phase-reversing switch is operating correctly, the output from the $(E'_R-E'_Y)$ detector during the burst consists of identical positive pulses.

The operation of the decoder phase-reversing switch is primarily carried out by means of line pulses but any mis-operation of the switch is sensed by the polarity of the pulses derived from the burst in the $(E'_R-E'_Y)$ synchronous detector. This form of decoder is relatively simple. In the presence of a chrominance phase shift the colour picture displayed may show horizontal stripes in which alternate lines of a field are of different colour; when viewed at a distance the combination of the two colours approximates to the intended colour.

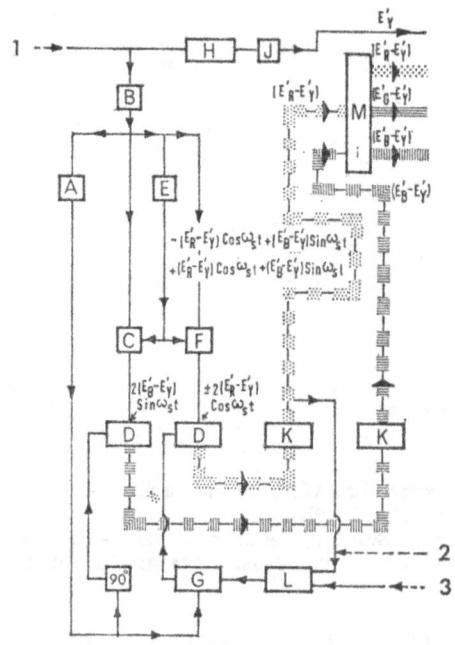

Fig. 16. Delay-line decoding for PAL. A: Burst-locked oscillator. B: Band-pass filter. C: Adder. D: Synchronous detector. E: One-line delay. F: Subtractor. G: Phase-reversing switch. H: Band-attenuating filter. J: Delay. K: Low-pass filter. L: Switch operating circuit. M: Matrix. 1: Composite signal. 2: Burst pulses. 3: Line pulses.

The second form of decoder performs electrically this process of averaging the positive and negative colour errors that may occur on successive lines. It incorporates a one-line delay which is also used to separate the $(E'_R - E'_Y)$ chrominance component from the $(E'_B - E'_Y)$ chrominance component. Fig. 16 shows a typical decoder of this type.

The luminance signal is derived, as before, from the composite colour signal by means of a band-attenuating filter. The complete chrominance signal, after extraction by a band-pass filter, passes to the burst-locked oscillator and to an arrangement for separating the $(E'_R-E'_Y)$ and $(E'_B-E'_Y)$ chrominance components. This arrangement consists of a one-line delay (e.g. a glass bar fitted with electroacoustic transducers) together with adding and subtracting circuits. If, during one line, the chrominance signal consists of $(E'_R-E'_Y)$ cos $\omega_s t + (E'_B-E'_Y)$ sin $\omega_s t$, the chrominance signal in the preceding line consists of $-(E'_R-E'_Y)$ cos $\omega_s t + (E'_B-E'_Y)$ sin $\omega_s t$. Thus, addition of the chrominance signals during successive lines results in $2(E'_B-E'_Y)$ sin $\omega_s t$; subtraction (i.e. addition with one of the contributions reversed in phase) results in $2(E'_R-E'_Y)$ cos $\omega_s t$ during one line followed by $-2(E'_R-E'_Y)$ cos $\omega_s t$ during the succeeding line. Synchronous detectors are used to derive $(E'_R-E'_Y)$ and $(E'_B-E'_Y)$ from the separated chrominance components. The periodic phase reversal of $2(E'_R-E'_Y)$ cos $\omega_s t$ is compensated by a corresponding phase reversal of the subcarrier fed to the detector. This latter reversal is carried out in step with line pulses; as before, any errors are sensed by the pulses derived from the burst in the $(E'_R-E'_Y)$ synchronous detector. $(E'_R-E'_Y)$ and $(E'_B-E'_Y)$, after suitable band limiting, are fed to the matrix.

It will be seen that, during any one line, the $(E'_R-E'_Y)$ and $(E'_B-E'_Y)$ chrominance signals are the average of the $(E'_R-E'_Y)$ and $(E'_B-E'_Y)$ chrominance signals transmitted during successive lines. This approximately corrects for the errors arising from chrominance phase shift; however, for large phase errors the average chrominance signals so obtained are reduced in amplitude and some desaturation of the picture results.

6.2 *The PAL subcarrier frequency.* In the NTSC system the subcarrier frequency is an odd multiple of half the line frequency. This results in minimum subcarrier visibility on the screen of the black-and-white receiver. However, if the same subcarrier frequency is used for the PAL system, the fact that the $(E'_R-E'_Y)$ chrominance component is reversed in phase on alternate lines prevents this condition of minimum visibility being maintained. This may be understood by considering the chrominance signal as the sum of two subcarriers having identical frequencies but a quadrature relationship, $(E'_R-E'_Y)$ cos $\omega_s t$ and $(E'_B-E'_Y)$ sin $\omega_s t$. Using the NTSC subcarrier frequency, the visibility of one subcarrier, $(E'_B-E'_Y)$ sin $\omega_s t$, will be a minimum. However, the process of reversing the phase of the other subcarrier, $(E'_R - E'_Y) \cos \omega_s t$, is similar to that of amplitude modulating it by a square wave at half the line frequency; thus side-bands are generated which have frequencies displaced from subcarrier frequency by odd multiples of half line-frequency. These sidebands have frequencies that are harmonics of line frequency and, therefore, have maximum visibility. From the above argument it can be seen that the use of the NTSC subcarrier frequency would result in a variation in the subcarrier visibility dependent upon the hue of the colour; the hue determines the relative contributions of $(E'_R - E'_Y)$ and $(E'_B - E'_Y)$.

As a consequence of the above, the PAL system employs a subcarrier frequency that is displaced in frequency, from the nearest harmonic of line frequency by about one quarter of the line frequency; in the case of the 625-line system, the displacement is one quarter the line frequency minus half field frequency. It can be shown that the patterns resulting from $(E'_R - E'_Y) \cos \omega_s t$ and $(E'_B - E'_Y) \sin \omega_s t$, using this frequency, are equally visible and that their visibilities lie about mid-way between the maximum and minimum values (these occur at line frequency harmonics and odd multiples of half the line frequency respectively).

6.3 *Summary of the PAL system to be used in the U.K. with the 625 line 50 field system**

The signal may be expressed as:

E'_M (excluding burst and sync pulses $= E'_Y + 0.493(E'_B - E'_Y) \sin \omega_s t \pm 0.877 (E'_R - E'_Y) \cos \omega_s t$

where the phase of the $(E'_R - E'_Y) \cos \omega_s t$ component is reversed during successive lines, and $E'_Y = 0.3 \, E'_R + 0.59 \, E'_G + 0.11 \, E'_B$ where $\gamma = 2.2$. (as in NTSC).

The subcarrier frequency:

$$f_s = \frac{\omega_s}{2\pi} = (284 - \tfrac{1}{4}) \cdot f_{LINE} + \tfrac{1}{2} \cdot f_{FIELD} = 4.43361875 \text{ Mc/s}.$$

The bandwidth of E'_Y is 5·5 Mc/s and the bandwidths of $(E'_R - E'_Y)$ and $(E'_B - E'_Y)$ lie within the range 1·0–1·5 Mc/s.

The burst signal consists of 10 cycles of subcarrier.

---

*Full details have been published in Doc. X1/174 of the CCIR, Oslo 1966.

7. The SECAM System

The SECAM system was devised in France by Henri de France who published his proposals in 1958. Since then the system has undergone considerable modification in order to improve its performance.

When compared with the NTSC and PAL systems, SECAM differs fundamentally in the way in which the colour-difference

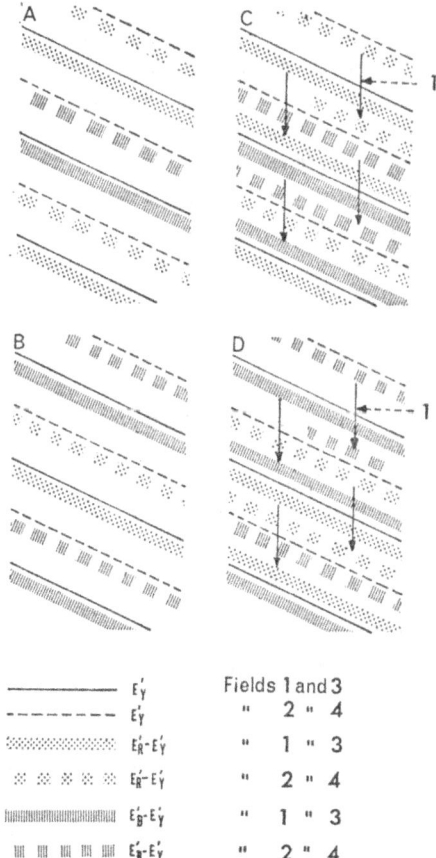

Fig. 17. Four fields of SECAM 5-line picture. A: Transmitted fields 1 and 2. B: Transmitted fields 3 and 4. C: Displayed fields 1 and 2. D: Displayed fields 3 and 4. 1: Downward displacement.

signals are conveyed from the coder to the decoder. It employs a luminance signal E'_Y identical to that used in NTSC and PAL but the colour-difference signals $(E'_R - E'_Y)$ and $(E'_B - E'_Y)$ are transmitted alternately during successive lines. Further, instead of quadrature-modulation, frequency modulation of the subcarrier is used.

7.1 *Sequential Colour-Difference Signals.* The fact that each colour-difference signal is transmitted on alternate lines, as shown in Fig. 17, has three consequences. First, in order to recover E'_R, E'_G and E'_B correctly in the receiver, it is necessary that both colour-difference signals and the luminance signal are available at the receiver decoder throughout every line period. This means that some form of store must be provided in the receiver in order to enable one colour-difference signal to be stored while the other is being received. The store consists of a delay device (e.g. a glass bar fitted with electro-acoustic transducers, as used in PAL) which has a delay of one line period. Thus when one colour-difference signal, say $(E'_R - E'_Y)$, occurs at the input to the receiver delay device, the output of the delay device consists of the other colour-difference signal, $(E'_B - E'_Y)$, which was transmitted during the previous line period. By means of simple switching arrangements, it is possible to obtain $(E'_R - E'_Y)$ and $(E'_B - E'_Y)$ simultaneously, although some of the information has been displaced downwards in the picture by the spacing of one line in a field.

Secondly, the vertical information carried by the colour-difference signals is less than that carried by the luminance signal. This occurs because samples of information, taken along a vertical strip of picture, are spaced in each field by one line pitch for the luminance signal and twice the line pitch for a colour-difference signal. When the E'_R, E'_G and E'_B signals are reconstituted at the receiver this, together with the fact that some of the colour-difference information is shifted downwards by one line spacing, leads to loss of vertical colour resolution and flicker effects on near-horizontal edges.

Thirdly, sequential transmission permits the two colour-difference signals to have the same bandwidth; the use of E'_I and E'_Q signals having different bandwidths offers no advantage.

7.2 *The Use of Frequency Modulation.* By using frequency

modulation of the subcarrier in order to convey colour-difference signals to the receiver, the phase of the subcarrier no longer determines the hue of the reproduced colour. However, when the colour-difference signals are zero (i.e. the grey-scale) the subcarrier amplitude is not zero; its frequency is merely undeviated.

The deviation of the subcarrier frequency is determined by the instantaneous value of the colour-difference signal applied to the frequency modulator.

The SECAM chrominance signal may be represented by:

$$E'_c = A \cos(\omega_s + D \cdot \Delta\omega_s)t$$

where A is the amplitude of the f.m. subcarrier, D is the modulating function causing deviation of the subcarrier frequency and has two values:

i.e. $D_R = K_R \cdot (E'_R - E'_Y)$ for those lines during which the $(E'_R - E'_Y)$ signal is transmitted.
and $D_B = K_B \cdot (E'_B - E'_Y)$ for those lines during which the $(E'_B - E'_Y)$ signal is transmitted.
Further, $\omega_s = 2\pi f_s$
and $\Delta\omega_s = 2\pi \Delta f_s$ and is the deviation of the subcarrier frequency resulting when D has unit amplitude.

As is normal practice in f.m. systems, the colour-difference signal is pre-emphasized before being fed to the frequency-modulator. A typical colour-difference signal pre-emphasis characteristic is shown in Fig. 18.

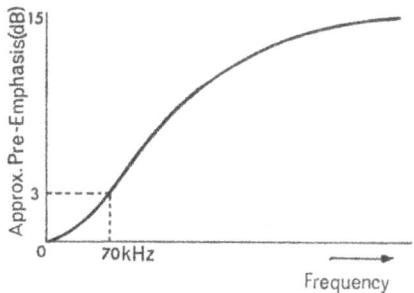

Fig. 18. Video pre-emphasis of colour-difference signals. Pre-emphasis defined as $20 \log_{10} |g_{v.f.}|$ where $g_{v.f.} = \dfrac{1+jf/f_1}{1+jf/kf_1}\left(\begin{matrix}f_1=70\text{ kHz}\\k=5\cdot 6\end{matrix}\right)$

The subcarrier is present throughout the active portion of each line period and may be visible to the black-and-white viewer even in those areas of the colour picture which are black, grey or white. Because of this the amplitude of the subcarrier is kept as low as possible, bearing in mind the problem of reception in fringe areas. The visibility of the pattern produced on the screen of the black-and-white receiver is further reduced by reversing the phase of the frequency-modulated subcarrier during every third successive line and every alternate field. This process exploits the frequency-interleaving principle somewhat less effectively than in the case of the NTSC system.

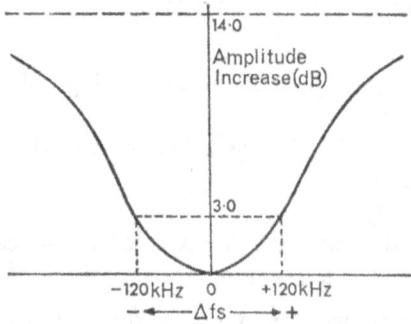

Fig. 19. H.F. pre-emphasis of F.M. subcarrier. Subcarrier H.F. pre-emphasis defined as $20 \log_{10} |g_{R.F.}|$ where $g_{R.F.} = \dfrac{1+j16F}{1+j1\cdot26F}$ $\left(F = \dfrac{fs}{fo} - \dfrac{fo}{fs}\right)$

An f.m. system tends to be more sensitive to interference towards the edge of the band than it is at the centre frequency. Thus better performance may be obtained if the subcarrier amplitude is increased as a function of frequency deviation. In the SECAM system the chrominance signal (i.e. the frequency-modulated subcarrier) is passed through a h.f. pre-emphasis circuit having a response similar to that shown in Fig. 19. As a result, the chrominance-signal amplitude increases with increase of colour-difference signal amplitude, which corresponds to an increase of colour saturation. Thus, in the aforementioned relationships describing the SECAM chrominance signal, the value of the parameter A is a function of D.

Finally, before the pre-emphasized chrominance signal is added to the luminance signal to form the composite colour signal, it is passed to a modulator that increases the chrominance-signal amplitude whenever the luminance signal contains components, of appreciable magnitude, having frequencies lying within the chrominance band. This process is carried out in order to ensure that the chrominance signal components in the composite colour signal have an amplitude which is sufficiently large in comparison with luminance-signal components having frequencies within the chrominance band; otherwise, spurious and unwanted effects can occur in the viewed colour picture due to the decoding process mistaking the luminance-signal components for chrominance.

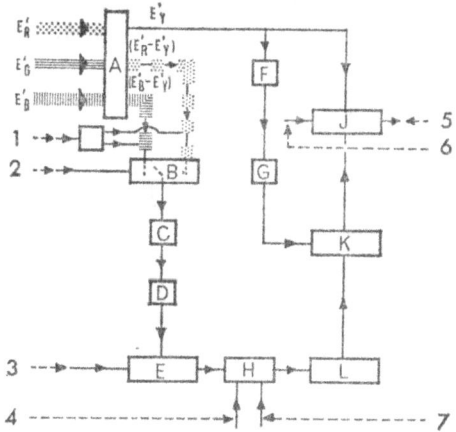

Fig. 20. SECAM coding. A: Matrix. B: Electronic switch. C: Low-pass filter. D: Video pre-emphasis. E: Frequency modulator. F: Band-pass filter. G: Rectifier. H: Phase reverser. J: Adder. K: Amplitude modulator. L: h.f. pre-emphasis. 1: Colour sync. 2: Line pulses. 3: Subcarrier. 4: Line pulses. 5: Composite signal. 6: Sync. 7: Field pulses.

7.3 *SECAM Coding and Decoding.* A typical SECAM coder is illustrated in Fig. 20.

The colour-difference signals $(E'_R - E'_Y)$ and $(E'_B - E'_Y)$ from the matrix together with colour synchronizing signals consisting of sawtooth colour-difference signals occurring during the field-blanking interval, are fed to an electronic switch, driven by line-frequency pulses, which connects them alternately to the input of the low-pass filter (typical bandwidth 1·0 Mc/s). The output of the filter is then fed, via the pre-emphasis circuit, to the subcarrier frequency modulator. After modulation, the phase of the modulated subcarrier is then reversed during every third line and every alternate field. h.f. pre-emphasis is applied and the chrominance signal is then amplitude modulated by a control signal consisting of the output of a rectifier; the rectifier is fed from the luminance signal via a band-pass filter selecting frequency components in the region of the subcarrier. Finally, the processed chrominance signal is added to the luminance and sync signals to form the composite colour signal.

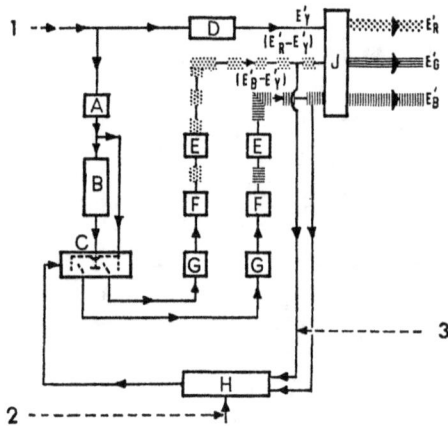

Fig. 21. SECAM decoding. A: Band-pass filter. B: One-line delay. C: Electronic switch. D: Band-attenuating filter. E: De-emphasis. F: Discriminator. G: Limiter. H: Switch-operating circuit. J: Matrix. 1: Composite signal. 2: Line pulses. 3: Colour sync.

A typical SECAM decoder is shown in Fig. 21. The composite signal input is fed to two signal paths. In the first, a band-attenuating filter attenuates the chrominance-signal components and provides a luminance signal for the matrix. At the input to the second path a band-pass filter selects the chrominance components of the composite signal; the filter characteristic is the inverse of the h.f. pre-emphasis characteristic of the coder.

The chrominance signal is now fed directly, and via the one-line delay device, to an electronic double-pole, double-throw switch operated by line pulses; any mis-operation of the switch due, say, to interference with the line pulses, is corrected at the end of each field by the colour-synchronizing pulses derived from the colour-difference signal detectors. Modulated subcarrier signals corresponding to $(E'_R - E'_Y)$ and $(E'_B - E'_Y)$ are thus made separately available and are fed to limiters and discriminators. The $(E'_R - E'_Y)$ and $(E'_B - E'_Y)$ signals obtained are subjected to de-emphasis (corresponding to the video pre-emphasis applied to the colour-difference signals in the coder) and are fed to the matrix where they are combined with E'_Y to form E'_R, E'_G and E'_B.

7.4 Specification of the SECAM signals to be used in France with the 625-line 50 field system*

The luminance signal:

$$E'_Y = 0\cdot3\ E'_R + 0\cdot59\ E'_G + 0\cdot11\ E'_B$$
where $\gamma = 2\cdot2$.

The SECAM composite signal is expressed as

$$E'_M = E'_Y + A \cos(\omega_s + D.\ \varDelta\omega_s)\ t$$
where $D_R = -1\cdot9\ (E'_R - E'_Y)$
and $D_B = 1\cdot5\ (E'_B - E'_Y)$

$\varDelta f_s$ is the subcarrier frequency deviation produced by unit amplitude of pre-emphasized colour-difference signal and is equal to 230 kc/s. (Unit amplitude of colour-difference signal is defined in terms of a scale in which, for white, E'_R, E'_G and E'_B have unit amplitude).

The bandwidth of each colour-difference signal is approximately 1·4 Mc/s (after pre-emphasis). The subcarrier frequency (undeviated) is equal to 4·4375 Mc/s (284 times line frequency). The value of A for undeviated subcarrier (i.e. colour-difference signal zero) is 0·1. The subcarrier is interrupted at the end of each line-blanking interval and recommences before the start of each active line period.

---

*Full details of the specifications for SECAM will be found in Doc. XI/164 (France and U.S.S.R.) of the CCIR, Oslo 1966.

The pre-emphasis characteristics (see Figs. 18 and 19) are defined by

$$g_{v.f.} = \frac{1+j\,f/f_1}{1+j\,f/kf_1} \quad k = 5\cdot6 \quad f_1 = 70 \text{ kc/s}$$

$$g_{r.f.} = \frac{1+j\,16F}{1+j\,1\cdot26F} \quad F = \frac{f}{f_o} - \frac{f_o}{f} \quad f_o = fs$$

The amplitude modulation of the chrominance signal which is related to the amplitude of luminance signal components $(E'_y)_{CH}$ within the chrominance band is defined by

Gain 0 dB for $(E'_y)_{CH} \leq 0\cdot2$
6 dB for $(E'_y)_{CH} = 0\cdot4$

The colour-synchronizing signal consists of subcarrier signals corresponding to trapezoidal colour-difference signals transmitted during six lines of each field-blanking interval.

The specification outlined above may be modified in order to permit the optimization of certain parameters.

These possible modifications include:

1. The use of different undeviated subcarrier frequencies during the lines in which $(E'_R - E'_y)$ and $(E'_B - E'_y)$ are transmitted. During the lines carrying $(E'_R - E'_y)$, $f_{sr} = 4\cdot40625$ Mc/s, while during the lines carrying $(E'_B - E'_y)$, $f_{sb} = 4\cdot25000$ Mc/s.
2. The number of lines of the field-blanking interval during which colour-synchronizing signals are transmitted is increased from six to nine.
3. The parameters of the video pre-emphasis applied to the colour-difference signals become:
$$k = 3$$
$$f = 85 \text{ kc/s}$$
4. The amplitude of the undeviated subcarrier becomes:
for f_{sr}, $A_R = 0\cdot144$
for f_{sb}, $A_B = 0\cdot116$
5. The nominal deviation is changed to:
280 kc/s for modulation by $D_R = \pm1$.
230 kc/s for modulation by $D_B = \pm1$.
6. The centre frequency of the r.f. pre-emphasis characteristic is 4·286 Mc/s.

8. Brief Comparison of NTSC, PAL and SECAM

During recent years the three systems, as applied to the 625-line, 50 field standard, have been intensively studied and tested by broadcasting and industrial organizations throughout Europe under the auspices of a special Ad-Hoc Group on Colour Television, set up by the European Broadcasting Union; the Ad-Hoc Group have issued a report* which summarizes the work carried out and the conclusions reached. The following sub-sections summarize some of the points made in the report.

8.1 *Compatibility.* Tests showed that, in general, NTSC is somewhat more compatible than PAL and SECAM. Little difference of compatibility was found between the latter two systems.

8.2 *Fundamental quality of the colour picture.* It was found that there is little significant difference between NTSC and PAL in this respect and that both these systems are slightly better than SECAM with regard to certain unwanted effects at horizontal boundaries between areas of different colour.

8.3 *Effects of distortions and signal errors.* Of the three systems, SECAM was found to be the most tolerant of chrominance-signal phase errors, although PAL with a delay-line receiver was found to be about twice or three times as tolerant as NTSC (and PAL with a simple receiver).

PAL was found to be more tolerant than NTSC with regard to unwanted attenuation of the chrominance-signal upper sideband.

In the simultaneous presence of certain distortions (amplitude non-linearity with loss of response at subcarrier frequency) and random noise, SECAM is not as good as NTSC and PAL.

8.4 *Receivers.* The NTSC receiver was generally considered as the cheapest. An NTSC or simple PAL receiver requires more colour controls than a PAL receiver with a delay-line or a SECAM receiver.

---

*Report of the E.B.U. Ad-Hoc Group on Colour Television, second edition, February 1965; also *Amendments to the Report of the Ad-Hoc Group,* second edition, February 1965, February 1966; published by E.B.U. Technical Centre, Brussels.

The NTSC system is the most suited to the use of a single-gun display tube; SECAM has less flexibility in this respect than either NTSC or PAL.

8.5 *Reception under adverse conditions.* With regard to the effects of co-channel interference, it was found that NTSC and SECAM are both slightly better than PAL (with a delay-line receiver) when the interference has zero offset; when the offset is about 250 Hz, NTSC is better than SECAM and slightly better than PAL (with a delay-line receiver).

The three systems are equally affected by weak echoes, as caused by multipath reception. When the echoes cause serious picture impairment, SECAM and PAL (with a delay-line receiver) are slightly better than NTSC.

In the presence of random noise NTSC is the same as PAL, and SECAM is almost as good as NTSC for signal-to-noise ratios giving rise to a picture quality better than "rather poor".

Appendices

Appendix A
Local TV Set Ownership

NIELSEN Station Index, local market audience measurement service of A.C. Nielsen Company, has gathered information on the extent of local color TV set ownership, market by market, since the fall of 1964.

The information illustrates the major growth of color TV in terms of the ability of the audience to receive the color signal, from percentages most generally less than 10 percent in late 1964 to percentages close to 20 and in some cases over 30 in early 1967. Among markets *not* listed on the following two pages, Lubbock, Tex., was high for the nation with 35 percent, with Akron, O., and Las Vegas, Nev., tied for second place with 33 percent each.

The 40 markets listed on the following two pages were selected by the editor as approximating the top 40 markets of the United States on a population basis. They were taken from NSI data as reported for 224 markets, and do *not* represent the selection of the Nielsen company.

The data provided are copyrighted in corresponding years by A.C. Nielsen Company, and used by permission; are gathered by telephone contact with households, during the process of soliciting diary keeping co-operation by those households. As such, they are subject to sampling and non-sampling errors as described at the end of the appendix and in NSI local market reports.

NIELSEN STATION INDEX MARKET BY MARKET COLOR TELEVISION OWNERSHIP ESTIMATES

Selected Markets (40)	% Color TV Ownership Nov. '64	% Color TV Ownership Nov. '65	% Color TV Ownership Oct.-Nov. '66	% Color TV Ownership Feb.-March '67
	%	%	%	%
Atlanta	4	11	15	18
Baltimore	4	9	15	16
Birmingham	4	6	14	17
Boston	3	9	15	17
Buffalo	4	7	13	20
Charleston—Huntington	*	10	14	17
Chicago	6	10	15	17
Cincinnati	9	15	21	26
Cleveland	6	12	19	26
Columbus, Ohio	11	17	24	27
Dallas—Fort Worth	4	7	14	21
Denver	6	12	18	23
Detroit	5	11	18	21
Grand Rapids—Kalamazoo	*	10	17	21
Hartford & New Haven	4	10	15	20
Houston	6	10	16	21
Indianapolis	7	13	19	25
Kansas City	3	7	11	14
Los Angeles	9	18	24	29
Louisville	4	11	12	15

APPENDICES

City			
Memphis	4	7	14
Miami—Ft. Lauderdale	6	12	23
Milwaukee	6	9	23
Minneapolis—St. Paul	2	6	13
Nashville	4	6	14
New Orleans	5	10	22
New York	5	7	17
Oklahoma City	5	8	15
Philadelphia	6	12	22
Pittsburgh	5	10	18
Portland, Oregon	7	11	21
Providence	3	8	17
Sacramento—Stockton	9	18	32
St. Louis	4	8	16
San Diego	9	15	28
San Francisco—Oakland	7	13	23
Seattle—Tacoma	6	11	22
Syracuse	3	9	19
Tampa—St. Petersburg	*	10	22
Washington	4	8	16

*Not reported for this period. NSI color ownership estimates are based upon responses obtained from telephoned households in the NSI areas of 224 markets and are subject to sampling and non-sampling errors. Readers are reminded that color TV ownership within the telephone universe tends to be somewhat higher than among all television households, and that telephone ownership levels vary between markets. The more appropriate usage of these data involves comparisons between markets or between measurements within the same market, rather than absolute appraisals of levels of color ownership.

Appendix B

Size and Characteristics of Television Audiences

THE Media Research Division of A.C. Nielsen Company publishes an annual report outlining the size and characteristics of the television audience, using estimates of TV usage gathered during the preceding year.

Television '67, current with the publication of this text, provides data for comparison of color growth, 1966 to 1967; also graphs the heavier use of TV by color set owners.

The following two pages of Appendix B, under the headline of "Color TV Ownership Increases Dramatically", chart the percent of U.S. TV households having one or more color TV sets, March, 1966 to March, 1967, with demographic categories of *household size*, *age of head of house* and *household income* amplifying the estimate for *total U.S. households*. (Nielsen defines the three income categories as: *lower*—below $5,000; *middle*—$5,000–9,999; *upper*—$10,000 and over.)

The fourth page, under the heading of "Color Set Households Watch More TV", uses viewing estimates from January-February, 1967, to point up heavier use of sets in color households—in dayparts including weekday and weekend daytime, early evening and prime evening viewing periods.

> (Data from *Television '67* copyright 1967 by A. C. Nielsen Company and used by permission. Estimates are based on the NTI sample; are subject to the definitions and statistical limitations set forth in regular NTI Reports.)

Color TV Ownership Increases Dramatically

Percent of TV Households

Color television has jumped from 9% of U.S. TV households in March, 1966 to 16% March, 1967, according to the latest estimates. Upper income households have the highest color TV ownership figure: 31%.

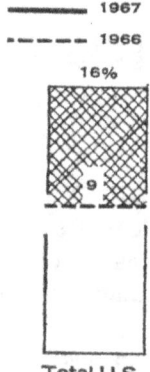

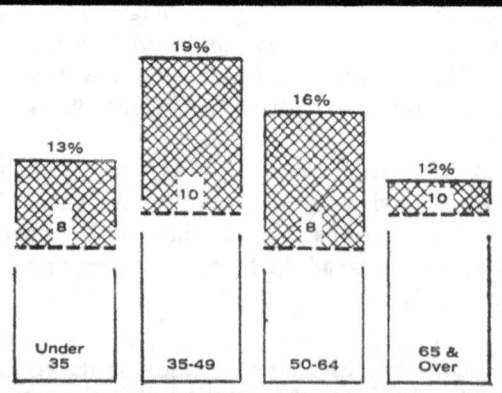

By Age of Head of House

Having One or More Color TV Sets (March 1, 1967)

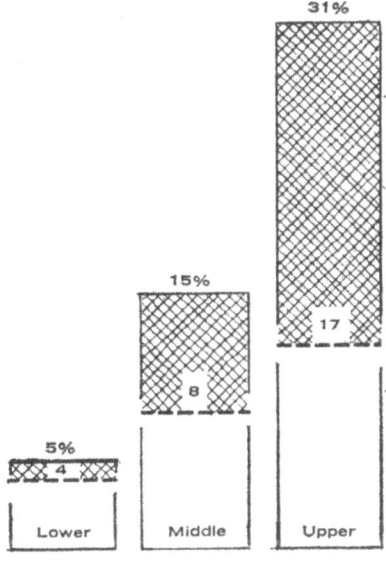

By Household Income

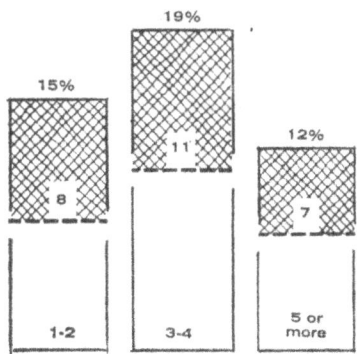

By Household Size (Persons)

Color Set Households Watch More TV

Percent of Households Using TV*
Black & White Only Vs. Color TV Set Owners
(January-February, 1967)

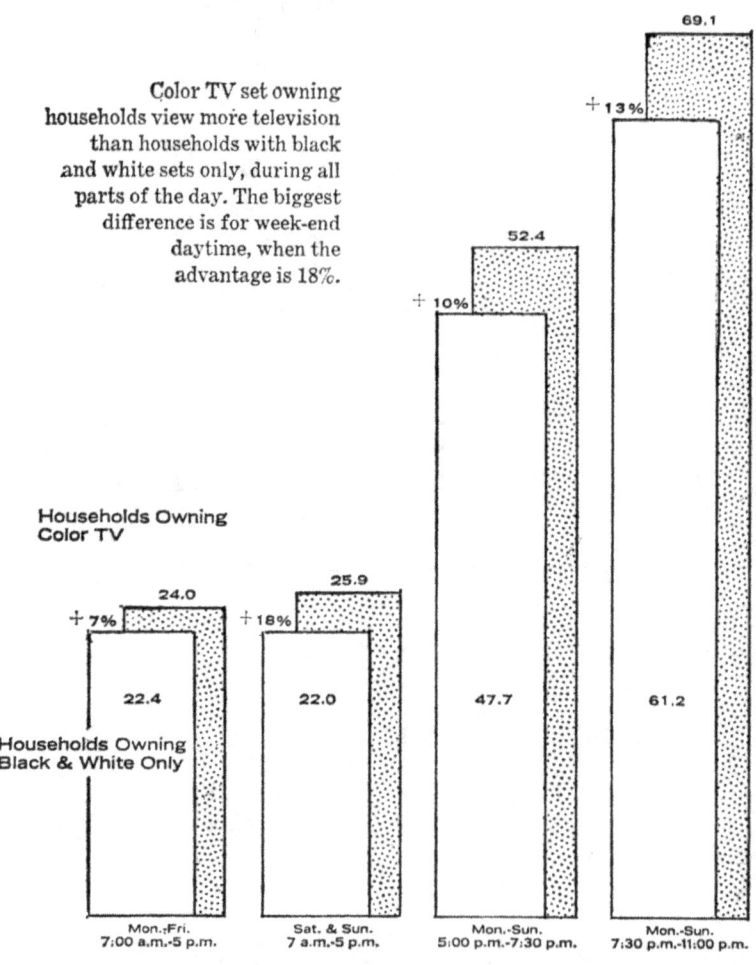

Color TV set owning households view more television than households with black and white sets only, during all parts of the day. The biggest difference is for week-end daytime, when the advantage is 18%.

*During Average Minute

Appendix C

Color Versus Black-and-White
Comparison of set production and sales

FROM the more important items of the times (1930: radios and vacuum tubes) to the present, the Electronic Industries Association (Washington, D.C.) has produced a great variety of data, reporting economic, production, sales and related information and services covering the entire U.S. electronic industries group.

The Marketing Services Department of EIA has provided materials detailing television set production and sales, for both monochrome and color units. The following represents excerpts from that data.

In the overall period of 1955 through 1966, the total U.S. television receiver market has absorbed 10·9 million color TV sets, on a scale beginning with 20,000 units in 1955, rising dramatically a decade later to 2·7 million units in 1965, then almost doubling the 1965 output with 5 million units in 1966.

For the final month of 1966, EIA reported that "At 632,000 units valued at $280 million, sales of color TV receivers during December, 1966 climbed 79 percent and 86·9 percent, respectively, from unit and dollar sales during this month a year earlier."

Comparing the calendar year 1966 to 1965, EIA reported: "Color TV receiver sales rose 71·2 percent and 78·4 percent in unit and dollar sales, respectively, during 1966, to reach 4·7 million units valued at $2 billion."

Comparisons to black-and-white TV set production and sales are of interest:

In the same 11-year period (1955–1966), the total U.S. monochrome receiver market approximates 83·4 million units; coupled with earlier available estimates (1952–1954), the total is estimated at 104 million black-and-white units. *If* all were in working order, this would represent better than one set for every two people in the United States!

For the final month of 1966, EIA reported monochrome set activity as "Down 27·8 percent and 31·3 percent in unit and dollar sales respectively during December, 1966—553,000 units with a value of $61 million."

For the year 1966, EIA reported "Monochrome TV receiver sales were off 13·4 percent and 18·2 percent, respectively, from unit and dollar sales during the previous year, to reach 7 million units valued at $813 million."

Impact of color during 1966 is documented in the EIA summation of *total* receiver sales (monochrome and color): "Sales amounted to 11·7 million units valued at $2·9 billion during 1966, increasing 8·1 percent and 33·5 percent, respectively, from unit and dollar sales during 1965." In terms of *average value per unit sold* in 1966, EIA listed color units at $435·20; monochrome units at $116·99. (It should be noted that both of these categories include table and portable units, consoles, and radio and phonograph combinations.)

TOTAL U.S. TELEVISION RECEIVER MARKET*
(add 000 units)

Year	Monochrome	Color
1955	7,738	20
1956	7,351	100
1957	6,388	85
1958	5,051	80
1959	6,278	90
1960	5,709	120
1961	6,168	147
1962	6,696	438
1963	7,236	747
1964	8,361	1,404
1965	8,753	2,694
1966	7,702	5,012

Source: Marketing Services Department, Electronic Industries Association.

The data on the previous page reflect estimates supplied by the EIA in the *Total U.S. Market* category (includes import and export activity) for the years indicated, and is identified as the "Total U.S. Television Receiver Market". This is pointed out in anticipation of the realization that these data for 1966 will be ahead of actual sales figures as reported in the preceding material.

Glossary

A star * following word signifies British terminology.

A
ABC. American Broadcasting Company—in radio days the "Blue" network of the National Broadcasting Company (1927–45), it was split from NBC and its parent Radio Corporation of America ownership in 1942; became known as ABC in June 1945. From radio networking, ABC expanded to television in the 1950s, with an ownership of stations in major markets and a grouping of affiliated stations that, by 1967, could be considered only slightly less than that of its major competitors, NBC and CBS.

ABERRATION. Color or image distortion in a lens or optical system.

AC SHIFT. Alternating current (phase) shift.

AGC. Automatic gain control. This ensures that the chrominance output remains practically constant as the chrominance input level changes.

AMBIENT LIGHT. Illumination from sources other than planned lighting. Ambient light falling on a TV receiver screen may appear as annoying "hot spots".

ANSWER PRINT. The first print where picture and sound are married into one unit. Until the answer print is correct, additional quantities of print are not requested.

AUDILOG (R) (also see *NSI, NTI*). A. C. Nielsen-developed diary for household use in recording TV viewing by household members and visitors. As a part of Nielsen's National Audience Composition service (NAC), members of a permanent Audilog panel record household member viewing during designated weeks. For Nielsen Station Index (NSI), randomly-selected households perform a similar diary-keeping service on a one-week-only basis. This information provides local market viewing data, from two to seven times annually depending upon size of market.

AUDIMETER (R) (also see *NTI*). A patented device developed by the A. C. Nielsen Company; records the minute-by-minute usage of the television set in the household. A randomly-selected national panel of approximately 1,200 Audimeter households sends in cartridges of film on which the machine has recorded this information; the results are tabulated and projected to form the Nielsen Television Index weekly and bi-weekly reports.

(In England, the Nielsen company is part owner of the TV audience measurement system commonly known as *Tammeter*; similar methodology produces minute-by-minute audience projections of viewing in the areas of the British Isles covered by the BBC and its commercial "competitors".)

In other Audimeter applications, a New York area *Instantaneous Audimeter* system "reads" the TV set usage of selected households; makes instant records of same and projects audience data for each 15-minute viewing period. It is anticipated that this instantaneous method will be projected to the entire national NTI sample in the near future, enabling "morning-after" national reports on the viewing of network programs.

AUDIO. Involves auditory effects or the components of a system handling the sound frequencies.

B BACK LIGHT. Lighting more or less aimed toward the camera. This gives the subject a better silhouette and a more three dimensional appearance. Apart from adding naturalism to the picture it also gives a sheen. Presents certain problems in color television.

BANDWIDTH (of antenna, of aerial*). Range of frequencies within which performance, in respect to some characteristic, conforms to a specified standard.

BANDSHAPING. Regulating of bandwidth.

BBC. British Broadcasting Corporation. The British Broadcasting Corporation was given its original charter for sound broadcasting in 1927, and was a monopoly controlling all broadcasting in Britain. This monopoly was maintained until the charter was revised in 1952 when planning for the Independent Television Authority was under way. Regular transmissions of television programs began in 1936 (the first in the world), ceased during World War II and began again in 1946. The BBC is now operating 2 networks designed to complement one another. BBC-1 is available to more than 99 per cent of the population and BBC-2, catering for "minority interests", was available to more than 66 per cent of the population when color television made its debut in 1967 on that channel. More transmitters for wider coverage are being erected. The BBC has been experimenting with color television for 19 years and has been putting out color test transmissions for over 10 years.

B & W. Black-and-white: monochrome television or film.

BLACK-BODY. An ideally perfect absorber and emitter of radiation.

BLACK-BODY RADIATION. Illumination of a continuous type from a light source such as a tungsten lamp.

BLACK LEVEL. Minimal voltage of video signal establishing blackness of transmitted image.

BLANKING. Replacement of picture signal by a signal of constant amplitude other than black level.

BRI. Brand Rating Index—a market research service that reports multi-media (newspaper, magazine, as well as TV) usage related to major consumer item product preferences.

BURN (in/through). A camera tube focused on a static object tends to retain the image of the object for some time, faintly superimposed on succeeding pictures.

C

CARRIER WAVE. A wave with the properties to enable it to be transmitted through a selected system after it has been modulated.

CASCADE. A chain of amplifiers in which the output of the first supplies the input to the second and so on.

CBS. Columbia Broadcasting System. CBS entered radio in 1927 as a program service to stations competing with NBC outlets. First titled the Columbia Phonograph Broadcasting Company, the network went through two changes of ownership before being identified in 1929 as the Columbia Broadcasting System. As the major competitor to NBC, CBS competed in talent bidding and raids during post-World War II radio; was for a time in competition with RCA Victor (NBC's parent company) in the manufacture of record players and TV sets; plunged into (and lost) the debate regarding compatible versus non-compatible home receivers for color TV; entered early black-and-white television on a firm footing, to continue a neck-and-neck race for dominance with NBC for top position in *total* television audience reached.

CELLS. Transparent, celluloid overlays carrying a drawing and revealing to the camera other cells and/or a background drawing below. By changing cells between exposures of individual frames, the effect of animation is achieved.

CHROMA CONTROL. A control for adjusting saturation of colors in the reproduced picture.

CHROMATICITY. The hue and saturation of a color.

CHROMINANCE. The colorimetric difference between a color and a reference white of the same luminance.

CINEX. A short test strip of print supplied by the laboratories with the day's rushes. It indicates the possible printing range from the negative.

CLAMPING (circuit). Process which establishes a fixed level for the repetitive components of the video signal.

COAXIAL CABLE. Will carry many radio, telephone and television signals simultaneously. Composed of a central conductor or wire surrounded by some type of insulation over which a wire mesh or tube is placed. The central wire and outside conductor are concentric.

COLOR (also see *Hue, Shade, Tint, Tone*). *Color* consists of light waves to which the human eye is sensitive: light or color wavelengths are very short, from 400 billionths to more than 700 billionths of a meter.

In color television, the producer works with a double vocabulary: *light* color, in which the primary colors are orange-red, green, and violet-blue; and *paint* color, where the primaries are yellow, green-blue, and magenta red.

As substances, *paint* colors are exactly opposite from *light* colors. The secondary colors in one are the primaries in the other.

In addition, the producer balances complementary colors (two colors that produce white light are complementary). Light, composed of three primary colors, demands that one of the two complementary colors must be a secondary color, e.g. magenta red with green, or yellow plus violet-blue.

Which complementary color is primary, which secondary? It depends on whether you mean *light* colors or *paint* colors. Magenta red, a secondary color in light, is a paint primary; green (its complementary color) is a primary in light but a secondary in paint.

In other words, a primary paint color is complementary to a primary light color—which is, however, a secondary paint color.

Out of this seeming semantic confusion, the color TV producer and his technical associates then use the vocabulary and techniques of *paint* color in relation to backgrounds, costumes, make-up, etc.; for special effects blend all of this with *light* color in adding hues, shades, tints and tones to the total visual image—and offer it to a sophisticated, *light*-color-primary electronic system for broadcast—at the same time keeping in mind the problems of compatibility along the gray-scale for black-and-white reception.

COLOR BURST. The color burst is a special color synchronizing signal sent out by the transmitter to enable the color receiver to separate the electrical signals which are carrying the coloring information.

COLORCAST. To transmit color television images.

COLORIMETER. Mechanical aid for matching colors visually. The observer looks into an eyepiece and sees the color to be matched in one half of a split circle. In the other half he sees a mixture of red, green and blue lights, called the reference stimuli. The amounts of light can be adjusted until the mixture matches the test color.

COLOR CORRECTION. The pictorial translation from the natural colors in the design of a product or package into tones of gray for what was felt to be better transmission on B & W television.

COLORPLEXER. The encoding device which produces a single 3-variable signal, which is then decoded at the receiver.

COLOR SUBCARRIER. The coloring information is transmitted by modifying the color difference signals I and Q, and modulating both signals on to a subcarrier. The modulated subcarrier is added to the brightness signal and both are modulated on to the vision carrier and transmitted together.

COLOR TEMPERATURE. A measure of the color value of light recorded in degrees Kelvin. The blue end of the spectrum gives the high reading by meter. Stock and processing are balanced for a certain color temperature. Color temperature is completely unrelated to the degree of illumination.

COMPRESSION. Progressive reduction in amplitude in both sound and video. There may be a linear relationship (more likely in the case of sound) which is sought and achieved. There may be an unwanted effect or distortion in the case of video signals. In some sound techniques compression is subsequently followed by expansion and the original condition is restored.

COST PER THOUSAND. The basic measurement tool for the buyer of television advertising. The insertion of the rating figure (number of households reached) into the cost of advertising, produces the cost-per-thousand-households-reached; program-by-program or individual spot announcement-by-announcement, comparisons can then be made that offer some evaluation of advertising efficiency.

With the increasing flow of *demographic* (see note) information, it is possible to evaluate specialized "target" audiences—*men, ladies of the house, teenagers,* as they are separated from the total audience. Thus *cost-per-thousand* can be applied to those desired "target" audiences; while obviously higher than overall CPM figures, the concept has the advantage of providing data comparable to similar information from other programs and announcement schedules.

In color TV, CPM has increasing usage as costs increase and the dollar value of the expenditures must be assessed in ever-greater detail.

CRAWL. A long sheet of paper suspended between rollers, containing a list of titles or credits relating to a program. When placed in an opaque projector connected to a film chain, the credits appear on the receiver in sequence as the roller is turned.

CUT-BACK. When editing a film, to return to a main scene after a number of interpolated close-ups.

CUT BAR OPERATION (Cut Bank Operation*). The switching from one video (picture source) to another on the cut bank without using a fade to black and often with no arrangements for cut in blanking. Simple cuts of this nature are likely to cause the picture to roll. The cut could be associated with a sound changeover also.

D DAILIES (or *rushes*). First ungraded prints made overnight from a day's filming work. They are viewed at once; if unsatisfactory, retakes may be necessary.

d.b. Decibel—by definition, 1/10th of a *bel*. The decibel is the normal unit for measuring loudness of sound; equal to the loss in power in a mile of standard cable at 860 cycles.

DECODING. At the color receiver the signals are separated again, or *decoded* into their red, green and blue values. (See *Encoding*.)

DEMOGRAPHICS. In audience measurement research (in simplest form, "ratings") the term refers to the many divisions of the broadcast audience resulting from detailed research into the *who* as well as the *how many* present in the audience. At both national and local levels, TV audience measurement companies presently offer about 30 "demographic breaks"—households by income levels (lower, middle, upper); by education of the head of the house (elementary only, some high school, high school diploma, one-or-more years of college); by age of lady of the house (18–34, 35–49, 50 or older).
In relation to color television, the concept of demographics has increasing importance (see Coffin-Tuchman chapter). Higher levels of viewing by households in higher education, upper income, larger family brackets, mean a "plus" audience for the advertiser of merchandise with special sales appeal in those demographic areas.

DENSITY. Degree of opacity or darkness of a film image.

DEPTH OF FIELD. Range of distance from a camera at a particular lens setting, over which all objects will be reasonably in focus.

DIFFERENTIAL GAIN. Ratio of the high frequency signal at various parts of the modulation characteristic.

DIFFERENTIAL PHASE. The change of phase of a video signal as it is varied from black level to peak white level. Best measured by observing the behaviour of a burst of high frequency at the appropriate levels. An important property of any equipment and circuits in color television and an undesirable effect. Particularly in the NTSC system. Less important in PAL and SECAM.

DIMMER. Electrical variable-resistance unit used to adjust light intensity.

DISH. Parabolic reflector generally used to direct signals in the receiving or transmitting unit of a microwave relay.

DRIVE DELAY. Delays put in the various sync drive circuits when timing pulses in a television studio. In general short lines are delayed to have the same delay time as the longest lines on the station. The delay can be carried out by means of lengths of cable or by adjustable networks.

E

ENCODING. The modification of the red, green and blue signals before transmission, so that they can be sent in only one channel. (See *Decoding*.)

ENVELOPE DELAY. The delay of the envelope of a modulated waveform caused by the delay of the carrier frequency. Some distortion of the envelope may also be involved.

F

FADE. Gradual dimming of picture to blank screen. The same effect can be achieved in sound.

FAX. Abbreviation for facsimile.

FCC. Federal Communications Commission—regulatory agency of U.S. government; duties include licensing of all broadcast stations.

FEEDBACK. Part of an amplifier's own output may be deliberately fed back to reduce inherent sound distortion.

FILL LIGHT. General lighting of a set, often unfocused. It "fills" the shadows cast by key light. (See note.)

FILTER. (1) Toned transparency used in front of camera lens to vary photographic value of shot.
(2) Device incorporated in sound recording circuit to eliminate certain frequencies.

FILM CHAIN. An equipment arrangement in which one or more 16 mm film projectors are directed in turn to provide image pick-up for a television camera. This may include the projector, multiplexer and TV camera.

FLARE. Halo-like bright light appearing as a streak across a shot, usually caused by a highly reflective surface placed at a bad angle to the camera lens.

FREQUENCY INTERLACE. Technique which makes possible the addition of the I and Q signals to the M signal without objectionable interference between the several signal components.

f/STOP. Refers to "speed" or ability of a lens to pass light. Calculated by dividing the focal length of the lens by its diameter.

G GENLOCK. Proprietary device for interlocking synchronism between originating and remote signal sources.

GRAIN. The small particles of which a film image is composed after developing. If these are too large they may be individually visible.

GRAY-SCALE. Variations in value from white, through shades of gray, to black on a television screen. The gradations approximate the tonal values of the original image picked up by the camera.

H HUE. A color that is brilliant and has no black or white in it. Red, blue, green, yellow, etc., are *hues*.

I I SYMBOL. Another signal produced by a matrix circuit. Three signals must be produced in all, each of which must be a different combination of red, blue and green. The I and Q signals convey color difference information, indicating how the colors being transmitted differ from a neutral or gray of the luminance value designated by the M signal.

ID. Station identification symbol—stations are required to identify themselves hourly, including call letters, frequency (channel number) and city of license. Promotional announcements are often included.

IMAGE ORTHICON. A highly sensitive TV camera tube used extensively in studio cameras, as well as for field applications.

INTERCUT. To edit two or more sequences of film or tape alternately into a sequence.

ITV. U.S. abbreviation for instructional television. (In the U.K. the same abbreviation stands for Independent Television.) Instructional television is called educational television in the U.K.—ETV.

K k.c. Kilocycle. A unit of measurement equal to 1,000 cycles per second and used to express frequency of radio and other electromagnetic waves.

KELVIN TEMPERATURE. See *Color temperature*.

KEY LIGHT. Main illumination of centre of interest in a set. It is a hard light to throw hard shadows which give the shot depth because they indicate the shape of the subject. The ideal key light angle for an artist is approximately 30 degrees to the horizontal.

L **LIGHTING CONSOLE.** This control board, more sophisticated than a simple switching system, permits pre-setting of light intensities so that scene changes can be made during programming without undue manipulation.

LUMEN. The amount of light which produces illumination of one foot candle over an area of one square foot.

LUMINAIRES. Lighting units, sometimes called lanterns.

LUMINANCE. The objective measurement of the brightness of an emitting surface.

M **M OR Y SYMBOL.** This designates the signal put out by a matrix circuit. The M stands for monochrome. Sometimes called the Y symbol.

MAGNETIC SOUND TRACK. Much sound recording is now made on to stock carrying a magnetically sensitive coating instead of emulsion. It is simple to edit, processing costs are cheaper and the quality of sound is higher.

MATRIXING. This technique solves the basic compatibility problem by adding the three primary color signals in a matrix circuit in the proportion of 30 percent red, 59 percent green and 11 percent blue. This combination produces a luminance signal which is equivalent to the output of a monochrome camera.

MATTE. Specially photographed mask which, when run in an optical printer leaves blanks which can be correspondingly filled in with something else at a second print.

m.c. Megacycle. Unit equal to 1,000,000 cycles persecond; used to express the frequency of radio, television and other electromagnetic waves. One megacycle is equal to 1,000 kilocycles.

MEMORY SYSTEM. In recording instruments, a device into which information can be fed and later extracted.

MICROWAVE (link). Combination of TV transmitters and receivers used to convey picture or sound information from one station to another.

"MIXED-HIGHS" PRINCIPLE. Process which permits color television to be realized in a frequency band hardly wider than necessary in black-and-white transmission.

MONOCHROME. Images reproduced on a black-and-white television system are in monochrome. The picture appears in black-and-white with gradations of gray.

MULTIPLEXING. The processing of the primary color signals so as to share a common transmission channel. Microwave relays are often multiplexed to carry video and audio signals simultaneously.

MUNSELL COLOR SCALE (evolved by A. H. Munsell). A system of color definition, based on *hue, saturation* and *brilliance* in *light* colors (see *Color*). Definition is in terms of arbitrary scales as defined by a series of visual charts. The *hue* scale includes five principal and five intermediate hues; the *brilliance* scale, ten hues from black to white—both designed to represent equal visual intervals.

mv. Millivolt—by definition, the thousandth of a volt.

N NAB. National Association of Broadcasters. The major trade association of the broadcast industry in the United States; includes most commercial TV and over half of commercial radio stations in membership. Establishes codes of acceptable industry practices, represents industry in national and local policy matters relating to governmental regulation, legislation, etc.; provides many legal and research services for membership. Annual NAB Convention, held in March or April, is considered definitive conclave of U.S. broadcasters.

NASA. National Aeronautics & Space Authority.

NBC. National Broadcasting Company. The first major radio network in the United States, incorporated in 1926 as a wholly-owned subsidiary of the Radio Corporation of America. From 1927 to 1942, NBC operated two networks: the "Red", which has continued as NBC, and the "Blue", which by Federal Communications Commission edict was separated from NBC in 1942, to become a separate corporation. In June, 1945, the "Blue" became known officially as ABC—the American Broadcasting Company. With the advent of television, NBC became one of the three major video networks.

NEUTRAL DENSITY FILTER. Filter for reducing exposures without altering relative values of tone or color, to give softness to harshly lit objects.

NSI. Nielsen Station Index. Offers local market audience measurement detail for approximately 225 United States urban areas. Originally an adjunct of NTI methodology, NSI in 1964 developed a series of techniques based on computer flexibility, from the initial selection of households to be sampled to the final output of viewing data.

These data are gathered by use of diaries placed in randomly-selected households, with initial telephone contact as the major means of securing diary-keeping co-operation. As a part of the telephone contact, NSI gathers information on the penetration of color TV set ownership, the number of multi-set (two or more) households, and the ability to receive UHF TV signals.

In further steps, NSI has offered a wider range of demographic information in its local market reports—which run from two "all market" periods of information-taking, in middle Fall and late winter—to 70-market measurement cycles for Spring and summer. In the largest U.S. market areas, NSI conducts additional three and four week rating periods, covering all major calendar periods of advertising interest.

NTI. Nielsen Television Index. Identifies the basic national audience measurement service of A. C. Nielsen Company. NTI bi-weekly and weekly reports from sample households offer projections of total TV households viewing the major networks' programming; in key rating periods, the bi-weekly reports are augmented by Audilog (diary) information, offering viewing estimates of major demographic groups, e.g. men, women, teens, children; men and women by various age categories, etc.

NTSC SYSTEM. Compatible color system devised by the U.S. National Television Systems Committee in the early 1950s and adopted as the standard system in the U.S.A. at the end of 1953. Also used by Japan and Canada, and six other countries.

O   O & O. "Owned and operated" stations in a television network. Network ownership of TV outlets is subject to federal communications law as it applies to all group ownerships—a maximum of seven stations, of which no more than five may be in the very high frequency (VHF) range, with others in the ultra high frequency (UHF) band. Each of the three major networks operates its full complement of five VHF stations (in the middle and late 1950s, NBC and CBS made unsuccessful attempts to operate UHF stations).

OPTICAL FILTER. Transparent frame around the television picture in a receiver to prevent undesired reflection.

OSCILLOSCOPE. Test instrument, similar in some ways to a television receiver, which shows visually the patterns of voltage and current characteristics.

P   PAL. Compatible color television system used in Germany and the United Kingdom and thirteen other countries. PAL stands for *phase alternate line*.

PAN. To move the camera in the horizontal plane.

PARAMETER. A dictionary definition gives: "Quantity constant in the case considered but varying in different cases". The practical case usually met is the possible variation of components, voltages, signals, etc. which will still produce an acceptable result in a piece of apparatus.

PHOTOFLOOD. A simple source of strong illumination used largely by amateurs or for close shots on location.

PLUMBICON. This tube is a development of the vidicon. Its sensitivity is high, nearly equal to the image orthicon, but with the simple and robust characteristics of the vidicon.

POLARITY. The sense of the potential of a portion of the signal representing a dark area of the scene, relative to the potential of a portion of the signal representing a light area. Polarity is stated to be "black negative" or "black positive".

Q QUARTER WAVE PLATE. This term has been applied in a variety of ways. At its broadest it involves a relative delay of a quarter wavelength, of light of defined frequency with respect to some other reference. Hence plates of birefringent material have been cut (e.g. quartz) in which polarized light beams of the ordinary and extraordinary ray have been changed one-quarter of a wavelength with respect to each other in passage through the plate.

Q SYMBOL. Another signal produced by a matrix circuit. Three signals must be produced in all, each being a different combination of red, blue and green. The Q and I signals convey color difference information, indicating how the colors being transmitted differ from a neutral or gray of the luminance value designated by the M signal.

R RADIO FREQUENCY/RF (system, stage). Part of the electromagnetic spectrum where bands of frequencies, or channels, are allocated for radio and television use.

RATING (also see *Share*). The term *rating*, established as a unit of measurement in radio broadcasting and later applied to TV, has one commonly-accepted definition: the percentage of households in the geographic universe, *able to receive* and tuning to a program at a given point in time. Example: an estimate (by sampling techniques) of 20 percent of the television households in the United States tuned to a program is a *rating* of 20. The approximate number of those households may be found by calculating 20 percent of the total estimated U.S. TV households (as of the 1967–68 season, 60.0 million).

The above is an example of a *national* rating, with the United States as the measured universe. In local audience measurement activity the concept of the term is identical, but the measured universe is then limited to those counties or other geographic boundaries generally reached by the broadcast outlets licensed to and serving the local area (and, again, with households equipped to receive the broadcast signals). Thus a rating of 20 in the New York area reflects an estimated 20 percent of TV households *within that area* tuned to the program.

(Data from the U.S. Bureau of the Census is most generally accepted for definitions of TV households within commonly-accepted geographic areas.)

RCA. Radio Corporation of America, parent organization of National Broadcasting Company (see *NBC*).

REAR SCREEN PROJECTION/RP (Back Projection*/BP). A method of projecting transparencies or cine film on to a screen placed behind artists to represent a still or moving background.

REEL. (1) 1,000 feet of 35 mm film or 400 feet of 16 mm film. Both lengths run for approximately 11 minutes.
(2) Unit of completed film.

REFERENCE BLACK. Almost any scene has a shadowed or dark area—this will be the "reference black" of the scene and will be adjusted by the video operator to zero percent signal voltage. A minimum reflectance value of 3 percent is recommended.

REFERENCE WHITE. The brightest element in a scene becomes the "reference white" for that scene and is adjusted by the video operator to 100 percent signal voltage. A maximum reflectance value of 60 percent is recommended for the reference white.

RTNDA. Radio-Television News Directors Association. Professional association of electronic journalists, representing both local station and network news activity; works to establish newsfilm standards, offers advice on college curricula in electronic journalism, campaigns for access to news sources equal to print media for news broadcasters and cameramen.

REFLECTANCE VALUE SCALE (Munsell/Ostwald). A commercial series of standard tones.

S

SATURATION. The intensity, depth and richness of a color image. Some developing processes reduce saturation in the prints, while increasing contrast: a wide range of brightness variation should therefore be avoided.

SECAM. Compatible color television system used in France, U.S.S.R. and 28 other countries. SECAM stands for *sequential à mémoire*.

SHADE. A color mixed from a *hue* and black is called a *shade*. The brilliance of the *hue* is cut down by the addition of black, e.g. deep brown.

SHADOW MASK TUBE. A special color display "three gun" tube which reproduces separately the red, green and blue primary images which are then combined optically. It can produce a very good 405-line color picture.

SHARE (also see *Rating*). *Share*, although seldom considered "fair share" by broadcast executives, very simply defines the portion of the total TV audience *tuned in* at a specific time to each of the available television signals in the measured universe.

In a simplified example, the ratings at a designated half-hour period in prime evening time are: 25 for network *A*, 20 for net *B*, and 15 for net *C*. Together, these ratings (percentages of total U.S. TV households) represent a HUT (Households Using Television) of 60. This HUT of 60 then represents 100 percent of the *viewing* households for this time period. Network *A* has garnered a 42 percent *share* of the TV audience, net *B* 33 percent, net *C* 25 percent.

A *rating* of 20, 25 or any other numeral can be recognized as constant, representing a percentage of total TV households in the measured area, national or local. Its *relationship* to other ratings may be evaluated by its conversion to a *share*, which indicates its relative worth against competition at a specific time. Thus in prime evening viewing, a *rating* of 20 might in turn represent less than a 33 percent *share* of the audience tuned in during that time period; a rating of six during late evening hours might in turn be evaluated as a 60 percent *share* of the TV audience.

SMEAR. An effect particularly experienced with vidicon cameras. When the camera pans on a bright object, or if the subject itself is moving, a smearing or trailing effect may appear behind it.

SMPTE. Society of Motion Picture & Television Engineers. A professional organization of specialists in the closely-allied visual arts; does major work in establishing technical standards for lighting, equipment, film, etc.

STAIR STEP GENERATOR (Staircase Generator*). A test instrument which produces a video signal which increases in discrete steps, usually from black level to peak white or vice versa, when the signal is displayed on a waveform monitor. Useful for measuring compression and overloads.

STOPPING DOWN. Reducing the diameter of the iris in order to admit less light into a camera.

STORYBOARD. A series of 15 to 30 pictures in miniature, usually hand-drawn, indicating the action of the commercial. Under each picture the copywriter adds appropriate dialogue. Camera movements are also indicated.

SUN GUN. Trade name for a series of portable, often battery driven lamps, of high efficiency. Used in television and in filming.

SWEEP ALIGNMENT. To align or adjust a piece of apparatus using a sweep and display method. The sweep of frequencies for example, is carried out continuously and automatically, as opposed to a spot frequency check at agreed points.

SYNC GENERATOR. An electronic generator which supplies pulse patterns for control of television circuits.

T TINT. White added to a *hue* produces a *tint*. Pink—red with white added, and ivory—yellow with white added, are *tints*.

TIO. Television Information Office. A public relations office interconnected with the National Association of Broadcasters by board and by financial support; acts to put forth a favorable image of the TV industry at all levels. Contact—by selective advertising in "quality" magazines, by frequent mailings, by personal relationships —is maintained with government spokesmen, thought leaders, educational groups, offices of religious bodies, etc., with the financial support of the NAB plus the major networks and the individual TV stations and their group offices.

TIP PENETRATION. The movement on a videotape head tip from just touching the tape to its position of use. The tips of the head are pressed into the tape during operation and it is necessary to define the amount in recording and reproduction to get the best results.

TONE. A color that is a combination of a pure *hue*, plus black *and* white, is a *tone*. Beige, tan, straw, and the many variations of gray, are tones.

TRANSMITTER. The general equipment which radiates radio or television signals for reception at locations within the service area.

TvB. Television Bureau of Advertising. A promotional bureau supported by commercial broadcast interests, with the purpose of promoting the sale of television advertising time. Provides extensive promotional and research tools for membership; acts as aggressive voice of commercial telecasting in competition with other media groups (e.g. newspapers, magazines, outdoor advertising, etc.).

U UHF (also see *VHF*). Ultrahigh frequencies; by definition from 300 to 3,000 megacycles. To augment the limited number of VHF channels available, the FCC allocated the UHF range from 470 to 890 megacycles to commercial and educational TV—U.S. TV channels 14 to 83. Since UHF signals have limited range, stations in this part of the spectrum are permitted up to 5,000 kilowatts of visual power.

V VECTORSCOPE. Instrument for measuring the amplitude and phase of the modulation carried by the quadrature modulated subcarrier. Checks the accuracy of transmitter encoders.

VERTICAL BLANKING (Line Blanking*). Suppression of the vision signal at the end of each line.

GLOSSARY 281

VHF (also see *UHF*). Very high frequencies, by definition from 30 to 300 megacycles. In establishing wavelengths for television transmission, the FCC first allocated the VHF bands from 54 to 88 megacycles (VHF channels two through six), and from 174 to 216 mc. (channels seven through thirteen). To compensate for reach-of-signal differences in the low and high parts of the overall VHF span, stations operating on channels two through six are limited to 100 kilowatts of visual power; those on channels seven through thirteen are permitted 316 kw.

VIDEO (control, operator, etc.). Refers to visual components of a television system.

VIDEOTAPE RECORDER/VTR. Device which can record both audio and video signals of a television production on special magnetic tape. It can be edited at leisure and played back later.

VIDEO SWITCHER. Control panel which allows selection of TV images from any of several cameras. The selected image is then fed into a broadcast transmitter.

VIDICON. This tube is less sensitive than the image orthicon and is generally used in small studios or for industrial purposes. However, the sensitivity is extremely variable depending on the electrical adjustment of the camera. It is simple and robust.

VIEWFINDER. The miniature television monitor incorporated in a camera which shows the operator the picture being picked up by that camera.

VTVM. Abbreviation for vacuum-tube valve voltmeter, which uses a thermionic valve to measure either direct or alternating voltages.

W WRATTEN FILTER. Proprietary series of film camera filters.

WIRE (Scrim, Jelly*). Wire mesh suspended in gelatine compound which can be inserted in front of a lamp to reduce the intensity of light from it.

Y Y SYMBOL. See *M Symbol*.

Z ZOOM LENS. A lens with multiple moveable elements, with variable focal length. Operation of the lens produces the effect of moving in and out from a scene—zooming in and zooming out.

Index

ABC 14, 53, 139, 202
AC shift 38
Ad Hoc Group on Colour Television (EBU) 251
Advertisers 152
Advertising Federation of America 172
Advertising in color 21-7, 141-5, 160-71, 181
   rates 166, 183
Advertising Research Foundation 126
AFL 11
After-images 23, 24
Agencies, advertising 152, 161
American Dairy Association 159
Amplitude modulation 220, 223
Ancona, Edward P. Jr. 82
Answer prints 165
Associated Press 115
Atlantic 122
Audience: "class" 122, 135, 142
   "mass" 122, 135
Audilog (R) 14
Audimeter (R) 12

Back light 68, 69, 71, 90, 92
Back porch 41
Bacus, Roy 147, 172, 187
Baird, J. L. 210
Bandshaping 32
Bandsharing 219
Bandwidth 32, 38
BBC 9, 66, 207
Big Ideas 187

Black-body 70, 110
   radiation 70, 92, 110
Black-level voltage 84
Blanking 44, 47
Brand Rating Index 123, 135
Broadcasters Promotion Association 9, 146, 187, 197
Bruch, Dr. W. 236
Buck, Max 160
"Burn in" titles 93
Burst 44, 220, 233
Burst, black 43
Burst flag 47
Byron, James A. 113

Campbell, Chet 146, 147, 197
Cash, Norman E. (Pete) 139, 162
CBS 14, 37, 53, 54, 202, 210
CCIR 204
CCSE Program 28
Chicago Art Institute 98
Chromaticity 87
Chrominance 38, 45
   signal 219
Churvis, Arthur (Bud) 102, 104
Cinex tests 89
Clamping circuit 41
Coffin, Thomas E. 121
Coleman, Donald F. 159
Coleman, Howard W. 197
Color as Seen and Photographed 110
Color Association of the U.S. 205
Color balance 83-6, 104
"Color bars" 225
Color burst 43

Color camera 44–6, 55, 56
  modular construction 44–5
  sensitivity 67, 81
  techniques 78
Color contrast 26
Color correction 168
Color difference signals 32, 221–9
Color distortions 23
Color engineering 21
Color moods 27, 77
Color Motion Picture Film and Color Television Seminar 110
Color pick-up tubes 30
Color Planning for Business and Industry 21
Colorplexer 31
Color print 89, 94
Color production costs, 81
Color programming promotion 140, 147–58, 186, 198
  costs 156–7
Color reception 22
Color reproduction 22
Color saturation 25, 38, 39, 50, 58, 84, 85, 88, 209, 213, 227
Color separation signals 213–18, 224, 227
Color set owners 123
  age 124
  household size 126
  income 123
  location 126–7
  personality characteristics 128, 130
  product usage patterns 127–8
Color set penetration 13, 17, 170, 199, 255–65
Color set sales 151–2, 184
Color signal swing 42
Color television equipment 175–7, 188, 191–2
  recurring costs 192
Color Television Engineering 28
Color television systems 30, 208–52
Color Television Week, Chicago 153
Color temperature 63, 70, 76, 91, 110
Color testing 57
Commercials 26, 27, 63, 64, 85, 139, 161, 168–70, 192
  cost 162, 164, 165
  videotape color 168

Compatible television systems 33, 211
Compatibility 31, 69, 77–9, 89, 96, 116, 219
Composite-signal spectrum 227
Compression 38–9
Constant luminance principle 211, 215
Contrast range 59, 60
Costume for color TV 24, 62, 73–4, 86, 89, 116, 192, 205
Crane, Woodrow 97
Crawl 105
Crosley Broadcasting Group 95, 139
Cut bar operation 44

Dailies 89
Day scenes 90
  exterior 91
  interior 94
Dealers, color sets 150–1
Decoder 237, 248
Decoding 31, 231–4, 238, 247–8
Demodulation 226
Design 74–7
Differential gain and phase 38, 39, 41, 42, 47, 48
Differential phase distortion 235
Dimmer 70, 71
Documentaries 97, 101–6
Drive delay 43

Eastman Kodak Company 82, 111, 170
Electronics at Work 28
Electronics Industries Association 263, 264, 265
Elements of Color in Professional Motion Pictures 90
Encoder 43, 47
Encoding 31, 247–8
Envelope delay 38, 41–2
ETV 203
European Broadcasting Union 251

FCC 30, 35, 37, 188
Fill light 90, 91
Film
  for color television 83–6, 109
  tungsten 111
Film chain 176–7

INDEX

Film processing laboratories 112–14, 166, 193
Film sequences 80
Film stock 80
Filming
  abroad 100–103
  on location 97, 101–5
Filters
  analysis 210
  band-pass 233
  bandshaping 42
  graduated neutral 93
  low-pass 233
  neutral density 89
  optical 210
  polarizing 92, 105
Flare 84
Frequency
  interlace 35
  interleaving 228
  response 38, 41, 42, 47, 49
Front screen projection 115
Front porch 47

Gallup and Robinson Report 161
Gamma, effect of, 78, 216
General Aniline and Film Corporation 111
Genlock 47
Graphics 116, 155
Gray-scale 61, 83, 87
Goldmark, Dr. P. C. 37
Goldwyn, Sam 7, 207

Harper's Bazaar 122
Hart, Frank 96, 98, 99
Hearst Corporation 37
Hue 39, 50, 209, 213

I signal 32, 33, 34, 35
ID 155, 156, 158
Image orthicon 45
International Radio-TV Society 9
Interpublic GmbH 159

Jamison, Jett 113, 114

Katz Agency 187, 188
Katz Color Survey 189
Kaufman, Lionel 166, 167
Kelly test set 48
Kelvin degrees 70, 110

Kennedy, John F. 117
Ketcham, Howard 21
Key light 68, 69, 90, 91
KLZ 107

Lemoine, Jacques 164
Lens flare 69
Life 122
Lighting 26, 57, 60, 63, 67–71, 75, 90–94, 98, 109, 179, 192
  fluorescent 62, 92, 109, 110
  incandescent 76, 109, 110
  quartz iodine 68, 110, 111
  tungsten 70, 110, 111
Local station color 172–186
Lord, A. V. 207
Luminaire 70
Luminance 45, 69, 87, 209, 214
  signal 32

M signal 32–5
Make-up 24, 71–3, 89, 179, 192
Matrix 213, 214
Matrixing 32
Mills, Kenneth A. 16, 187
Mixed-highs principle 211, 213
Monitor 50
  color 47
Monochrome TV systems 30
Multiplexing 31, 33
Munsell Color Notation System 61, 74, 88

NAB 8, 146, 154, 197
NAB Code Office 167
NASA 99
National Educational Television 203
National Survey of Television Sets in U.S. Households 126
National Television Systems Committee 223
NBC 8, 14, 107, 108, 121, 139, 146, 153, 160, 172, 197, 202
NCAA 11
Newhart, Bob 160
News on color TV 107–11, 178
The Newsroom and the Newscast 114
New Yorker 122
NFL 11
Nielsen, Arthur C. Jr. 10

Nielsen Company 7, 10, 197, 255, 259
Nielsen Product-Media Service 16
Nielsen Station Index 14, 253
Nielsen TV Index 13, 122
Night scenes 64, 90, 91, 92
NTSC color TV system 37, 40, 47, 204, 207, 219–23, 229
  color synchronizing 231
  comparison with PAL and SECAM 236, 237, 243, 251
  compatibility 235, 251
  decoding 231–4
  distortions and signal errors 235, 251
  E'_I and E'_Q signals 229–231
  good features 235
  quality of picture 251
  receivers 251
  reception 252
  subcarrier frequency, choice of 227–9
  summary 234
  weaknesses 235

O & O's 95
Ostwald scale of reflectance values 88
Outside broadcast 97–101
Overload 39
Oxberry still camera 157

PAL color TV system 204, 207, 219–22, 236
  coding and decoding 237, 238
  comparison with NTSC and SECAM 236, 237, 243, 251
  compatibility 251
  distortions and signal errors 251
  quality of picture 251
  receivers 251
  reception 252
  subcarrier frequency 241
Paul, Sol 204
"Persistence of vision" 35
Peterson, Sheldon W. 107
Phase characteristics 38
Phase distortion 42
Playboy 201
Plumbicon 45, 68, 75
Polarization error 68
Primary colors 29, 208

Primary color signals 31, 32
Print density 85
Print media 143, 157, 161, 182, 199
  advertising 157, 199–201
  Hi-Fi 200, 201
  R.O.P. color 200
  Spectacolor 201
Processing color film 113
Processors 113
  newsfilm color 177
Props 76
Public service programming 95

Q signal 32–5
Quaal, Ward L. 95
Quadrature a.m. 220
Quadrature modulate 234
Quarter wave plate 68

RCA 28, 153, 202
Radio, decline of 12
Radio-TV News Directors Association 107, 113
Rathman, Mel 104
Rear projection 80, 115
Reel-to-reel balance 85
Reference black 88, 93, 94
Reference white 87–8, 90–1, 93–4
Reflectance values 87, 88
Royal Television Society 8, 53

Sarnoff, General David 11, 153, 202
Sarnoff, Robert W. 153, 202
Saturday Evening Post 162
Saturday Review 122
Schickel, Steve 100, 101
Schwerin Research Corporation 161, 171
SECAM color TV system 204, 207, 219, 221, 222
  coding and decoding 247–8
  comparison with NTSC and PAL 236, 243, 251
  compatibility 251
  distortions and signal errors 251
  quality of picture 251
  receivers 251
  reception 252
  sequential color difference signals 244
  specification of signals 249
  use of frequency modulation 244–7

Set 75, 87, 192
Sequential color analysis 210
Sequential color television systems 210-11
Shadow 63, 84
Shadow density 84
Shadow-mask tube 30, 210
Significance of Some Receiver Errors to Color Reproduction 40
Sine square pulse 48
Skin tone 57-8, 64, 71-3, 75, 87, 89-90, 104-5
Slides, color 115
Society of Motion Picture and Television Engineers 82
Sound Off 187
Sound track
  magnetic 112
  optical 112
Spectrum 208
Spot photometer 93
Stair-step generator 48
Stair-step signal 39
Stanley, A. R. 66
Stein, Gertrude 207
Stevenson, Robert Louis 173
Stills, color 115
Storyboard 167
Stroboscopic action 229
Subcarrier 34, 41, 219
  amplitude 40
  frequency, choice of (NTSC) 227-9
  oscillator 34
Sun Gun 103
Sweep alignment 48
Sync compression 41
Sync generator 41, 43, 50
Synchronous detectors 233
Synchronous noise 41

Telefunken A. G. 236
Television '67 259
Television Age 21, 204
Television Bureau of Advertising 121, 139, 144
Television Station Management 197
Television white 59
Test equipment 48-9
Three color simultaneous system 209

Time 200, 202, 203
Time delay 38
Time-Life Broadcast 107, 113, 114
Tip penetration 45
Tommy Tint 149-50
Trailer 85
Transient response 48
Transmitter 50
Tuchman, Sam 121
TVA Groups Inc. 164
TV Film Trends 170
TV Guide 149
Two-phase modulation 33

United Press-International 115
United States Bureau of the Census 126

Variety 199
Vectorscope 48
Video equipment 24, 43-8
Video switcher 43-4
Videotape, color 62, 114, 168
Videotape editor 176-7
Videotape recorder 44-6, 50, 115, 176-7
Vidicon 45

Waner, John M. 82
WBAL 37
WBAP 113, 147, 172
Wentworth, John W. 28
WFGA 166
WGN 159
WGN Continental Broadcasting Company 95, 99
WHEN 166
White signal level 224
Wilner, John T. 37
Wilson, Midge 205
Winckler, E. Carlton 53
Wire 70
WMAQ 146, 149, 151, 152, 153 197
WNDT 203
WTCN 107

Zoom lens 176-7, 179

For Product Safety Concerns and Information please contact our EU
representative GPSR@taylorandfrancis.com
Taylor & Francis Verlag GmbH, Kaufingerstraße 24, 80331 München, Germany

www.ingramcontent.com/pod-product-compliance
Lightning Source LLC
Chambersburg PA
CBHW061435300426
44114CB00014B/1691